RICHARD TO MINNA WAGNER

Richard to Minna Wagner

LETTERS TO HIS FIRST WIFE

TRANSLATED, PREFACED, ETC.

By William Ashton Ellis

VOL. I

VIENNA HOUSE
New York

Originally published by H. Grevel & Company
London, 1909

First VIENNA HOUSE edition published 1972

International Standard Book Number:
Volume I . . . 0-8443-0012-8
Volume II . . . 0-8443-0013-6

Library of Congress Catalogue Card Number: 75-163797

Manufactured in the United States of America

TRANSLATOR'S PREFACE

In my Introduction to the letters of RICHARD WAGNER TO MATHILDE WESENDONCK (Eng. ed. 1905) I dealt so fully with the home-relations of his first marriage, that, apart from the more intimate light now thrown on them by the present collection itself, I need do little more than recall to mind the barest skeleton of material facts.

WILHELM RICHARD WAGNER, youngest of nine children, was born to his father, Magistrates' Clerk at Leipzig,* May 22, 1813. At the age of 21, beyond a few smaller pieces, there stood to his credit four overtures, one of them performed once at the Leipzig Gewandhaus, a Symphony, likewise played once there, and an opera, *Die Feen*, destined never to be mounted until five years after his death ; he had held the position of chorus-master at the Wurzburg theatre for the best part of a twelve-month, and just secured that of operatic conductor at

---

* Even though a passage in one of Richard Wagner's own "family letters" of considerably later date than the present collection suggests a sentimental preference for the idea that Ludwig Geyer, his mother's second husband and father of sister Cecilie (to whom the letter is addressed), may have been his actual progenitor—a fancy first blurted into the public ear as fact by F. Nietzsche a few years after the master's death—the *best* authorities have never lent it serious credence; the like-ness to his eldest brother, Albert, and through him to his *paternal* uncle, is far too striking for such a theory, whereas there is not one line of resemblance in the portraits of either Albert or Richard Wagner to the almost effeminate features of their artist stepfather.—W. A. E.

Magdeburg, entering on his duties in that town in the autumn of 1834. Here he first met "Minna," a pretty actress then engaged for "young heroine" parts at the same theatre.

CHRISTINE WILHELMINE PLANER, described as her parents' "3rd daughter," was born at Oederan, half-way between Dresden and Zwickau, the 5th of September 1809, her father being a mechanic of some sort and, as we learn from page 496, so ignorantly opposed to the march of education that he refused to have his daughters taught to write. Though Minna, as she always was called, must have acquired that elementary art in his despite at some period of her adolescence, or she could scarcely have obtained the various stage engagements we know she did, yet this early illiterateness is of equal ultimate importance with her three-and-a-half-year seniority to the husband she married at Königsberg, while he was temporarily out of employment, on the 24th of November 1836. In letter 172—which I strongly recommend for prompt perusal— we shall find Richard Wagner alluding to his "young wife," whilst certain other references in these letters (e.g., no. 239) suggest that even so late as the early 'sixties she left him under the delusion that her birth had occurred in the year 1813, as stated on the marriage certificate ; which would have made her a few months younger than her husband, and only just turned 23, instead of the actual relation of $27\frac{1}{4}$ years on Minna's side to $23\frac{1}{2}$ on Richard's. A man of his eternal "juvenility" (cf. p. 505) ought never to have married at so "in-experienced" an age (p. 502), as he recognised himself in

later life ; and when he did marry, his bride should have
been some years his junior, not one whose character and
narrow views were already set past all transmuting.   But
a still greater misfortune was the barrenness of this wedlock ; there was nothing in the home, beyond the husband,
to keep or turn the woman's heart young, and it is plain
as day that from the first she arrogated to herself the part
of mentor.

True, quite early in the history of Richard and Minna
Wagner's wedded life we catch glimpses of a juvenile
third member of the household, and her name is of
constant recurrence down to the end of the 'fifties ; but
how little this NETTE, or Natalie, contributed toward
brightening the home, at least for its head, these pages
will eventually reveal.   Strange to say, however, in themselves they never afford us the smallest direct hint as to
who this Nette really was.   Once, and only once, Wagner
refers to "my N." (p. 23), but that is obviously a mere
façon de parler; for he follows it up in a sense that
proves Minna the young girl's accepted guardian, whilst
we know for certain, even did these letters not clearly
imply it, that Nette was no blood-relation of *his*.   Her
relationship to Minna is much more puzzling.   Though
Richard writes to his half-sister Cecilie at the same
conjuncture, that a provisional home has been " found for
Natalie with her sister Charlotte," and six years later
denotes her to friend Uhlig " my sister-in-law," yet not
one of the numberless allusions in our present collection
styles Natalie either " your sister " or—if I may broach
a now current tradition—" your child " ; the nearest we

get to a suggestion of kinship is that on page 592, where Minna is told that, "if one could manage with N.," and "provided it were offered her," this young person "could have no other choice whatever, than to attend to you and share our home. In the case supposed, that is her plainly-destined natural vocation, from which she at utmost could escape by marriage." But not even Minna, indisputably her relative in some way, "could manage with Nette" for long at a stretch when the girl turned to termagant woman; and as to exactly what became of Nette after the second migration to Paris we are left in darkness, albeit Minna's husband magnanimously undertook to pay a modest annual stipend to this Natalie Planer who had come into the world at least a year or two before he first met Minna herself.

In the same connection, another reference in the first edition of my Introduction aforesaid needs a trifling amendment. There I called Natalie "the youngest of the old Planers' three daughters"; but, whether she was their actual daughter or not, it is now evident that, besides a married son who died in early manhood (pp. 29 and 409), they had *four* other children: viz. our Minna and her sisters Charlotte Tröger, Amalie von Meck, and "Jette," the last-named apparently dying a spinster (p. 116).

Beyond the above small corrections, there is not a syllable to retract from that Introduction; in fact, I can honestly say that our present collection of letters proves me rather to have under-rated Wagner's kindness and affection toward a helpmate who really would have been happier, not "with a lesser man," but with a sterner and less indulgent. Had *she* only chosen, no childless union could ever have been cheerier than theirs ; whilst, the first promptings of a natural jealousy once subdued, even the blameless episode with Madame Wesendonck might have shewn poor peevish Minna what a treasure of love she had spurned at her feet, and how she had only to stretch forth her hand, to gather it into her bosom,—for her husband's letters to her from *after* that episode should have melted any save a heart of stone. No : it certainly was not the fault of RICHARD Wagner, that this first marriage of his became more and more of a chastisement as years rolled on, till finally that year which might have seen the joyful celebration of a Silver Wedding, saw nothing but one forlorn attempt to re-establish a hearth the foundations of which had been sapped by the wife's own lack of sympathy long, long before those emotional events which led to abandonment of the Asyl near Zurich. In January 1866, just three weeks before Minna's sudden demise after a virtual separation of something like four years, Wagner tells his eldest surviving sister, Luise Brockhaus, that he has begun to write his private Memoirs, and already reached his one-and-twentieth year with them : " Down to that epoch in my life I have been able to employ a cheerful tone, even while recording my errors ; from that time forth (and this is still reserved for me !) my life becomes serious and bitter, and I'm afraid the cheerful tone will now forsake me,—my marriage looms ! Not a soul knows what I have suffered through that ! " How wise was his friend Pusinelli, the Dresden physician who had studied Minna's mental condition at close quarters, when he set his face against this ill-matched pair's reunion in 1859 (letter 194) ! With a wife who, after an absence of fifteen months, could suspect her husband of merely "studying his own convenience" in an itinerary thoughtfully drawn up for her journey to Paris in comfort (see pp. 596, 599), what hope was there of any further dwelling together in peace and concord? That one little trait is even more convincing than any of the big.

Let it not be presupposed, however, that these volumes constitute a chronicle of marital laments and reproaches ; only at rare intervals, thrown off his kindly guard by some particularly wounding "thrust" (*cf.* p. 692), does Richard Wagner lay his bosom bare : but then we see, as under an electric flash, the misery inflicted on a temperament so keenly sensitive by a wife who had next to no personal knowledge of "the feeling of true love" (*cf.* pp. 502, 715). I have already suggested that letter 172 should be read *first* of this whole collection : it gives an illuminating glimpse of their courtship and marriage, with its first fatal breach, in language whose every sentence bears the stamp of charitably-mitigated truth. Then let the reader take letter 3, and he will find the story briefly brought, in more attractive colours, down to the commencement of the Dresden period, when Minna suddenly shews restive-ness again, perhaps to be explained by fears for her own health. Letter 36, with which should be combined letter 28 of eight months earlier, will then carry the tale of domestic variance (under Natalie's malign influence now, be it said) down to the first year of exile, more than a twelvemonth *before* the Wesendoncks set foot in Zurich ; whilst letter 46—written at the time when the new-fledged plan of the RING DES NIBELUNGEN was under discussion on paper with Liszt and Uhlig, and *must* have been mooted by mouth to the wife, though it is conspicuous by its total absence from the Albisbrunn group—will shew that the same domestic opposition to all his views and projects, which had embittered the latter half of the Dresden period, is still rife at Zurich.

Letter 50, of July 1853, is matched by letter 71, of Sept. '54, and letters 82 and 90, April and May '55 (from London), with the same tale of doubt and suspicion in quite ordinary matters on Minna's part. Then we come to no. 104, with its revelation of such " eternal scoldings " between Minna and Nette, that Richard insists on the latter's departure,—a letter which should be taken in conjunction with no. 195, of three years later, when Minna actually proposes re-introducing that undesirable female into the household by bringing her to Paris, but luckily changes her unstable mind. The next landmark of importance, and indeed of such importance as to form a watershed, is supplied by letters 120 to 123 : a specific jealousy foretokened in no. 88, of three years previously, though meantime lulled to rest, has broken out at last in fullest fury ; and how entirely imbecile was Minna's handling of a very plausible weapon, is proved by no. 134, where her husband bids her "Be gentle, kind and patient ; you

can't believe what power it gives you over me. Your
tears and laments that last night in our house touched
me more than any argument." She had only to appeal
to his pity, and no more devoted husband could be
found on earth, as evidenced by the last two letters
in vol. I. ; but she could neither forgive nor forget,
except her own shortcomings, and behind the whole
remainder of the correspondence—her side of which we
can 'reconstitute' almost as though it lay before us,
especially with the aid of those few letters of hers
addressed to others which we do possess—there lurks
the spectre of that Asyl episode, ready at any moment
to scare away a patched-up peace. Thus when they
came together in Paris again, it was a foregone conclusion
that domestic concord would never last for long ; and
to what a terrible pitch the poison of unreasoning
jealousy still rankled in the woman's breast, is demon-
strated by that profoundly sad and eloquent epistle from
Vienna 1861, no. **217,** which at the same time supplies
the last possible word on Richard Wagner's relations with
Mathilde Wesendonck,—little though Minna allowed it
to pass as such, as will be seen from no. 247, of the
ensuing summer.

If letter 242 proves that even in the matter of choice
of residence the wife's social tastes were no longer
compatible with the husband's creative needs, our crucial
no. **248** attests that after her ill-fated flying visit to his
temporary retreat at Biebrich, end of winter 1861-2,
Wagner's farthest-sighted friend and Minna's doctor saw
still more plainly than himself that the breach had now

become irreparable. And yet it was not without another desperate effort, November 1862, between letters 260 and 261, the long-suffering husband finally convinced himself that even the spending of two nights beneath the same roof as his wife spelt ruin to his peace of mind henceforth, the devastation of his art. In the previous May he plaintively had told her : " My child, decidedly you have too few real cares, too little occupation, since you always find so much leisure to think of yourself and wrongs done or possibly still to be done you," and entreated her not to be " for ever upsetting the mind of your husband, who does not belong to you alone, but to his art, to the world and posterity " (pp. 736, 738) ; yet in December 1862, their brief Dresden meeting past, he again has to beg her : " Ah, good Minna, you really ought to take a little thought to make things lighter for me . ., but you abide by a constant illusion about me and my mode of life, from which nothing seems able to tear you " (p. 775) ; whilst in the ensuing month the conclusive situation is thus summed up in words impossible for any unbiassed reader not to countersign : " That you should always put the worst construction on what I do or leave undone, as also on my motives for it, is your misfortune ; I am used to it. But how you can dream of drawing me to you thereby, would be a marvel to anyone who did not know you " (p. 778).

There was one excuse for Minna ; only one. Richard Wagner repeatedly advances it, but nowhere more heroically than in that dreary Paris winter of his solitude when the signal fiasco of his French *Tannhäuser* had

been capped with a Viennese frustration of his certain
hopes of *Tristan*, and he was already engaged on the
poem for a "lighter, easier work," *Die Meistersinger*, to
mend his lot : "Allow me this time, surely, to excuse
your reprimand on the sole plea that you still are
ailing ; for which I profoundly pity you—and more
than you'll believe !" (p. 691). Her health—his
solicitude for which is testified even by the space it
fills up in my Index—had gone from bad to worse
in one direction, that of uncontrollable nerve-storms :
and really we can but infer that her reason had
begun to totter, when we see how often in the later
years she reads into his letters the diametric opposite
of their plain and obvious meaning.   And to be mated
with this poor wreck and wrecker, was the fate of
the genius who cries from that forsaken Paris winter :
"A quiet home-life ! !—nothing beyond on this earth !—
why should it not be granted me, of all men, who
need it so?" (see page 680) !—

I have thus drawn attention to the more tragic
passages and letters in our collection since they are
liable to be missed on a mere hasty perusal, buried as
they often are beneath a mass of business and domestic
details of great biographic, but far less psychologic or
intellectual interest than is furnished by most other
published volumes of the master's correspondence.   For,
in itself it is symptomatic of the recipient's mental
calibre, that her husband very rarely touches deeper
subjects than those concerning personal relations and

worldly fortunes in his letters to Minna. One by one, she had erected a pale round all such loftier or deeper topics, until we find him writing to Cornelius in that letter from which I quote on pages 714-5 : " My good will was so great, that I gladly resumed towards her that peculiarly simpering language one uses to a child, and listened with ostensible interest to things quite off my plane and often most distasteful to me." We see him constantly in search of things on *her* plane wherewith to fill those copious letters she manifestly grumbled at unless they brought the flattering tribute of uncommon length. Thus the gaiety exhibited is often forced, and we must be on our guard against taking too much in earnest many a remark merely meant as a joke. Yet there are two letters, seventeen years apart, nos. 16 and 205, in which the spontaneous overflow of joy is supremely moving, and in each of these instances the strongest note is one of wistful sorrow that the wife should not be at his side to share it. His *Flying Dutchman's* first performance in Berlin, his own first hearing of long-famous *Lohengrin*, are the occasions of these letters, which surely none can read with eye unmoistened or heart that does not leap out to their writer. Yes, reader, neglect awhile my previous admonition, and take *those* letters first.

A word in conclusion on the more technical aspect.

The German issue of the present collection, first published March last year, bears neither name of editor nor preface, neither elucidative notes nor index. One can understand the delicacy of feeling which prompted Wahnfried to so unusual a course, though the German publisher's prospectus had pre-announced the work as edited by Baron Hans von Wolzogen, and in fact the immediately succeeding issue of the *Bayreuther Blätter* (Spring 1908) contained a supplementary word of introduction by Wolzogen himself to its reprint of letter 36. From that supplement we learn this one material fact, and this alone, that "there are no more of these letters in the archive," in other words, that these are *all* the master's letters to Frau Minna at present possessed by his heirs. It is remarkable indeed, and to the world at large quite unexpected, that so great a number should have been procurable. However they may have passed into the Wahnfried strong-box, whether as a whole restored to Richard Wagner after Minna's death, or by instalments slowly gathered since his own, the fact that Minna preserved such cogent testimony without a self-protective weeding-out goes far to exalt her inmost character : it is as though she dimly foresaw the day when herself she might be instrumental in triumphantly clearing her husband's name from calumnies reposing on a false assumption of her "martyrdom."

But let me restrict my few remaining lines, as said, to technique. In sundry instances I have noted on the following pages their indications of letters still missing from the sequence. Those lacking at its latter end could scarcely add much to our fund of knowledge ; but those from the time of her first Soden cure (see p. 610), still more from the first three months of his expatriation, and most of all from the period before our collection so much as commences (e.g. from the month or so when he was in a Paris debtors' prison, or the time of her own escapade), would be a welcome addition, should the originals still exist. On the other hand we must remember that, except at the epochs represented by the main divisions into which this correspondence naturally falls, Richard and Minna were very little away from each other, even at the time of their courtship, and therefore no numerous accession is to be anticipated, though wellnigh the most interesting document of all, his final proposal of marriage, was actually seen some years ago by Mr. H. E. Krehbiel before its presumable plunge into the recesses of a secretive collector's portfolio. For those few truants we therefore may possess our souls in patience.

As to the German editing, with so conscientious a scholar as Hans von Wolzogen to attend to it, we may be sure that the infinitesimal number of dots represent all the omissions effected. Indeed, he might have gone a little farther in the case of a few particulars anent the operation of domestic medicines, which my publishers have preferred me to dot out between square brackets. Further, it would have been as well if the use of square brackets for editorial *additions* had been adopted in the German issue, from which that typographic artifice is absent. I merely refer to such obvious additions as a few non-original dates or the interpolation of a stray subsidiary word to complete the sense ; where the matter within curved brackets is, after all, not very apt to be confused with an author's own parentheses. Those curved brackets I have therefore deemed best to retain, even where their source was quite palpable, reserving the conventional squares for my own elucidations.

Finally, a remark on the mode of translation. It may seem a little incongruous, to find " Thy " etc. as signature to a letter whose main body abides by the accustomed " your " ; but—remembering what a point Wagner makes of his " Du " on page 90—I really could devise no other method of preserving the peculiar intimacy of tone, while avoiding the poetic flavour associated in our English tongue with the second person singular. Even if that discrepance should offend at first, experience has convinced me that the reader will scarcely notice it after a longer familiarity. A more burning question is that of the colloquial style I have deliberately aimed at ; my sole apology for which must be, that the diction of the originals for the most part is idiomatic and colloquial in the extreme, far more so than that of any other collection of the master's letters with which I am as yet acquainted.

And now it largely rests in the reader's own hands, whether the present volumes shall soon be supplemented by an English rendering of the delightful *Familienbriefe*, i.e. letters from Richard Wagner to his mother, sisters, nieces, and so on.

WM ASHTON ELLIS.

PRESTON PARK, *January* 1909.

CORRIGENDA

Page	6, line 13,	*for*	" Bechmann "	*read*	" Bochmann "
,,	14, ,, 19,	,,	" Strusse's "	,,	" Struwe's "
,,	36, 37 and 39, *passim*,	for	" Cornel "	,,	" Cornet "
,,	58, line 15,	,,	" Erner "	,,	" Exner "
,,	398, ,, 8,	,,	" Zcohinsky's "	,,	" Zschinsky's ".

Richard to Minna Wagner

1.

DRESDEN, *Thursday morning.*
[*July* 21, 1842.]

DEAR GOOD WIFE,

My opera [*Rienzi*] will be given *the end of September*—that is to say, about 12 days later than originally fixed.—I set this chief item of news at the top of my letter that you mayn't have to read far in uncertainty. Had I got here the commencement of this month, my opera would have been given as early as the end of August ; for—only fancy!—the Devrient, Tichatscheck and Reissiger have been back *three* weeks already, without the least thing being done. It is abominable! On the day of my arrival I did not catch Fischer till evening, at the theatre, and after I had looked at him, could lay no blame on *him*,—the poor man looks quite pinched and haggard, for his most strenuous activity has singly to make good the laziness of all the rest, to keep business even half going. Now the play-manager, Dittmarsch, has also been ill for some time, and poor Fischer has to stage-manage the Play as well.—To the point, however ! The mischief is that Tichatscheck goes to Salzburg for 12 days, not at the end of September—as we supposed—but at its *beginning :* in fact he starts the last of August. So it's quite impossible to bring my opera out *before* his journey. However, I have hit on the following plan, and it has met with everyone's approval :—We will begin the study of my opera *at once*, and if by the end of August we have got through with all the chamber-rehearsals, so that everybody is letter-perfect—*then* it won't much matter if Tichatscheck leaves us for 12 days. As soon as he gets back, we'll have another week of chamber-rehearsals, to rub off any rust ; then will come 8 days of stage rehearsals, so that the opera can be given about the 26th.of September, and there will be no more need of a break in its representations. Tichatscheck has begged me to give him a diligent coaching—the Devrient has declared her readiness for anything—and the only obstacle, as all agree, is Reissiger's sloth, which *I'll* soon remedy ! The rehearsals begin next week.—So much for my opera : they all say, " It's lucky you came ! "

I have put up here in the same house with your mother, and occupy a room vacated for me by the landlord's sister. They obliged me at once, only it has been impossible to find out what they want for it: " The merest trifle—make no bones about *that*—it would arrange itself," and so forth.—I don't fancy they'll be grasping.— The first night was awful—although very tired, I couldn't sleep a wink. Beds a mile high, in which I baked ; mice, watchmen—a general conspiracy ;—yesterday I was a complete wreck, but, for all that, neglected nothing. To-day I have to go to Reissiger at 10, to see to the parts being given out ! Just think !—the parts have been in the office a fortnight, for Reissiger to sign—and out of pure indolence the man hasn't arrived at it yet. I have taken steps to get them sent to him this morning ; then *I* shall be there, and he shall sign them in my presence. Then I'll go on to Lüttichau, to get every-thing confirmed—which will be rather melting work in my black clothes.

Naturally I have been unable to give a thought to our lodgings as yet ; I'll commence this afternoon, though. What is to be done with my good Mama, as things have turned, I hardly know :—please write me quickly what she thinks about it. Anyhow I will find her somewhere to alight, and try to get it in the same house as ourselves ; only—of course !—for an undetermined period. In any case, I'll write you both, the instant I have found an apartment.—

However, I must hurry up to get this letter off to-day, that you may not have to wait for news too long.—

I enclose a few lines for Dr. Ullrich :—How are things really going? Is the Mama out of bed yet? Grant God that her illness is over !——May you only not be short of money ! ——Write as soon as you can ; you know my address.—I found your parents quite well and cheerful—I gave your mother a thaler to lay out—as soon as it is spent, she's to tell me and I'll give her another.—

No doubt you have heard the awful tidings of the sad death of the poor Duke of Orleans ! Isn't it horrible ?—I couldn't help weeping for him.—

God grant us a better ending ! In the meantime, though, we'll live another brief half century in health and joy !—Farewell, my dear, dear wifie ! Heartiest love to my mother, and tell her everything. Farewell and don't forget

Thy
good HUBBIE.

Regards to Jette !
Regards to Türk !

2.

Monday,
DRESDEN, 25. *July,* 1842.

DEAR, DEAR MINNA,

Well? When are you coming? Everything is arranged, and luckily with time enough left to report to you at leisure. First for the apartments, then. — I've been fairly round the whole city, looked at 21 apartments, and found many among them that would have suited us quite well, but the cheapest were 20 thaler. That's how the new houses run : it is impossible for us to take rooms in one of them just yet, and besides, they offer us no convenience whatever in the way of kitchen and the like, but for the most part are merely arranged for the Deputies, who are assembling here now and make house-room very dear. So I considered it quite a stroke of luck, when I found at last the lodging I have taken. It lies on the Promenade, by what is called the Johannis-Allee, to the *right* of the Promenade if you go down the Seegasse from the Market, about 3 or 4 houses before the corner-house in which you say the Emil Devrients live. It is no new house, to be sure, two flights up, and the rooms a trifle low, but will do well enough : 5 windows looking on to the Promenade, 2 decent rooms with 2 windows apiece, and one with 1 ; quite nicely furnished, 2 beds with mattresses, etc. ; also use of a kitchen. The rent comes to 12 thr, it's true, but everyone advised me to close with it, as it would be impossible, they said, to get a lodging like it cheaper. What particularly determined me to take this abode, moreover, was that on the same floor there is another very *beautiful* lodging with sitting-room and bed-room, which is let to someone who doesn't take possession till the end of August ; consequently my mother can put up there for one or two weeks, as she pleases, and it will be left to her generosity what she pays, since the people can't well ask for rent, of course, when another person is already paying. She therefore will be let off cheap, and as she will scarcely remain a *whole* month at Dresden under present conditions, my opera not being given before the end of September, *this* kind of halting-place can only be what she would like.——That ends the apartments story ; rest assured I *couldn't* have managed better.

For the rest, my prospects here are looking brighter and brighter. My *personal* intervention seems to have really done my cause a heap of good. I really haven't time now to describe to you in *writing* all I've settled and put straight amid the shakiest circumstances ; only thus much : *all* are for me, and for a *speedy* production of my opera. Lortzing's *Casanova* (a little opera) was really to have been given first, with Tichatscheck to sing in it ; but he has asked Lüttichau to relieve him of the rôle, that he may study *Rienzi* the more diligently. Yesterday Koch told me that Tichatscheck had said to him that, if he could truly help my opera thereby, he possibly might decide on not leaving us for Salzburg at all !—

The Devrient seems extremely well disposed towards me. Yesterday I dined at [Ferd.] Heine's, who is attaching himself more cordially to me every day, and whom do you think he had invited ?—The *Devrient !*—She was in very good vein, and it was determined that right at the end of my opera (—where Adriano comes rushing in, to rescue Irene from the burning Capitol—) she shall gallop in on horseback—just fancy ! riding like a *man.*—That will raise a fine Halloh ! ! !—

Reissiger I have quite in my pocket—I've made him a present of my opera subject, the "*hohe Braut.*" When

I read it to him yesterday, he was beside himself, all fire and flame ; in return, he's to be nice and industrious !—

And now, my good, brave, charming wife, you're coming Thursday, aren't you ? Anyhow I shall wait for you outside the gate on Thursday—but in case you do not come till Friday, I herewith give you the address to which the coachman is to drive :

Waisenhausgasse, no. 5, *left side of the court,* that being the entrance from the *road.* I shall move in to-morrow afternoon, to get everything prepared for your and Mother's welcome.

With *money* I am provided : Luise came through here en route—as you know—and Bechmann, who was with her, offered me the money for next month straight off, to save him the bother [of sending it].—So that fell out exactly as I wished.—And so will everything, be sure of it !——For that matter, I was quite delighted with Luise, she said so many nice things about you.—But now for something dull. On my return home last evening from the theatre, I find an unfranked letter from *Paris*, which costs me 16 groschen. It was from Troupenas, asking me as amicably as possible for the arrangement [*Reine de Chypre ?*]. I fell to at once, and worked till midnight to get the arrangement finished. I am packing it now, and shall send it off at once through the Leipzig firm.—

Now grant God you all are quite well !—The Mama must have recovered by now, I should think ; may she be feeling quite brisk after this crisis !—

Arrive safe and sound, and give me due praise if I've done the right thing.—Farewell, my dear Wife, be good to me, and come full soon to

Thy

How's Türk ?   charming RICHEL.

Postscript. I had just sealed up this letter, dear Minna, when I received your own. I therefore am breaking it open again, to reply in haste to what you write me. It is *very disagreeable* to me, that you two won't come till Monday ; for, besides my longing for yourself, I have already hired the apartment for a quarter till the end of October. Notwithstanding that I can move in as early as tomorrow, I shall have no more to pay than if I entered on the 1st of August ; so I *don't lose* by it—still, it goes very much against my grain, for many reasons, to be left alone so long. Only don't alarm yourself about the lodgings ; I made the agreement in such a form that I believe I shall have to pay no rent before the end of October—when the quarter expires—for I said : " I will take the rooms till the end of October, and then pay you 36 thr." The people are in good circumstances, too, and won't be wanting money earlier. This was a prudent move of mine, as it will make it easier for us to pull along till the production of my opera.—If it's only Mother's *nervousness*, perhaps, do persuade her in my name rather to choose Thursday for travelling.—My God, what a mite of a journey ! and she shall find everything handy here. Do see if you can't coax Mother round. For the rest, *you're to remain in Dresden yourself*, you understand ? My prospects are *good !*

In great haste, as I must be off to Tichatscheck. Farewell ; see if you cannot come *soon !*

3.

Thursday, 9 *in the morning.*
DRESDEN, 28. *July* 1842.

BEST WIFE OF MINE,

I was just busied with my moving in yesterday, when I received your letter in the new apartments. It makes me very sad, to think you mean to leave me still alone so long ! Dear Minna, we absolutely ought not to be parted for long ; that I feel afresh once more, both deeply and sincerely. What you are to me, a whole capital of 70,000 inhabitants cannot replace. If I've no business on hand, I fret the more for being alone ; but when I have been tiring myself out all day long, and evening comes to find you not indoors, I take a violent dislike to all the home comforts so grateful to me otherwise, and what I find outside the house indeed is not in the position to compensate me for a single minute. I haven't yet quite understood one passage in your letter : you speak of a necessity for our being parted still longer, perhaps !—Where is that necessity ? When, to pursue my soaring plans and hopes (which you did not even share with me), in circumstances that might well have scared the stoutest-hearted man, I prepared to set out from Russia ; when amid perils of every kind I embarked at Pillau, to commence a fearfully uncertain journey that was to bring me to a still more doubtful goal—did you *then* speak of any necessity to leave me ? By God, I should have been obliged to agree with you then ! But it never entered your head. When storm and danger were at their greatest, when you saw a hideous death before you as reward for all the hardships you had shared with me, you simply begged me then to lock you faster in my arms, that we only might not sink into the deep *asunder !* When we were hovering on the brink of starvation in Paris, many an opportunity was offered *you* to save yourself : one word, and Frau v. Zech, who was so heartily fond of you, would have taken you with her to Gotha,—the Leplay herself, forgetting her stinginess for your sake, would have conducted you back to your home as her travelling-companion :—why did you not speak of a necessity *then* for us to part ? Look you, I could have found nothing to reply to you then. But now that I feel I have my future more and more in my own hands, I ask you, why are you talking now of this necessity ? Tell me, what makes you so faint-hearted ?——See, all is arranged for the best. Lodging and piano hire I have deferred to the end of October ;—till the production of my opera it is nothing but a question of our board, and we can defray that well enough with what I have still to receive. Consequently I shall be a burden on *no one* any longer, least of all on my family. So rid yourself of this anxiety ; for, were I really to run short of money, now I know that in the midst of strangers I'm a *stranger* here no longer : I have convinced myself I've won new friends here who merely fall short of my *old* as yet in that they haven't yet had time to prove their friendship. Really and truly, dear Minna, to me it looks as if I were of some account here ; this moment, for instance, I have obtained 200 thaler from the Devrient for Kietz. She is an artist, you see, and so are Kietz and I, and artists ought to have to do with none but one another : no *trader* ought to come between, or it leads to odious conflicts.

Enough ! I won't tell you much more, though I should have matter in plenty. At least you'll soon be coming, after all, so I'll save up everything for word of mouth !—

Till then, though, merely this :

How glad I am at your assuring me dear Mama's health is restored, except for a weakness in her feet :—as this weakness is a natural result in any case, one must make one's mind easy about it. As for her quarters here, things have altered a little ; it's a very fine place, true enough—only she will have to pay 2 Rthr a week, without bedding ; it couldn't be managed otherwise, and Mother will readily understand it too, when she gets here —so I have only taken it for a week, to begin with,—for I'm a little timid, you know, at this kind of commission. Anyhow, everything is ready, and all I cry to both of you, is Come, do come !—

As for yourself, dear child, everybody is asking after you with the warmest interest. They are all very fond of you, and I shall have a hard job with my convenient excuses if you refuse to call on them. Well, that will all arrange itself, and you shan't find me compelling you to anything.—

Be at ease about Ulrich : in your timidity you probably saw more than there was to see. I have written him exactly as we had agreed.

—Farewell. Father and Mother send love. Your mother keeps giving me too big helpings ; I'm terrified every time she serves up !

You shall pay for the lodging I have occupied till now —you'll soon settle it, whereas they beat about too much with me !—

Come soon ! Monday, Monday ! Ah, if only it were Monday now !

> You darling south-wind, blow still more !
> For my dear Minna my heart is sore !

Hearty greetings ! Adé, my good Wife,
                              Thy
                                   RICHARD.

When *will* they clear that cursed youngster out, that Matz ?—-
Türk ! Türk !

4.

DRESDEN, [*Friday*] 2. *June* 1843.

DEAREST, BEST WIFE OF MY HEART,

Though I shall write you again the day after tomorrow, to send you your allowance, I cannot refrain from heralding it with these few lines to-day. Our first letters must have crossed, and apparently we both received them at the same time. I found yours after an evening of adventures : At noon on Tuesday I suddenly received a command from the King, through Lord Steward v. Minkwitz, to arrange a little court-concert for Pillnitz posthaste ; remarkable to say, everything fitted in, everyone turned up, and so three carriage-loads of us started at 5 o'clock, Lipinski, Kummer and two others from the Kapelle for a quartet, Bielzizki and the Gentiluomo for songs. On our arrival at Pillnitz all the doors are nailed up, so to speak, not a flunkey knows anything about us ; we glare at one another, and the Gentiluomo begins to scold. Then Grand Marshal v. Reitzenstein is called on the scene ; he takes us at least into a room, and explains that a messenger had been despatched to countermand us, since the Grand Duchess Helene had not come to Pillnitz as invited, and consequently the whole Court had gone off to the Weinberg : the messenger must therefore have missed us. The Gentiluomo flew at the Grand Marshal so like a true comedian that we men sought to make ourselves scarce, and abandoned her to her fate ; she drove back to Dresden alone, whilst we went to the hotel to stave off hunger, where we amused ourselves quite well till half-past 10, and I really was glad of the opportunity of mingling with these leaders of the orchestra for once. Lipinski turned all fire and flame for me again ; with a quite heartily-meant embrace he made full amends for the wrong he had done me. So we drove home in the best of spirits, and there I found your letter, which I read in bed with great content. Yes, a letter like that does one real good ; for even the shade of sadness in it strictly reposes on nothing but love, and to love and be loved remains ever a boon, even when yearning has to enter the bargain. See, at least we no longer need yearn in dread for one another now ! Schlankelino will comfort himself soon enough, if only he gets on more intimate terms with the phantom Spook !—

The 3rd. That's just the way ! I have been obliged to suspend writing a whole day ; but you know it of old. Yesterday I had only got just so far with my letter as to be meaning to tell you how it happened that, against my immediate intention, I did not forthwith answer yours which so delighted me, when all manner of things intervened to withhold me once more. *Lindenau* called again, and the Rottorf, who greatly dislikes my being disturbed when at work, mistook the Premier Minister for a vagabond, and denied me to him ; the poor man had to depart, leaving behind him a couple of lines in which he begged me to call on him as soon as possible. The Rottorf was frightened out of her wits when she learnt that it had been the Minister ; whilst I had to dress and make off to him myself. He had shewn my composition to the King, and the latter had sat down to the piano at once, played it straight through, and expressed his great delight with it. This business [see no. 5] gives me heaps to do, however, a hundred jobs to get things properly together.

The day before yesterday I made a fine day for myself. After finishing my work, I went to dine at the Waldschlösschen alone, thence over the Hirsch through all sorts of woods and byways to the Ziegengrund, past

Loschewitz to Blasewitz, and from there to the cemetery, where I gave orders for the restoration of my father's grave. It will not cost very much, and in the autumn we'll plant a couple of trees, shall we not?

—If you could only see me in my lovely summer costume! It's a perfect joy; only I made a bad choice with the violet gloves, for when I pulled them off for the first time, and was pointing with my finger on the bill of fare, the waiter bounded back in horror, for my whole hand looked just like a gigantic violet, the gloves had shed their dye so.—I've also been to the collector with the lottery coupon, and to my delight got 10 thaler, 26 ngr, for it, the whole ticket having won 50 thr; a thing that always strikes one as a present. In fact I meant at first to send it you forthwith, to buy yourself a pretty summer mantilla at Teplitz; as it occurred to me, however, that you probably could do that better in *Prague*, just hear how I have roughly planned the thing! You will surely come and visit me for once? Very good: you shall come for our Grand Choral festival, the 7th of July—(unfortunately I shall be unable to belong to you much at that season, as you may well imagine: Worse luck, you must think!—) and once you're here, I'll manage to get leave, perhaps for a fortnight, then travel back with you to Teplitz. We'll do all the excursions there, and go to Prague; then I'll leave you at Teplitz again, and return to Dresden, whither you shall follow me for good the end of August. But in July we'll discuss it all between ourselves; isn't that right, you good Mienel?—Pebs shall go with us, too, to Prague; it will not cost too much to travel in a carriage by ourselves, which makes a journey twice as agreeable,—and thus we'll dispose of the lottery prize!— I've had no further

letters yet, excepting from the Heinefetter in the matter
you know of, and from the editor of the *Theaterchronik*,
sending me a number in which I'm highly praised as
Kapellmeister.   Kietz's letter to you I enclose ; you will
see that you may make your mind quite easy now, so I'll
write you nothing more about it.——

I've just had to make another break, to write a letter
to the Minister ; you have no idea the mass of things
there are to see to.   And when the unveiling affair
[statue to the late King] is over, I shall have to put on seven-
league boots for the Grand Choral festival ; as soon as
I've finished the composition, the rehearsals will come,
and so on.   Added to which I now have all the operas ;
to-day—for a variety—*Freischütz ! ! !*   When I have got
the composition done, too, I shall have to sacrifice my
beloved morning hours for 3 weeks long (—I now rise
regularly by 5 *at latest*—) since I perceive I must do
something for my health.   Consequently I have decided
to go through a complete course of waters at Strusse's ;
much against my will, as one has to be very strict
with it.

Otherwise I'm very well, thank God—the lassitude
also has left me, and I am fit and fresh.   If only you
may get so, too ; you know what I mean, so thoroughly
well that one may expect something of you again,—but
don't let Dr. Ullrich help you overmuch, lest it go with
you as with the countess !——

Well, dear child, Eisold has just brought me my pay,
tomorrow being Sunday ; so it is exactly a week to-day
since you left.—Herewith you therefore receive your
month's money ; if it doesn't last out, you know well
enough to whom to apply ; for *you* there will always be
money.   Deny yourself nothing, and make an excursion

off and on ;—they're all too far for *you* on foot, so drive in comfort.—Best love to the Mama. Jette was here the day before yesterday, to receive her " week's wages " ; she gave herself such airs that she couldn't speak for lisping.—Fürstenau buttonholed me yesterday, Hadn't I any orders for Teplitz ? *No :* said I, you may imagine why.—Last night there was a new farce at the Bad [summer theatre] ; I went out to it, and ran into your butcher—what's-his-name, on the Ziegelgasse, your parents' landlord :—he also is going to Teplitz to-day, and asked if he could take anything for me. Again I said *No !* Everybody seems going to Teplitz, only I can't possibly contrive it ; each holiday, church duty twice ; and then the rehearsals : it's shameful !—Now, write again soon, and tell me a thousand things, even if just as pell-mell as in this letter of mine ; I'm continually interrupted. Write me a whole quantity, for you already are writing well and as I like. No doubt you've shaken down a little better, and things are pleasing you again. How goes it with the tiny garden ?—You dear good Mienel, at Pillnitz and Loschwitz I kept thinking, " You're nearer again to that foolish Minel ; would you were with her quite ! "—

God preserve you ! Farewell, farewell ! Get well and cheerful ! You have reason for it, since everything around us stands well, and it is a great thing to be able to say that. A thousand kisses from
Thy
R<small>ICHARD</small>.

I have heard nothing more of Avenarius, and have no desire to go to Leipzig ! As soon as he's there again, I shall write him [our] orders about N., either to bring her with him in case the whole establishment is leaving

Paris toward autumn, or in the contrary event to hand her over to a railway-guard on my behalf. In either case I'll send him the money he has disbursed for me till now.—

5.

DRESDEN, 6. *June* 1843.

MY BEST, DEAREST MIENEL,

In spite of the greatest rush and uproar, in which I now find myself on account of tomorrow's festivity, I must bid you Good-day in all haste and tell you a scrap about myself. Only this moment has my room been vacated by all the military bandsmen I had to call together ; I'm curious about tomorrow's result, though it probably will be no very great shakes !

However, that's a minor matter. Besides wanting to thank you with all my heart for your dear good letter—which exactly crossed my own again—and to give you 43,000 kisses for it, I have particularly to tell you something which has been most agreeable to me. Yesterday the 5th, about 6 in the evening, I ask you, were you not thinking hard of Cassel?—For *my* part I could have thought of the Holländer production there only with the greatest uneasiness, if the Dettmer, who had just returned from Cassel, hadn't given me the most encouraging reports the day before. She had attended a stage-rehearsal, to wit, and told me that both the basses, Biberhofer as Dutchman and Föppel as Daland, had sung the first act in such style already that she would scarcely have recognised it for the same as here : Biberhofer has a glorious voice, she says, and is a very handsome man ; Föppel quite excellent, sturdy and brisk. A young and very pretty singer, a Mlle Eder, uncommonly popular there, sang the Senta with the greatest zeal, and kept ask-

ing how the Devrient took things. The orchestra already
went capitally, for Spohr was in love with this music and
had taken the greatest of pains. Everyone shewed the
greatest affection.—Now, isn't that highly encouraging?
The Dettmer could never bring her story to an end. The
whole place had been on tenterhooks for my arrival, as
it had got noised about that I was coming myself.—

The overture to Rienzi was played on the Brühl Terrace
yesterday ; I was among the crowd, and at the end of the
overture, which was very well executed, a regular Hurrah
went up : *Bravo! Bravo!*—One may hear it every day
now, sometimes on the Terrace, sometimes in the Grosser
Garten ;—a very good joke to me !

Lord, if tomorrow's affair were only over ; I've so
much to compose still, and time is pressing fearfully !
I must give up my contemplated spa-cure ; if I cannot
be very strict with it, and over-exert myself even a little,
it may do me more harm than good.—I'll see if I can't
get longer leave next month perhaps ; then I'll stay with
you at Teplitz, and we'll drink and promenade together.
That would be fine, would it not ?

Ach Jesus! I must go and dress now,—the Minister
etc. expect me at the Zwinger, which already is enclosed
to-day, to make an inspection of everything.—

Be content with this morsel to-day, little Wife of
my heart ! You shall shortly have news from me again ;
were I to keep waiting until I had plenty of time, it
would come off very seldom !—My good child, entertain
yourself well, build up your health, and stay fond of me.
Adieu, you dear, good chick !   Thy

Best greetings to the Mama.   RICHARD.
Pebs is not to bite Türk's legs.

6.

BEST MINEL,

A tiny report in hot haste!—Yesterday's fête went off very well, *my* chorus decidedly bearing off the victory over Mendelssohn's, which had no effect and remained unintelligible.—Lindenau confessed this to me to-day quite candidly, and assured me the whole Court was of the same opinion.—The Lord Steward has just conveyed me in the name of the King a

gold snuffbox,

very solid, with splendid embossing.—So—a *gold* snuffbox too, now—out of that you'll always have to take a pinch, however strong the tobacco, you good foolish, very best Minel, you!

You don't write me at all! What can be the meaning of it? Have you already struck up with another? Just wait, and you'll catch it!—

Full speed ahead for the Apostles [*Liebesmahl*] now! This evening we have *Norma*, with the Werthmüller,— the rubbish!—

Kindest regards to the Mama!—Pebs is to behave himself nicely, or I shan't shew him my gold snuffbox.

Adieu, you dear, dear, good Wife! I am ever and always near you with my whole full heart!

Thy

RICHARD.

7.

See, Minel of my heart, already I must write you again, for I've received something to-day of still more value than yesterday's snuffbox, namely a letter from *Spohr*, from Cassel, which really has made me extraordinarily happy. I'm going to send it to the musical journal at Leipzig at once, that extracts may be printed from it ; so I have hurriedly made a copy to send on to yourself, my dear wife. From this copy you may see what *great* good fortune came my way when just *this* opera fell into *such* hands for its production at a second theatre ! It has touched me to the quick ; everything seems to have combined to give *this* opera more admirably at Cassel than anywhere else. However, you will be able to judge that from the letter itself. Immediately I had received it, I dressed and called on Fischer, who was as pleased as a child, fell on my neck, and covered me with kisses, crying, " Just as it ought to be ! *Cassel* was the very place for *this* opera to be brought out next. What luck ! Good news ; it *is* good ! "—Then on to *Heine ;* the same tale there !—Yes, dear wife, it really is an extraordinary stroke of luck ; I'm too delighted—I don't know what I'd take from anyone for these good tidings ! ! Only, rejoice with me too, dance and shout ! have no more fear now ; everything is bound to go ; and even if it should go slowly—I'm marching with you toward a *glorious* future, no *tinsel* fortune, but solid and enduring !—

Now I must go and sound the alarm ! Laube is floored already by such successes, as they so flatly contradict his prophecies ! Forward, ever onward on my road !

Farewell, my angel, my good Wife ! Be glad and merry ; luck and Heaven are with us, you see !

Thy

RICHARD.

8.

DRESDEN, 14. *June* 1843.

MY DEAREST, BEST MIENEL,

I can't possibly tell you how sorry I am for your happening on such detestable weather for the start of your cure. Really it worries me daily and hourly, as often as I see it rain ; and as often as a friendly gleam of sunshine shews itself, I'm delighted for your sake. Put up with it, though, as best you can ! People who understand have assured me it would go on raining all this week, but *then* would come settled fine weather. God grant it !— Heartiest thanks for your letters.—I always receive them on my return home at night, for they are never delivered till between 6 and 7 o'clock, at which time I'm always occupied, with rare exceptions. I could well imagine you'd be glad, and I wrote back to Spohr that the only grief his letter had occasioned me was the impossibility of embracing you, dear wife, in my delight ! That we must defer for the nonce, but *what* a hug we'll give each other when the time comes !—With this Spohr, for that matter, I really have made a remarkable conquest ; all who know him, represent him as the coldest, brusquest and most inaccessible of men, one who gives everything strange the cold shoulder. My having won him over to this extent, and purely through my work, is accounted to me a great merit by everyone.—This fortunate result at Cassel lends me great advantages.—I have written to Küstner, Berlin, redemanding my original score, as I at least may presume that the *copy* is finished now ; for the rest, I informed him that this opera had now been given at Cassel with marked success, but proudly mentioned nothing further.—For that matter, all are coming to the opinion that it perhaps would be better if the

Holländer were given precedence at other places, because if people don't yet know the brilliant subject of *Rienzi*, the *Höllander* will interest more and whet their appetite, which *Rienzi* then will satisfy far better than the other way about. Well, I shall let things happen as God wills! As for the *unveiling* ceremony of the 7th inst., I'll merely add the following : I had over 200 singers for the festal choruses ; my composition was set quite simply for men's voices in four parts, without accompaniment, so that the tenors had a brilliant field. It was a windless day, and all sang with the greatest affection ; the effect was solemn and stirring. Mendelssohn's composition was quite another thing : brass instruments accompanied it, and " God save the King " was woven in ; the chorus sang *in unison* throughout, and moreover in the deep bass register, so that the tenors made no effect at all, and hardly could even join in : the result being, that at most points one heard nothing but the brass, scarcely anywhere the voices, and as it all sounded like " God save the King," nobody could make head or tail of it. With mine, on the contrary, almost every word was positively understood ; and the whole town speaks of my chorus alone, whilst Mendelssohn's gets nothing but a head-shake. That's the truth.—For the rest, the ceremony was really *very* brilliant, and I'll describe it to you circumstantially by mouth.—

Should you be fretting about my health, you'd be doing wrong : I'm brisk and well, my head is clear ; even my lower regions are behaving well again now, I hardly suffer at all from gripe. Nevertheless, I should like to take a cure with you.—The nuisance is, that this bad weather often debars me from my walks now. I have a deal to do ; when I've no opera, there's some shindy or other with the Liedertafel. My composition is all but finished now, and I count on a great, an inspiring effect for it.

The day before yesterday the King commanded me to the *Bastei*, with a few singers and bandsmen ; luckily the weather turned out so bad, that the party was put off again.—Tomorrow is the feast of *Corpus Christi*, and I must conduct at church in *uniform*, as it is the highest of saint's-days and every one appears in *gala*. We had never given that a thought.—

Our operas are going excellently, and since for *my own* part I'm holding next to no rehearsals now [after Lipinski's protest—see *Life* ii, 21] the band is perfectly amazed at my aplomb, as with the *Stumme*, besides thanking me for saving it trouble.

The other day I dined at Flemming's.—Yesterday we, the Heines, Tichatscheck, and so on, were at the Wüst's, who had much exerted herself for her dinner-party. For that matter, her health's in a very bad way ; at any moment she cannot sing, and all believe she won't be able to much longer. They speak of—consumption of the windpipe : isn't that dreadful !—Lüttichau, for another thing, is expected back very soon ; I am thoroughly glad of it, for sake of my leave too.

And now I must conclude, as we have a rehearsal. Reconcile yourself to the bad weather with the thought that it's bound to improve soon !—If you remark any sort of progress in your health, you may easily imagine how happy it will make me ! Do everything for it, and write me in plenty of time if money runs short, do you hear !— Farewell, my dear good Wife ! Take my thanks for your love, and rest assured of mine for ever !

Thy RICHARD.

Kindest regards to the Mama.

Don't you despise my *snuffbox*! People value it at about 100 thaler—particularly the work.—

9.

My very best Mienel,

A great confusion has arisen, and I'm sorry to say, it hasn't even yet resolved itself into my being able to report to you duly to-day. I received a note from *Cecilie*, to wit, telling me that N. was leaving Paris the 12th of this month, and would travel to Dresden without any halt. This piece of news so plumped upon me that there naturally was nothing else to do than fold my hands till N. arrived here. Two evenings running has your father been to the railway to receive N., and I instructed Jette to come and tell me at 7 this morning in case N. came last night, so that I might inform you at once ; only—the person who doesn't appear to have come is my N., since *Jette* hasn't shewn her face yet—and now it's half past 8. We needn't grow uneasy, all the same, for I can only suppose that N.'s departure from Paris has been delayed a little—and that no doubt will prove to be so. As soon as N. arrives, she is to have a day's rest at the old man's, and then I shall give her a few thaler to go on with, also a letter, and despatch her to Lotte at Zwickau per post :—that will be right, will it not? After your return, you know, you can go and see her there.

For the rest, though cordially enough, Cecilie writes rather touchily—and—perhaps she's not quite wrong.— I enclose you her couple of lines.

Avenarius wrote me, before leaving Leipzig, that he would no longer be able to come to Dresden : if I had anything more to say to him, would I put it in writing. So I just forwarded him his out-of-pockets, and there's an end !

After another talk with Frau Wächter, I have just engaged the maid-servant. She is contented with all your conditions ; I gave her a thaler as earnest, and she will put in her appearance a week before Michaelmas.

—The fine weather now set in has heartily delighted me for your sake. You will go for good walks now, no doubt, and help Peps hunt for bones !—Your last letter, my good child, I read at 2 on Sunday morning ! ! Just fancy ! After rising at 4 on Saturday again, to finish my big composition, about 8 I received orders to beat up singers and horn-players for an excursion to the Bastei with the Court. Everything went right ; at Pillnitz, dinner with the Court ; back again there from the Bastei by water, now singing, now blowing. The King was as pleased as Punch,—but it was nearly 2 before we got home again !—

Then I found your letter, and read it with the greatest joy—but I was so fatigued that it was not until I rose that I discovered I had gone to bed in my cravat and stick-up collar.—

That old donkey, Reissiger, has just interrupted me— and now I must dress for the rehearsal of *Sonnambula.*

—As I shall probably be writing you again by next post, about N., I'll conclude for to-day, and salute and kiss you, my dear wife, from my whole, whole heart !— The time when we shall meet again is drawing ever nearer—how happy we shall be !—

Best love, and keep good to me !

Thy

RICHARD.

I had almost forgotten it. My mother is coming to Teplitz on Thursday, and begs you to order her old room, or the next one, at the Blue Angel, also a bedroom at the back for the servant and Kläre's children (—who are coming with her) ; it wasn't to cost more than 4 thaler a week !

Do *me* the kindness of attending to it.

10.

DRESDEN, 30. *June* 1843.

MY VERY BEST MINEL,

Best thanks for your dear letters. Your quite unwonted writing-fit is proof to me what heartfelt love can bring to pass. For my part, I finished my instrumentation also yesterday, and to-day at least may take a rest from writing ! Last Tuesday I rehearsed the vocal part of my new composition for the first time : already it went better than I expected ; immediately it had been sung through once, a general outburst of enthusiasm among the 200 singers present found vent in prolonged applause. We rehearse in a large hall in the Brühl Garden, so several of us went off to the restaurant to take a little something after the rehearsal ; upon my entry I was greeted by the Peace chorus from Rienzi, performed by the band : when it was over, the whole audience applauded quite alarmingly ; then I learnt that it had just been played a third time by desire. Directly after, they played the overture to Rienzi again, now hackneyed every day, and from all sides there went up the same hurrah. Hartung afterwards told me, he had got up this overture to his own misfortune, for it killed his people through continually being asked for ; thus it had just been redemanded for the third time.—

I shan't go out at all to-day, but take a rest ; for I'm
quite knocked up and my nerves are very agitated, in
spite of my looking so *stout* and *fat* as you are always
told. But that comes of this respectable life, you see, of
no-excess, of going " to bed at 10, often in fact as early
as half-past 9.''—At any rate my constitution must be
fairly tough now, or I couldn't keep going with my nerves
in this excited state ; even when I'm quite done up
through some over-exertion, precisely through my sound
constitution I rapidly recover.——

The *Cassel* operatic regisseur has been here ; he told
me a lot, and had never done impressing on me *what* it
meant for my Holländer to have been received still more
warmly on its second performance, since the Cassel public
was fully 5 times colder than the Dresden, for instance.
Spohr, too, has written me again very cordially, indeed
affectionately, and informed me of the fresh success.—*Lüttichau* is taking *Cassel* en route, and arrives here the 5th.—

Enough of myself for to-day ; now for you ! At
yesterday's rehearsal a singer brought me compliments
from Dr. Ullrich, who sent word you were getting on
very well. Exactly what you had written me yourself.
See, that delights me more than anything !—

It likewise is a great delight to me that you mean to
arrive by the 4th, and suits me in every respect ; though
in no event could you have heard the general rehearsal
before the 6th, at 8 in the morning.—I hope to be able to
come and meet you, and am looking forward as a god to
finding you quite well again !—I have no anxiety about my
leave, as I fancy Lüttichau will now begin to shew some
true consideration for me.—That's my opinion, and if at
last we have really good weather into the bargain, I think
we may enjoy ourselves nicely for once !—

All your orders shall be obeyed, and I've forwarded the letter to Lotte.—But it has just struck 9, and it's high time this letter went off to the post, if *it's* to catch it too. God preserve you, and keep you in health ! Give my best regards to all, and hold me dear until we meet again ! Perhaps I shall be writing once again, before ; for certain, I am always thinking of you ! Farewell, my good Wife,
Thy
RICHARD.

11.

DRESDEN, 1. *July* 1843.

MY VERY BEST WIFE,

I have just received the accompanying letters to yourself as enclosure to a couple of lines from Tröger ; they must have been posted before Tröger received your last letter, which I despatched at once, however. They still speak of nothing but silver, and I do not even yet know if the watch is also there ; but that, no doubt, will soon transpire.—This moment it occurs to me that you won't get this letter till Monday, and as you'll be here yourself by Tuesday evening, you would receive the enclosures time enough if I kept them to give to you here. But why so stingy, when I can take this opportunity of breathing a few hearty words to assure you how fond I am of you, and how much I'm looking forward to your speedy advent ?—

I haven't arrived yet at writing to Cecilie, so I shall postpone it altogether now until after the Choral festival. Before then I should like to have ended another job, which I didn't want to put off any longer, namely the reduction of Rienzi to one evening ; I have made a beginning already, and expect to finish it in a few days. It will be well, you see—in case I do obtain my leave, as I hope—

to have everything behind me, so as to be able to devote all my attention to my *new* opera [*Tannhäuser*].

Now I shall soon be able to convince myself whether you're really so well and jolly as I am assured ! So you will get here on *Tuesday* the 4th ? That's fine !—Everything is prepared, and most longingly awaits you.

Thy
RICHARD.

12.

DRESDEN, 12. *July, afternoon.*
1843.

Mienel, Mienel, I've *got my leave !* I really must say I've been very pleased with Lüttichau again, and especially with his whole manner of treating me.—At first, when I spoke up for the singer that cur . . d Mme Könneritz had recommended so, there was nothing to be done with him at all—he was a perfect goat ;—but when I began about myself, and asked if I might entertain any hope of doing something for my health this summer, his face simply beamed, and with the utmost graciousness said he : "Dear Wagner, you know how fond I am of you, and therefore can easily imagine that your health is of even more account to me than the benefit you are to the institute committed to me. People like yourself must be kept in good spirits and health before all things, so merely tell me, From when do you wish to be free?" "From the middle of this month," said I—"And for how long ?"— "Until the middle of next month again "— "Good ! Just dispose of your time at your pleasure !" etc. That completely touched me, and I didn't disguise it from him :—for you must remember, there's *very much* to do just now—two new operas to be got up with Moriani in a jiffy.—

So I'm coming, my chick ! Only I shall be unable
to come before Monday or Tuesday next week. Firstly,
I want to conduct yesterday's opera once more,—then I'm
invited to Lüttichau's for Sunday ; and lastly, my Rienzi
scribbling won't be finished earlier, and I do so want to
have everything done and behind me, to be able to lead
as careless a life with you as if there were nothing in all
the world to weigh us down. Indeed I'm looking forward
to it *very*, *very much*—to ease and repose after labours
ended, and strengthening for fresh.—
    I hope you got back comfortably to Teplitz. Poor
woman, you are certain to be having no good day to-day,
through the news [death of Minna's brother] you had to bring
the Mama !—Nor can I possibly tell you how grieved I
was in general for you here ! Make up for it all well
now, through rest and comfort in the way you live. See,
to-day's tidings must surely cheer you up again, for they
prove how well I stand here, and with what distinction
I'm treated.
    Now, goodbye for to-day. Heartiest love to good
Kläre, and console your Mama to the best of your
power !—
    I shall write you again the exact date of my coming.
Till then, my dear brave wife, fare as well as you can,
and fondly remember

Thy
RICHARD.

13.

DRESDEN, 16. *July* 1843.

DEAREST MIENEL,
    In all haste I must tell you my intense surprise
at your not having yet written me at all ! Say, are you

cross with me, perhaps? Have I done anything to you? Or—are you unwell?—You make me most uneasy!—

Then I also wanted to tell you, I cannot get away from here till *Wednesday*,—I have to conduct once more on *Tuesday:* also the *Rienzi* scribbling won't be done before.—So I shall come in any case on Wednesday evening:—dress Peps in his best, and build the archlet of triumph. Do you hear?—*Wednesday!* I have leave then till the 15th August.

There was a very fine article on my "Liebesmahl" in the Leipziger Zeitung.—

I must send this letter off at once, or it won't leave till tomorrow.—

Adieu, Wife of my heart! Get well and cheerful! There'll soon be altogether with you, heart and body,

Thy

Best love!   RICHARD.

14.
BERLIN, 4. *January* 1844.

MY VERY BEST MIENEL,

I feel sure this letter will still find you, which it really oughtn't to have, had you complied with my wish and left Dresden by Thursday morning [same date]. So listen, dear Child—I'm all right, and have already taken various steps to-day, though I didn't reach my hotel till getting on for 3 in the afternoon. In any event you must come now, for my opera [*Holländer*] is not to be till *Sunday*, instead of Saturday,—it was all a mistake of the secretary's, who wrote "6th" in mere error for "7th." As a fact, it suits me better, for I shall be present at *three* grand stage-rehearsals this way: there have already been *four* band-rehearsals, and Küstner has assured me the opera was already going very well. Tomorrow, accordingly, I shall listen and not conduct ; but if the conductor doesn't satisfy me, on *Friday* and *Saturday* I shall hold the rehearsals myself. From the band's side I've been told fine things already by Conzertmeister Ganz.—Meyerbeer also returned here yesterday ; I haven't succeeded in catching him yet ; shall try again at 8 tomorrow morning. He may be of great service to me, after all—particularly with the King.

So listen, dear infant ! It's no good your objecting any more :—you shall still see *Rienzi* at Dresden on *Friday*—if it really comes off ; but, *Saturday* morning you must just arise at half past 4, get to the station at half past five—or half past 6, I'm not sure which—and travel direct in one day to Berlin, where you'll put up at the *Hôtel de Russie* with me ;—I have settled everything about the room already. If there is a *human possibility*, I shall meet you myself at the station ; if not—merely ask for the *Hôtel de Russie's carriage*, which will drive you to me ;—but I shall be there myself in any case.

So—I expect you *for certain*. Don't go and spoil my great delight !—I have the best hopes of success for my opera. It must have made a hit even at the rehearsals, to judge by Küstner's smirking face.—

Na—you're coming, aren't you ? !—

Kindest regards to the good assistant [August Roeckel] and Tichatscheck.—Tell Fischer I couldn't get back before *Tuesday* or *Wednesday* :—ought I to write as much to Lüttichau ? Perhaps not ! Farewell. Greetings and kisses from the whole heart of

Thy

faithful, fond, good

RICHEL.

15.

DEAR MINNA,

You have no idea how sad you made me yesterday through not coming ; and now I have just returned from the railway again, where I went to await you a second time—and *again* you hadn't come !—Now I find your letter [waiting for me] and see that I'm right, after all, in being a little *quick* in everything : something really comes off with it ; whilst *hesitation* leads to *nothing.*— Get along, I'm very cross with you. If there were any chance of this letter reaching you by *midday Monday*, I should just have one more try, — namely, to induce you to take the express to *Jüterbock* on Monday evening and get here Tuesday noon. For Tuesday is my opera's *second* performance, which I've been pressingly invited to conduct as well. I have held the two full rehearsals myself, and also am to conduct this evening ; the representation will go *very well*, Bötticher, Ziesche and Mantius are *excellent ;* in spite of the house's smallness, you wouldn't recognise the machinery again, after Dresden :— I am expecting a good success—God grant it !—I shall write to Lüttichau tomorrow morning, [that] I cannot return before Thursday noon !—

Amend your ways !—I'm very cross with you, because I'm much too fond of you and miss you too unwillingly !

Kind regards to the assistant !

Farewell !

Thy RICHARD.

16.

God knows whether you will receive this letter, dear Minna, or whether you really did receive my yesterday's in time to start for here. Anyhow I'm writing, since I want to have a chat with you that way at least. Yesterday I did not get to bed till after midnight, and at 5 this morning I had lights brought and the stove lit, as I couldn't lie sleepless any longer. Had *you* been here, you see, we should have sat up chattering the whole night through,—but there was only me !

Lord, what doesn't one experience on such an evening as this last ; what hasn't my mind gone through again ! It was one of the most critical nights for me !—Just think, —with this fantastic opera, completely off the beaten track, and offering from the outset so little that is grateful or attractive, I was making my bow before a public *entirely strange* to me ! I felt that keenly : in all this audience there wasn't a single personal friend of mine, not a soul prepossessed in my favour,—everybody sitting in ordinary cold curiosity, thinking : H'm, what sort of a thing will it be, this Flying Dutchman ?—After the overture, not a hand stirs ; the melancholy first act is listened to with strained and wondering attention, without any one knowing which way to take it ; with difficulty is the singer a little rewarded here and there ;—in short, I grow aware of my position— but don't despair, for I see that the representation itself is going extraordinarily well. The second act commences, and I gradually convince myself that my aim is attained : I have cast a spell about the audience, and the first act has attuned it to a key which makes it capable of follow- ing me whithersoever I will. The interest increases, suspense is changed to agitation, exaltation—enthusiasm ; and before the curtain falls a second time, I celebrate a triumph such as certainly but few have reaped. Never, not even at Dresden with *Rienzi*, have I seen or heard such a prolonged outburst of enthusiasm as that which followed the curtain's fall here :—one could see and hear that among the whole assembly, high and low, prince, lord and beggar, there was not a single person who didn't cheer like mad. And when at last I appeared with the singers, you would have thought the house was coming down !—

So I had an easy job with the last act : the scenery went as excellently as its effect ; everything was sung and acted very briskly, and came to a surprisingly rapid close, which itself was represented very well. Long ere the curtain fell the tumult broke loose afresh, and it roared for an eternity before I could thread my way out from the orchestra and come forward with the singers, who were waiting for me once more.—In brief, my dear wife, I have scored a remarkable triumph : those alone can judge the extraordinary and unprecedented nature of my victory here, who are in a position to weigh exactly all the circumstances, the present state of our operas, the complete and startling variance of my departure in this Holländer.—

The representation was entrancingly fine ;—all sang and acted like gods—I could have eaten them ;—the Marx quite turned my head : if there was anyone I expected little from, it was she—and how she cheated and surpassed my expectations ! I'll say no more to you, than—insane as it sounds—the Devrient will have to look to her laurels.—The only opportunity I had of letting off a little steam after the performance, was supplied me by the Devrient. She had sent for me some hours before the theatre,—I called, and found her with her lover ; you know what she is, but for all her unconventionality she greatly cheered me by her sympathy. After the performance I spent another hour with her ; she had suffered and rejoiced with me, and was highly pleased with the success. Then, when I got back to my hotel, the landlord received me with a congratulation : his guests had sounded the alarm already, and trumpeted their enthusiasm.—How I wish you had been there ! ! Nay, don't you think I need be cross with you ?—I sat up in bed all night alone, and babbled to myself. I'm to dine at Meyerbeer's to-day, at Küstner's tomorrow. I haven't seen Meyerbeer yet since the performance. The King was present, and somebody who kept his eyes on him assured me it pleased him uncommonly. Mendelssohn, at whose table I have also been once, quite made me glad :—after the performance he came on the stage, embraced me, and congratulated me very cordially.—

I am writing to Lüttichau by the same post, [that] I shall reach Dresden on Thursday.

Adieu, you horrid Wifie ! If I'm cross with you, don't .let that make you cross with me ; it's all because I'm so fond of you !—

Kind regards to the assistant. Farewell ; I shall soon be back with you.

Thy RICHARD.

Address :
    Ihrer Wohlgeboren
      Madame
        MINNA WAGNER
          Ostra-Allee Nr. 6 in Dresden.

Should Madame Wagner be away, this letter is to be delivered to Königl. Musikdirektor, Herr Röckel, who is authorised to open it.

17.

HAMBURG, *the 15th March* 1844.

MY GOOD DEAR MIENEL,

My earliest occupation here, after half sleeping off my journey, is to write to you. I've been prattling with you all the time, even when I awoke last night and wanted to set my travel-heated blood in order by a strong effervescent powder ; I had no candle, and meant to *feel* out the inscription on the different packets : it was unnecessary, though, since you prudently had made them up of different sizes, so that I could recognise your forethought even in the dark. In the morning I at once began my usual chat from bed with you and Peps, to pretend I still was with you. It's *nicer* at home, however ! ! ! And all things considered, the Devil take our quitting one another !—

I had good luck with my journey's connections : at Leipzig I caught the Magdeburg, at Magdeburg the Brunswick train ; from Brunswick per the evening mail at 9 direct to Hamburg, which I reached yesterday, Thursday, at 7 P.M. Fatigued I was, and all to pieces, particularly through what I suffered in the crowded diligence, where any stretching of one's legs was not to be thought of, so that at last they not merely hummed, but almost howled. Arrived at my inn, I had a good rest, and simply sent for Cornel. He came, had forty minutes' talk with me, then left me alone and to sleep. All's well, dear child ; it was a particular relief to Cornel that I didn't arrive on a *Friday*. To-day we shall merely discuss and arrange this and that ; tomorrow, Saturday, will come the first stage-rehearsal, Thursday 21st the first performance, and Sunday the second, so that I can leave again on Monday and be back with you by Tuesday evening. They've already been rehearsing with the orchestra ; and the bandsmen too, so Cornel says, are all fire and flame for the thing. In short, he counts upon an unusual success ; which God grant !

I shall chiefly pass to-day with Krebs and Cornel, and so find my way about. —I know of nothing else here yet to write you of.—

The brief glimpse I had of Magdeburg made a great impression on me ;—the railway comes straight to the rampart where we so often took our hopeless promenades in times of becalming. Lord, when I think of that rag-fair ! For that, it's nearly 10 years now, since we two first came together there, we ancient love-birds !— Have you slept in my bed ? In thought I lay both nights in yours : had you fumbled, perhaps you'd have found me in it,—if Peps didn't get there before me.

Na, greet my friends, hold me dear, and take good care the children [imaginary] don't throw the bed-clothes off at night ! Farewell, you good old sweetheart, be of good cheer, and reflect that not everything in the world is as bad as this villainous pen which the waiter has brought me ! Adieu, Mienel ; many, many kisses from

Thy
RICHARD.

Oh, be so good as to beg Pusinelli, in my name, to send Concertmeister David of Leipzig a textbook of my oratorio too, that one may be printed in accordance there.

18.

HAMBURG, 22. March 1844.

Na, Mienel, Rienzi came yesterday and triumphed anew. It really is no trifle, to give the opera so that it makes a furore without a true Rienzi. After the first act such frantic applause still continued long after the music had ceased, that, having bowed already several times from the conductor's desk and then left it, I was obliged to return there to acknowledge yet another salvo. Then with the second act the greatest tumult broke loose, and after I had likewise made my obeisances from the orchestra, I had to appear upon the stage as well, where I again was received with an unspeakable Hurrah. After the 3rd act, which had a great effect here, the same proceedings as after the 2nd : I had to appear again. The 4th act had the same effect as its first time at Dresden ; after the 5th I was called again with jubilation.

—That will do for you, on the outer success ! I cannot comprehend to-day, how a success of this extent was possible without Tichatscheck. With Wurda, I may say I triumphed purely through the thing itself, since he wasn't a patch upon Tichatscheck, although he sang portions quite well ; but the whole fellow is shockingly *wooden!* How many thousand times I muttered, "Heavenly Father, had I only my Tichatscheck here ! "—The more unequal to it Wurda was, however, the greater the true honour to me, and I confess I'm rather proud of it. All the rest was very well sung for the most part, with exception of the *Envoy of Peace*, who was very dozy. The choruses went excellently, and the most enraptured of all were the bandsmen and singers themselves ; which is a very good token of lasting. *Adriano*, as I expected, was capital ; the two demagogues—excellent ! The stage arrangements were still a little shaky, though much was mounted very well, some things decidedly better than at Dresden, especially the ballet. Confusion still prevailed in the processions, off and on : no great mischief, however, since the general effect was capital.—I could desire nothing more, than to see the jubilation if Tichatscheck gives the Rienzi here !

—I'm a wee bit run down, my good Mienel, as you may easily imagine, but feel well here on the whole.— Now you have heard the main thing, tell my friends ! Cornel reckons on upwards of 20 Rienzi performances this year ; the *tantièmes* will be a relish, won't they ?— So *Sunday*, if no one falls ill, will be our second performance ; then I shall depart on Monday morning, and, God willing, be with you at Dresden *Tuesday* evening by the last train, and embrace and kiss you to our hearts' content.

The thing is going, good Wife, the ship speeding full sail.

May this letter find you well and hearty ! Adieu, for the present ; I shall be with you on *Tuesday* evening.

Thy
RICHARD.

19.

BERLIN, 10. *December* 1845.
Wednesday morning, 9 *o'clock*.

MY DEAR MIENEL,

It is the third day since I left you, and things have gone quite well with me ; how do they stand with yourself ?—God grant you no less passable a frame of mind than mine is now, for which I'm very simply indebted to an extraordinarily successful clearance which set in on my journey. Good Lord, on what things our inner and outer life often depends, when one observes it closer ! !—

I've hit off everything most happily, till now : Monday I saw the Stumme [*Masaniello*] at Leipzig, and Tuesday *Don Juan* with the Lind at Berlin. Could things have

fitted better ?—On Monday, after being thrown from the
arms of one relation to another, with one or other of them
running after me everywhere, I had to dine at Luise's,
and go to Cecilie's after the theatre ; all the rest were also
there each time, the Laubes too.   Lord, how pitiful I
thought the Leipzig theatre !   One will never do much
with its tenor ; a disgusting stick !   On the other hand,
Schmidt has already booked my *Holländer* for February ;
and that, at any rate, they should be able to give capitally :
I saw Kindermann as Pietro in the Stumme, and am very,
very pleased with the man—he has *everything* for the
Dutchman.

So my Leipzig affairs were soon settled, and to my
satisfaction ; the Berlin won't commence till to-day, as I
couldn't undertake anything yesterday.   I did not arrive till
getting on for 2 : had dinner, a wash and brush up, secured
a ticket for that evening's theatre, and had only just time
to call upon the Frommann, who is living with a well-to-
do lady in very fine style.   The Frommann could tell me
nothing of consequence regarding my affairs ; I'm to dine
with her to-day, however—that is to say, at her friend's—
and Professor Werder will be there, also the young *Göthe.*

At Don Juan I was terribly bored : Donna Anna,
moreover, isn't held to be the *Lind's* best part ; she sang
the last aria extraordinarily beautifully, for the first act she
lacks very much.   She has a curious pensive individuality,
which interests one much in itself, but cannot rise to a
great dramatic portrayal.   In the first act the Devrient
is incomparably more affecting.   But there : I can't
record my verdict on the Lind so briefly, and therefore
save it up.   All the rest were wooden, as we have got
accustomed to in Don Giovanni everywhere.   The
auditorium of the new Opera-house pleased me exceed-

ingly ; beyond question it is superior to our Dresden one ;
i.e. more roomy, not so low, nor with such a dead
acoustic.

Now, after passably sleeping it off last night (—it was
half past one before I got to bed at Leipzig, and I had to
be up again at 5—), I intend, God willing, to make a start
with my affairs to-day. I shall go to *Redern* in the first
place. Together with the result of my endeavours I then
shall also let you know the date of my return. Until
then, my ducky, fare as well as you can ! Best
love and kisses ! Hold me dear, as I you, and only
open up again ! Regards to our people, and farewell,
well !

Thy
RICHARD.

20.

BERLIN, Friday morning, 1845.

My dear good Wife, I'm simply longing to be home
again ; God only grant I may find all safe and sound !

My affairs here are ended for the present, and I'm
really only staying on to-day to see the Lind in Norma
and at last redeem my promise to spend an hour with the
Frommann and Professor Werder. Tomorrow, Saturday,
I go to Leipzig, where Hermann has arranged a little
party in my honour ; and at 11 on *Sunday* forenoon—
if God doesn't dispose of me otherwise—I shall be at
Dresden, with you !

Not to leave you in the dark till my arrival, my
dicky-bird, I'll tell you briefly the result of my endeavours :—

1. Küstner wants to give my *Rienzi* in September
next.

2. Count Redern wants the King to give me the commission to compose my next new opera for *Berlin*. To produce one of my operas here between now and Easter, is impossible, as I have *convinced* myself.

Redern, at whose house I dined in brilliant company last Wednesday (instead of at the Frommann's, to whom I therefore had to send regrets—), wished to arrange for me to read my new opera-text [*Lohengrin*] to the King himself. For that, however, I should have needed to remain here *all next week* at least, since the King left yesterday with Redern etc. for the chase, whence they do not return before Monday.

Mme Meyerbeer, who surprised me by great cordiality and interest, considers Redern's plan, that I should get Royal orders from Berlin for my next opera, the best of all ; her husband returns at Christmas, when everything is to be set to rights. If *Rienzi* can still be brought out in the interim, so much the better : Küstner has pledged me his word of honour, and struck hands on it ; but whether Küstner himself will still be Intendant after Easter, is very doubtful.—

I'm merely telling you the most important news ; much else by mouth ! Now grant God I find you safe and sound !

Farewell, my good Minna ! to our speedy reunion !

Thy

RICHARD.

21.

BERLIN, *Monday*, 20. *Septbr* 1847.

Well, my good old Minna, another greeting to you before I start my Berlin day's-work ! I feel quite lonely, and have a talk with you at every season of the day,

also dreamed of you both nights. How are you getting on? Are you thinking of me, or must Papo first
remind you?

I'm not quite straight with my abode yet : owing to
Werder's having stipulated that I should only be bound
for a week, the landlord went and let the rooms engaged
for me, along with others, to a family that turned up
afterwards and wanted the whole for a longer term.
However, I'm to have two other rooms this evening that
after all aren't bad ; only, I have the inconvenience of
not being able to unpack before I'm settled in my proper
quarters.—

Yesterday I dined at Meinhardt's hotel, where I happened on Pfister,—Stawinsky, too, is usually there. The
landlord seems to want to take no payment,—all the
better—I pocket the damage!—This Pfister is swimming
in rapture and enthusiasm about his part, and behaved
uncommonly modestly to me :—If I would take him in
hand and instruct him thoroughly, said he, I might make
his fortune, etc.—Everything else seems standing well,—
I was a deal with Taubert yesterday, and found him too
a decent, well-intentioned fellow who shewed much zeal.
For that matter, I am convincing myself that an unlimited
influence now stands at my command here ; all have
assured me the King's orders were so categoric, that I
might ask for whatever I liked and Küstner would have
to play up to my wishes : directly he opposed me in
anything, I had only to go straight to the Minister of the
Household, Prince Wittgenstein—nay, I merely need
threaten him to.—Well, that remains to be seen!
Whichever way,—nowhere have I been in such clover
as here. So—everything stands well! The Chorus is
to be introduced to me to-day ; tomorrow I mean to take

Pfister in hand alone ; Wednesday there's a string-rehearsal. Taubert has held eight rehearsals already. The Köster arrives tomorrow, and on Wednesday will join our rehearsals.—To-day I mean to polish off my calls. Such is my life.—

At Leipzig, where I got shaved and ate a beefsteak, I had a moment's talk with Julius [a brother of his] ; he bids me tell you the wine is quite ready and may be bottled in a month, even earlier if you chose :—another care the less, you see, for you poor harassed one !

Now don't forget the grapes, good Mienel ; indifferent though Küstner is to me, still I had promised him.— . Don't be cross at my having forgotten to leave you the money for them ! If yours won't last, as I shouldn't be at all surprised, I can send you more money from here ; for, judging by appearances, Berlin won't cost me much :—in fact, we shall even put a little by here.

God keep you well and in good heart ! You have more reason to be cheerful now than ever, if you reflect what a long-delayed good turning stands in front of us at last.—Things are bound to flourish with us, after all. What would you say to a pretty country-house ? Not bad, eh ?—

Greet your house-mates, our old pet animals. Keep well and write me some day ! For the matter of that, I can't at all see why you shouldn't come to me sooner. If your money is on the decline, just come : we shall be living at the King of Prussia's cost here !—

Adieu ! Farewell, and think of me as frequently as I of you, you good old Minna !

Thy
RICHARD.

Regards to Röckels too.

22.

To-day, my dear Mienel, I am able to report to you on sundry matters ; what I most should like, however, would be to report receipt of news from you ! The day after tomorrow it will be a week since I left you, and I may surely be pardoned for wishing to know how you are :—so write !—

The family which took rooms after me on the same floor, and drove me into others, has arrived ; it is the *Köster* family, and close beside me I can now hear *Adriano* being practised. Strange coincidence in this big Berlin!— Yesterday I was able to hold the first regular ensemble-rehearsal, and had much reason to be satisfied ; Taubert has been industrious, and even the Köster, who only reached here late the night before, came punctually to the rehearsal and shewed she had already been learning up. The choruses are splendid ! Ah, what good it does one after Dresden !—I had taken Pfister through his paces the day before : the fellow has no lack of good will, and his voice will pass muster if one doesn't think of Tichat-scheck ; but the misfortune is, the man has learnt nothing at all, lacks the merest *a b c.* All the same, he isn't clumsy, and I was surprised how fairly rapidly he followed this and that suggestion or example I set him. The part will probably pull him through, and he won't hear of a doubt of endurance ; he declares he could sing the whole of it and not break down. Good luck to him !

There are rehearsals every day now, and I've quite enough to do. The day slips by so soon here, that I haven't yet arrived at proper intercourse with stage-manager, scene-painter, or ballet-master ! All last evening I spent chatting with my neighbour, Köster ; a first-rate energetic poet-brain, with whom I went quite deep. He has an excellent influence on his wife ; her voice is very agreeable and pure—she will make a very good Elsa here.

Yesterday I also remembered it was highest time to announce myself to Meyerbeer, who is here. I didn't catch him, so left a card to go on with :—neither is he likely to be overjoyed about my Rienzi !—The Frommann is to arrive to-day ; I have seen no more acquaintances as yet, nor have I managed yet to call on Tieck at Potsdam.—

Dear child, the time of your arrival is still a long way off ; at times I fall into a thorough fit of anxiousness about you—when you do not write to me, I begin to fancy you are ill ! What a ghastly thought it is to me, that the leaves at home must now be yellowing and falling more and more !—On my walks through the streets here, when I meditate on this Berlin and what it possibly might have in store for me, that we even might remove here in the long run, a strange enough feeling comes over me ; I cannot form a notion of it yet at all, at all !—Neither will I vex my mind with it much, for doubtless I'm dreading without any need. Lord, how contented one might be with Dresden—if the nest had but a little higher standing ! That *this* place is more the right field for my artworks, is undeniable,—but a truce to these fantasies !—

I eat at Meinhard's—on a running account (—if the man takes any pay for it, which I still do not believe !) My landlord also keeps a restaurant, so that I can get anything I like at home, even dinner if I wanted.— Nothing paid him either yet ; so things are going very well, you see ! There's room to take in you, and even Kläre ; another point disposed of.

Now, write to me, you good old girl ; God grant

you're in good health ! Lonelier than me you are *not*—
for only when we two are *together*, are we also not lonely.
You cheerfully might come here even earlier, if you would
eke out with the Frommann when I can't be much at
home.—Just think it over.—

Farewell, and remain an atom good to me !

Greet—na, you know all about that,!—Adieu, good
Minna.

Thy

RICHARD.

X There's a Peps always haunting this street ;—it
surely can't be ours ?

Dear child, please tell Meser he's to send me *two*
textbooks of Tannhäuser immediately by post.

23.

BERLIN, *Sunday*, 26. *Sept.* 1847.

A thousand thanks, my good Wife, for your kind
letter, which has given me a veritable heart's-delight
such as I cannot possibly express ! You will hardly
believe how good, how lovable, you shew yourself in this
simple letter !—See now, it's quite splendid for us to be
calling each other " Old Minna," " Old Richard " ; what
is a young passion, beside so old a *love ?* Passion is only
beautiful when it ends in a love such as this,—in and for
itself it's a suffering ; but a love like ours is pure enjoyment—and a brief separation always makes that quite
plain,—from a long separation may a kind Fate preserve
it !—Isn't that so, good Wife ?—Your tiny mite of doubt,
too, I forgive you,—I can but smile at it, for it really
sounds too droll to think that I'd be casting eyes about
here in Berlin a bit because you were away !—You silly
girl !—

Now for a word on my affairs.—They're standing well ; I have been able to hold rehearsals 4 mornings running from 10 to 1 o'clock. Really I deem myself lucky to get the chance of holding such thorough rehearsals once more: the whole company always punctually on the spot and in earnest,—no chattering, but undivided attention. When I think how that ass of a Dettmer always gave himself the air of doing me a favour by singing this Colonna ! Even if I may have detected just a trace of such a sentiment in Bötticher and the others— they are always in deadly earnest with their work ; and in return I shall obtain a capital ensemble.—Naturally I have to expect the best *Irene* here [Frl. Tuczek],—the duet in the last act will be a gem such as we haven't known at Dresden for many a long day ! The Köster is almost too good for my Adriano : she has something very virginal about her, very womanly—much more than Johanna, who strikes me, on the contrary, as somewhat bluff,—and with it an uncommon gentle magic in the voice—in short, I'm looking forward to her *Elsa* (—Bötticher has asked me to revive the Holländer, also, with Frau Köster !) Pfister now takes the place of *Peps* with me, he dogs my footsteps so, and will not leave my side ;—not that I have any objection, since it makes me more familiar with him and lets me take him in hand with less ceremony. There can be no rehearsal of Rienzi for several days this coming week, on account of the Köster's début ; which offers me the advantage of concerning myself with Pfister alone. That will be the crucial time, and I have good reason to hope it will turn out well. From Monday week we shall pass on to the stage ; all the singers are well up in their music now.

The Frommann arrived on Wednesday, and sends

kindest regards. She is on the alert, and always has something of profit to tell one. She's looking forward to you immensely, and only begs you'll come as soon as possible.

And now I must accuse myself: I'm living very luxuriously here, which is rather disagreeable, than agreeable, to me. This Meinhard doesn't know *how* to shew me his esteem, and besides the most voluptuous feeding at his place (—for that is famous!) not a dinner passes off without champagne. We sit down to table at 3, and it regularly lasts till 5 ; deprecate as I may, he will declare it's good for my inside,—and thus much is certain, the aperitive effect is constant. At 5 o'clock a drive in Meinhard's *equipage*—then I go on to the Frommann, who always has tea served, though I never drink anything there but cold water.—You see, I'm accusing myself, and to speak candidly, however good these people are, and little as I may despise anything good, I honestly am pining for your cuisine—especially when you serve me yourself. Well, that will come to an end here in time ; though when *you* arrive, you will have to go through it yourself! There's no escaping it, as Meinhard has said,—for which matter, the man's a Berlin droll of a humour one can but envy him !—

Enough of chatter : it's my first altogether free day, and I mean spending it on a visit to *Tieck* at Potsdam ; the Frommann says he might be of more use to me than anybody, with the King !—Gracious, I haven't seen Meyerbeer even yet !—I've bought myself a hat, had boots made, etc. ; you shall be able to hold your head high when you come ! h'm ! h'm !

—Kind regards to Röckel ;—he is afraid my money won't last out, and has written me as much,—good fellow ! I'll answer him presently.—Certainly, when I look as far as the end of October, one must begin to think of something soon ; nevertheless, that will all come right.

Be as merry as you can, and don't make my heart so heavy with the good animals. I'm sorry for them, of course, when I think that you will soon be leaving them as well ; see how weak one is !—But—want to delay it as much as you like—by Saturday week you have got to be here, in any case ; and then we shall have been 3 weeks apart and have another 3 weeks here together, shan't we ?

Farewell, you good Minna ; I must go and dress, if I'm to catch the Potsdam train at 10 o'clock. If you write again soon, you'll make me *very happy !* Believe that, and be sure of it ! The joy of reunion will soon be upon us—Juchhé !—Adieu, adieu ! Write and come soon !—

Ever and always
Thy faithful RICHARD.

(For the *grapes*)

Sr Hochwohlgeboren
des Herrn E. von Küstner
Intendant der Königl. Schauspiele
pp. pp.
in Berlin.

24.

BERLIN, *Sunday*, 3. *Oct.* 1847.

My good Minna, don't be cross with me for leaving it so late before writing again ! I have only a couple of hours to myself in the morning, and if anything whatever crops up then, as has always been the case these last few

days, even that little is lost to me. —My homesickness is
as great as any such a thing can be : but my country is—
you and our small household ; I know of nothing in the
world that could compensate me for it ! Only reflect
how we live, and whether I indeed know any other
pleasure than my home ! You can't think how I'm
longing to be able to hug you to my breast again and
shake off that chill which freezes one's whole being at
last in a strange land like this, cut off from all affection !
No, my ambition does not carry far—to me a fair
heart's-country stands above all else ! And now, dear
child, our longest time of separation is surely past ?
Thank God ! ! !—

You always strike me in your letters as not quite
well ;—you can't think how peculiarly doleful that makes
me each time ! I was perfectly relieved when you wrote
me at last that you had really been having those horrible
headaches again ; for I know where I am then, and alarm
myself no farther. Poor little poppet !—

But tell me, what on earth have you been hearing, to
give me such strict warnings to be very careful ? You are
so exhaustive in these warnings, yet mention nothing that
has prompted them ! I expect it's nothing very serious,
after all.—You are completely right, that I bear my heart
too much upon my tongue, and should often do more
prudently to keep this and that to myself, or to ourselves ;
I will not contradict you in the slightest there, and can
only excuse myself by saying, that is how I'm made.
God will take care, however, that I do not come to grief
through empty chatter !—Nevertheless, *you are right !*—
What would you more ? ?—

I haven't much to report from here this time ; the
past week has been rather a medley. The Köster was to

have made her début in Euryanthe ; a sore throat prevented her,—so rehearsals of Rienzi were held again, but
chiefly with the orchestra alone, which latter gives me
great delight. Last night we had a grand rehearsal of
the scenery ; it will all do fairly, only Küstner committed
the stupidity of ordering the new scenes long before he had
had due consultations with the regisseur etc.,—therefore
sundry things have not turned out correct.—

Another matter. If you were meaning to arrive here
Saturday evening, you would exactly not find me in,
and I couldn't come and meet you,—for we have a big
rehearsal just that evening : on a Friday, again, you
probably won't wish to travel, and before then you're
unlikely to be ready ;—wherefore you perhaps had better
get here Sunday evening—if not on Thursday. So write
me *when* you mean to come for certain, and whether you
will travel direct in one day, as I then should meet you
at the station toward 7 in the evening.—My God, I'd
rather you were there already ! !

There is a possibility, however—you know the stage
way—of the performance not coming off at all on the
15th :—the Köster is unwell (? ?) on the 12th, 13th and
14th. However, I have hit on this expedient, that the
actual full rehearsal, particularly for the singers, shall
take place on Monday evening, the 11th,—Tuesday a
rest, and on Wednesday a repetition *without* tiring the
singers, and Thursday no rehearsal at all, so that everyone may come to the production nice and fresh ;—the
Köster has agreed to it, and *hopes* to cause no upset :—
yet, who knows ? !—Not that it would be so great a
misfortune,—for the *King never goes* to the theatre on
his birthday, and moreover they have a prologue etc.,
which makes the evening some half an hour longer ! !

So it strictly isn't very tempting to me ; but we shall
see. —Only *whatever betides*, come *you at latest* Sunday,—
the rest will soon be squared !—

I dine at *Meyerbeer's* to-day ! He is going away
soon ;—all the better !

Make your mind easy about Meinhard.—In the first
place he really is a jolly, decent fellow, who considers me
an honour to him ; and although he has a second reason,
it's of no harm to me : he is Pfister's bosom-friend, to wit,
and most anxious that I should give him a lift, train him
thoroughly in his part, etc., to obtain him promotion.—I
haven't seen the Frommann for a couple of days ; I can
only go there of *an evening*, and then she is often
engaged.—

Yet another thing, dear child. I have commissioned
Röckel to raise some more money and give it to you ;
firstly, in case you run short, and secondly, to make us
safe here. So take it !—

I have had a cold all the time such as I've
seldom experienced ; my head is always in a maze, and
that adds no little to the discomforts of my existence :
but it will do me good, and save me from severer
illness.—

Now, God grant you may have no more to complain
of, and that our reunion, for which I'm longing so with
all my heart, may find us both quite well and cheerful !
Why should it not ?—if we are not in the best of health
by then, we shall soon become so through the joy of
repossession !

When my thoughts fly home, I often have to cry
aloud for melancholy !—Home ! Home ! It tops all
else, for sure !—

Farewell, my dear good Wife. Love me as unconditionally as I love you, and then I'll ask no more! Farewell ; a thousand kisses from

Thy

RICHARD.

25.

BERLIN, *Wednesday, 6. Oct. forenoon,*
1847.

GOOD, DEAR WIFE—I have this moment returned from a conference at which I was informed that the doctor has declared the Tuczek can't sing for 6 days ; owing to that and other causes, the first performance of Rienzi would be postponed for a week—i.e. to the 22nd Oct. This didn't make much difference to me, as it would give me another week in Berlin to pursue my aims. Neither need it have any influence on your coming hither, for I most earnestly beg you to get here next Sunday notwithstanding :—let that therefore remain as arranged :—only you will have to tell Kläre about it, since she would probably be unable to stay here so long. Tichatscheck also, who intends coming here the 14th, you must inform how things stand, and that he should await another letter from me first, to make quite certain. For I perhaps may still find a means of making it possible on the 15th, after all,—whilst our rehearsals are proceeding without the Tuczek ;—but it is uncertain in the highest degree.—

Now I mean to see if this brief note can catch the midday train,—so excuse my haste.—

You dear good Wife, I can't possibly tell you how much I'm looking forward to you ! Farewell till then ! On Sunday, I hope, I shall see you !

Thy

RICHARD.

26.

BEST WIFE,

My heartiest love, to begin with, and the wish that this letter may find you in good health and spirits !

I've only just attained sufficient repose to sit down and write to you ; the first two days in Vienna set me in a regular turmoil, particularly through the quantity of running about. But now for my history !—The journey was a slow one : no farther than Görlitz I had to wait 4 hours (Hr. Laforgue was my companion). Not until 8 in the evening did I reach Breslau : after a hurried look at the town, I called on Mosewius, who was immensely delighted to see me ; we sat up together till 1.

Next day, Saturday, the train didn't start for Vienna till 2 P.M. : after an awful night—for 3rd class on the Austrian line was a torment of hell !—I reached Vienna at 8 on Sunday morning, and put up for the first at an inn. How many 100 stairs I climbed on Sunday in search of a suitable room, I know not ; all I do know, is that I nearly succumbed to fatigue. Finally, in a small side street leading to the Stephans-Platz I found a cheap room, 8 gulden the fortnight ; Monday forenoon I moved in, and now have slept my first night there. There you have my journey's calendar : now for the impressions !—

Good Minna, what would you not have said, if you had been with me this time ! Even at Breslau I believed I was in Paris again, as compared with Dresden : this magnificent folk-life ! Citizens with white staves ; instead of police, the National Guard in blouses and plumed hats ; public hawkers at every corner, selling placards, "There is no more Monarchy (with inauguration of the two-chamber system)," etc. At a station in Moravia we

met the new Federal Governor (*Reichsverweser*) ; every
station decorated with German flags.   But Vienna—I
avow !—seen for the first time again on a fine bright
Sunday, it quite bewitched me.   It was a rediscovered
Paris, only more beautiful, gayer and German.   During
the 16 years I hadn't seen Vienna the whole city has
been renovated : its half-million inhabitants, all bedecked
with German colours, marched through the streets on
Sunday as in triumph,—on Saturday, through the energy
of the National Committee, a feeble, incompetent ministry
had fallen !   You should have seen these people's
physiognomy ; everything that repels you in the Dresden
populace, would attract you here.   The National Guard,
dressed almost militarily, with broad 3-colour scarfs
of silk ; the students (8000) in old-German gowns, with
plumed caps on their heads, long bayonet-muskets and
sabres, keep watch : nearly all I saw were handsome
fellows.   And then this opulence, this life ! this original
garb of the women, an entirely new shape of bonnet with
feathers and German-tricolour ribbons.   On almost every
house a German flag.   And then the street-criers, men,
women, children : " Fall of the Pillersdorf ministry ! "
1 kreuzer ; " The Americans will not forsake the
Germans ! " 1 kreuzer.   " War on the Russians ! " 1
kreuzer.   " Final decease of the aristocracy ! " one kreuzer.
So it goes on.   But everything gay, serene and youthful !
Nothing ugly or low have I come across yet : everyone
amiable, noble and blithe !   God, how common and
greasy does a certain town compare in my eyes !—Sunday
night I was at the Theater an der Wien ; they gave
" Scenes from the Life of Napoleon "—Hr. Wohlbrück
starring as Napoleon !   A poor affair in every way.   One
thing amused me, however : not only had Pokorny

adorned the whole house from ceiling to floor with German banners, but even the waiters, who called out Ice etc. in the entr'actes, were dressed in black, red and yellow, from top to toe. All fudge, no doubt ; but it will shew you how things are looking here.

For my friend Müller I had to trudge to the Burg, where he was on guard. Yesterday I found Bauernfeld at last ; he's a downright hypochondriac now—for two months he was completely insane, so I've heard—he sees nothing but black, and deems the time entirely unfit for experimenting with the Theatre. Possibly he's right, but I shall not give my efforts up for all that ; I have a rendezvous at noon to-day with a Dr Frenkel, described and recommended to me by Bauernfeld himself as very active, intelligent and influential. —The theatres are in very low water now, a result of bad management. The Burg theatre has closed,—at the opera-house the singers etc. are going shares, without a director ; I haven't been there yet : perhaps to-night.—

Certainly politics take the wind out of everything here more than in a smaller town like ours. In a city where questions involving the continuance of large states have to be decided every day, other interests naturally dwindle. In such a throng I'm very lonely still,— almost as in Paris ; only to-day do I hope to make proper acquaintances. Yesterday it took me 4 hours to find out Bauernfeld alone ; nowhere could I ascertain where he dwelt, or even if he lived here at all. Moreover, it rained the whole day yesterday,—I moved out of my hotel, and so forth.—How it runs away with money ! I think I shall be able to live quite cheap, however, in private lodgings.—

This afternoon I'll write you more.

12. *July.*

I meant to resume my letter yesterday afternoon, but didn't get back to the house, as I now belong to Vienna hospitality. I have found my man—i.e. Professor Fischhof, a man who possesses my operas. I met him yesterday noon, and spent the whole day and part of the night with him. *There's* a man who appears to have understood me at once, lock, stock and barrel. Even before I unfolded my plan to him,* he expressed his great delight at Vienna's having pleased me, since it gave him hope I would soon remain here to occupy an important sphere of action. Then I laid my plan before him : he fell in with it at once, and sketched out the following plan of campaign. The new Minister of Education, Erner, a man of much talent to whom everyone looks for great things, is a friend of Fischhof's. He will introduce me to him : thereon we want the Minister to bring the whole proposal forward with his draft budget for Public Instruction, and to name a *commission* to decide how much of it can be carried into immediate execution as a commencement. One thing has to be remembered, however : the present great preoccupation of all statesmen with the weightiest political affairs. Nevertheless I shall go on urging that at least the principle be recognised officially, whilst whatever can be carried out at once, should be so ; and this chiefly concerns the Kärnthner-Thor theatre (Opera), which is without a director and in a state of dissolution. Fischhof himself conceived the greatest hope of the thing : there was *money* enough in Vienna, said he, and if the plan could be published

---

* *Cf* " Plan for organisation of a German National Theatre," *R. Wagner's Prose Works* VII.—Tr.

through print and proclamation, accompanied by a public appeal, he was sure 500,000 florins would be volunteered at once to set the matter going.—Well, that was our first discussion of the thing ; further results will follow : Fischhof will arrange a meeting of the most important litterateurs etc. at his house.

So I can tell you of a start—and even if the whole plan can't be carried out forthwith, still I am certain, after this uncommonly sympathetic reception, that my presence here will bear good fruit.

Last night I was at the Kärnthnerthor theatre with the attaché to the *Russian* embassy and Fischhof, his Liberal instructor ; a wretched ballet was played, " the Gamin of Paris."

Now, my dear good Wife, let this suffice for the nonce. I have saluted you morning and night ; you have returned it, no doubt? for we two old grown-into-one are always together ! You walk by my side all the day here ; I point you out this and that, and converse with you. Farewell, be of good health and courage, and hold me dear ! Many hearty long kisses from

Thy

RICHARD.

27.

VIENNA, 15. *July* 1848.

MY ENTIRELY GOOD DEAR MINNA,

I made a fool of myself, now I remember, in not giving you my address last time, since I probably have spoilt my chance of getting news from you, for which I'm longing so. To make it still possible, I'll write my address down at once : *Goldschmidgasse no.* 594, 1*st floor.*—As I think of staying on here till the end of next week, I now shall hope to get a letter from you yet in any case ; at least, I beg for one with all my heart.— My Vienna ship is answering the helm quite splendidly. At 4 next Monday afternoon there is a big meeting at Fischhof's, when my plan's to be broached for acceptance in general. Directly my name had appeared on the Visitors' list I had several callers, among others Dr Bacher (very rich and enthusiastic), who entered into my plan with delight. Very influential also is the acquisition of Staatsrath Vesque von Püttlingen (composer of the opera "Johanna d'Arc," under the name of " Hoven ") ; Fischhof and I dined with him yesterday at his villa in the country : my plan enraptured him, and he begged immediate copies for the Ministers, to make them provisionally acquainted with the thing. For the Kärnthnerthor Opera, however, all considered that one condition must be made : namely, that I should cut myself adrift from Dresden, to take over the direction of this theatre. I replied : At Dresden I certainly have a Royal appointment for life, with a good salary etc. ; nevertheless, if my wishes could be thoroughly fulfilled for Vienna, I have hopes of soon being released by my King. That satisfied them all, and on Monday, as said, a general meeting is to be held ; then the Minister is to be approached with all their signatures, asking for a commission to be named at once to draw up a suitable scheme for the introduction of my Theatre-organisation ; all that they regret, is that I must leave again now, and cannot take immediate part in this commission.

Dear Wife, this Vienna is a glorious city ; everything here gives me such an agreeable feeling of warmth ; the conditions are home-like and yet so colossal. What surroundings ! I had forgotten them all, and am truly bewitched with them now for the first time. One may enjoy it all fairly cheap, too ; for a 20-kreuzer [about 5d.] elegant coaches take you to the most beautiful spots in the neighbourhood. I have been most, in fact nearly all, of the time with Fischhof, as he conducts me everywhere. A capital fellow, that, of uncommonly wide acquaintance, standing in the highest esteem with everybody, high and low. Two of his pupils are the Russian attaché, with whom we have gone out several times already, and the son of the Turkish ambassador, with whom we are to drive to Baden to-day. Only think, I am keeping company with Turks and Egyptians here, for there is also a grandson of Mehemed Ali, the viceroy of Egypt. For the rest, Vienna is now distinguished from all other cities chiefly by its presenting no party-friction at all ; there is only *one* party here, the *radical:* at Inspruck sits the court-party, about which no one bothers any more. A fine fête took place yesterday : disquieting rumours had been spread, that the military intended to strike a blow at Vienna, and so forth. Well, a deputation from the army came to the Committee of Public Safety the day before yesterday, and declared its wish to quash any such rumours by organising a meeting of the National Guard and Army next morning in the Brigittenau, there to vow brotherhood. It came to pass, too, and amid cheering and music the National Guard, students, army with officers, 12 Generals etc., workmen and the like, all marched through the city mingled anyhow and arm in arm. It really was exalting. —It will be many a long day before Vienna falls to the ground ; what wealth abounds here ! Nobody asks after the Emperor now, no one wants him ; one is quite sufficient for oneself.—

Enough for to-day, dear good Wife : I have to be

at Fischhof's at 9, to go to Baden with the company aforesaid.—

You shall soon have another report from me ; God grant you're as well as myself ; only be of good cheer and good spirits !   After all our manifold experiences, I fancy things will go quite comfortably with us at last.—Yes, yes—one has really learnt something for the future from it all.

Now, many, many hearty kisses from

Thy

RICHARD.

28.

ZURICH, 11. August 1849.

MY GOOD MINNA,

It is very disagreeable to me to have to *write* to you again, firstly because I hope to have you soon with me again yourself, and secondly because I fully understand that no amount of my writing will suffice to revive in you a single spark of moral courage (*Lebensmuth*).   That is natural enough, and as I certainly am unable to write you just yet the *only* thing to please and reassure you, namely that I have secured another appointment for life—nothing remains but to prove to you by experience that your lot won't really be so cheerless at my side as it is bound to appear to you now from a distance.   The most cheerless thing at any rate is separation, at least for me, since it sets me in hourly *uncertainty* about you and your health : not to know how things are standing, is the worst of all, and you must therefore forgive me if I only think of *you* when I think of Dresden, not of our animal pets, dear as they are to me also.   For my part I've experienced again in person, and conclusively, that the *human being* is the main affair, outtops all else ; your heart, alas—through habit—

often seems almost more attached to furniture, houses and so on, than to the living man.

However—even this will surely all clear up for both of us when we're only together again. Your profound dejection is so natural and explicable, that it leaves nothing to say, neither will *words* dispel it ; here *life* itself must exert its healing power, and with certainty I hope—not through argument—but through life itself to succeed in reconciling you to it again. Your chief anxiety, about our maintenance, will also soon be laid ; you have only to gain the conviction that things can't *all* conform at once and in such hurry to our wish, that we perhaps may need a little spell of patience ere the new and future takes firm shape. And even as regards your own poor parents, for whom I certainly am sorriest, the hardship is only just for now and the immediate future—something better will soon turn up for them as well, be sure.—

How active is *Liszt* in my behalf, his last letter to me has proved, in which he also intimated that he had sent you 100 thaler : this money, he wrote, was from an admirer of Tannhäuser for the enjoyment that work had given him, but who didn't wish to be named. At the same time he invited me to add to the pianoforte score of Tannhäuser a dedication to the Hereditary Grand Duke of Weimar ; which I attended to at once, and indeed with a couple of verses that—without compromising my free-thought principles in any way—will make a due effect. Liszt is certain to collect the desired modest yearly stipend for my works before long—at bottom it needs no juggling —only he cannot batter in the door like that at present (after all that has happened), but must proceed a little warily : which means a *delaying* of the thing, but not its giving up. That you will recognise, dear Wife, yourself?

So pluck up heart : our time will come ! And even should it drag a little, I'm arranging for immediate needs already. The 300 gulden, which I shall not have to repay till I make them by Lohengrin takings, are the *only thing* I'm borrowing ; I shall *earn* the rest. A few friends, to whom I had read something of mine, have offered to beat up for me this autumn a select small audience of private subscribers at a high rate, before whom I'm to recite my new poems in a course of three evenings. I shall then give a concert of excerpts from my operas also,—the receipts from both enterprises, which will cause me no trouble whatever, will last us all the winter.—So it's merely a question of gaining time, and everything will straighten ; but we must pass that time together, or else it certainly will not be bearable—for me at least. I have already sent my big article on Art to Paris ; after it has appeared in the *National*, Belloni will get it published separately in brochure form, and transmit me the fee. Through Liszt I have also despatched this long essay to a German book-seller, who is to publish it as a brochure in German ; if it catches on, I shall then write more—for pay, of course.— Have no fear ; I shall be keeping myself,—but you must be with me.

If you only would write me you're coming at last ; I deplore each fine day you are missing here !—By all means bring N. with you ; I have thought that over, too. But what is all this about a situation for her ? She is simply to come to be with you, to help you in every respect, and—as you also very justly remark—that you may have someone about you, should I have to go travelling. In short, she's indispensable to you, and costs next to nothing ; would your worry about her be smaller, if you left her behind ? If she wants to earn something besides, she can do that better here than at Dresden, for work is *better paid* here. So bring her in any case.

As regards our residence in Switzerland, don't entertain any fear ! The fugitives are nothing to me, and moreover are so dispersed throughout the whole of Switzerland, that one scarcely remarks them at all in single places ; any eventual reclamations, also, will only apply to those who took part in the last insurrection in Baden and the Palatinate ;—*I* don't rank here at all as a fugitive, for I have my full Swiss pass and permit for a year's residence, i.e. as good as for ever. To people outside, no doubt, such a state of things always looks worse than it is in reality ; war isn't so much as to be dreamt of, and I'm threatened with no other kind of disagreeables, as I have sponsors and sureties enough here to enable me to be fully naturalised in the Canton [at any moment]. I mix with none but Switzers, as you'll soon be able to convince yourself.

What do I want you to bring me ? You will surely be best judge of that yourself : include in your packing those scribblings of mine which you found in my desk, also the bound music and scores which stood in the pillar-cabinet in my study ; of the other things you'll be able to form your own opinion what would be of need to me. The scores on the floor, also whatever lay loose in the cupboards, just give to somebody at Dresden to take care of. I have no further orders. I wrote to Uhlig a day or two back, asking him to go on with the pianoforte score of *Lohengrin* he had already begun from the theatre's full score ; I also enclosed a few lines to Fischer, who will doubtless have conveyed you my request by now.

Liszt wrote me, Heinrich Brockhaus had lately called

on him and offered, from himself and the family, to do everything possible for me.   On that I don't particularly reckon—in fact, I'm disregarding it completely.—

The main thing is, for you to come here quickly : if N. is with you, Peps will give no trouble even on the railway ; only you must conceal him skilfully when you get in.   Do try, however, to let me know as precisely as possible *when* you will be arriving at Rorschach, the first Swiss station on the Lake of Constance, as I should very much like to come and meet you there.   I shall not take *weekly lodgings* before I know exactly from when.

Once again, I'm quite crestfallen at having to keep on writing you ; my impatience to have you here at last is growing daily, and my vexation at the long delay prevents my finding zest for anything.   When I drew the comfort from your letters that you were coming soon, my work at once put on a spurt,—now everything hobbles again.—And then you're surrounded by the cholera too ; what everlasting dread and pain that causes me !   Up, up ! Minna, dear wife !   Make haste and come, and my whole heart could wish that this letter itself no longer might catch you !   How gladly would I have written it in vain !   Pluck up courage and be with me soon !   All else I'll keep for word of mouth.   Farewell, a pleasant journey, and *hope !*

Soon to embrace you most ardently,

Thy RICHARD.

I can find no words to tell you how beside myself I am at your deliberately *choosing* to start on your journey so late !   In this way it may last a fortnight yet ! !   Fie, that is horrid of you !   At first I believed the fault was simply Liszt's delay in sending money, that you would be waiting for it, all impatience to carry out your decision at last. But no, I was mistaken,—arrival of the money has altered absolutely nothing in your purpose ! !

Only upon reading your letter through once more, have I distinctly made out that you do not think of leaving Chemnitz until *Saturday*, i.e. to-day, the day I'm writing, 11th of August ; and this you wrote me on the 5th ! ! notwithstanding that you had received news of the money's arrival ! ! ! I confess, dear Wife, this quite intentional delay has turned me rather bitter. So, only to-day are you starting from Chemnitz—where there are no preparations at all to make for your departure—to go to Dresden, where it will last another while before you've seen to everything, which you cannot at Chemnitz ! And I am counting the days and hours ! So you were simply staying on because you had made up your mind to. Naturally, then, you're in no hurry to come to me ! Why should you be ? Every Chemnitzer, etc., of course is better than your—husband ! Ah me, ah me ! God alone knows when you'll come now !

29.

PARIS, 3. *February* 1850.

MY GOOD MINNA,

I'm writing you a few lines to-day just to prevent your getting anxious ; I cannot write a proper letter yet, I've not yet settled down. So, merely the following in brief, to ease your mind.

As you will already have heard from me from Mühlhausen, I didn't meet the least obstruction at the frontier ; my pass was all in order. The remainder of the journey certainly fatigued me greatly ; I don't think, however, it did me any further harm. Arrived in Paris, I rushed

off to Belloni : by divine dispensation, he hadn't returned
from Weimar yet : and Liszt had sent me a bill of exchange on Paris " payable in 14 days " !   On the strength
of my letter, however, Belloni's mother had secured me
a lodging, and for no less than 60 *fr.* [per month] in the
Faubourg Montmartre. The room was dark and uninviting, blocked up with cupboards and lumber ; nevertheless I submitted, though I remarked at once that there
was a deal of street-noise even here.   At last—done up
and tired as a dog, I go to bed at 10, when a female
singer immediately above me commences practising an
aria from the Puritani !   That lasted until half past 11 :
imagine my sufferings !—Next day—dog-tired as I was
—I started lodging-hunting ; I chased around the so-
called quiet quarters till I nearly dropped—and found
nothing !   The whole of my day thereby went to the
Devil, and at night again I couldn't really sleep.   Finally
to-day—in fact I've only just returned from hunting—
I have hired another apartment on the 4th floor of a
Cité (*Cité d'Antin*)—65 *fr.* ! !   It's the quietest of any
I have seen, however.   Tomorrow midday I move out,
so think of coming to a rest at last, and starting my
business and labours—especially the translation of my
scenario [*Wieland*].   Otherwise the delay in Belloni's
return is no hindrance to me whatever ; I have spoken
with Franck, and he told me Belloni had set my affairs
well in order.

Now I must lie down a bit ; you won't be cross with
me for that, dear wife ? Ease, ease ! To ease your
mind as well, however, I assure you that, despite my
tiredness, I'm feeling somewhat better ; once I have had
a thorough sleep, I expect to be in good trim again.   If
I had anything to fear, it must already have seized me

by now ; but the mere fact of my not feeling worse to me is a sign I shall soon be quite well. So—farewell for to-day, dear Minel ; you shall soon have a longer and better-written letter. I have seen no one but Franck yet, I had too much to do with the lodgings.

Once more, farewell ! Keep in good health, and be good to me ! Heartiest greetings to our steadfast friends, especially to Boom and Sulzer.

Ah, how I'm longing to leave already !

Farewell,

Thy

RICHARD.

30.

PARIS, 9. February 1850.

MY DEAR MINNA,

Without exactly much material, I am writing you to-day again, instead of waiting for your news first, just to tell you how I'm getting on. My last letter to you was written under influence of the greatest exhaustion,— no doubt you'll have remarked that in its slipshod style,— but since last Monday I'm in another lodging, about which I wrote you before, and gradually am getting better ; my room looks on to a *Cité* (large courtyard), and at least has the advantage of there being no piano and no lady singer near. It passes my comprehension, how dear everything has become here ; or was it so before as well, only we didn't know it ? I am paying 65 *fr.*, and need say no more than that I envy Brix, in recollection, the room he had from us for 40, which was far more comfortable, and better in every way, than my present one at 25 *fr.* dearer.—In order to recover, I spend nearly all the day indoors ; you may imagine what that costs for wood, with this firing tariff ! Moreover, I have already been obliged to rig myself out a little : 1., hat ; 2., umbrella (indispensable !) ; 3., black tie ; 4., gloves ; 5., 2 pairs of under-garments ; 6., a purse,—finally 7., a ready-made paletot. In addition, I have been to Loizeau, whom I unfortunately still owe something (as you know), and he complained of having had great losses and being much thrown back. I got measured for a coat, a pair of out-door trousers, a black velvet and an ordinary cloth waist-coat. I must try and pay Loizeau off during my present stay in Paris ; but what I have just ordered was absolutely necessary : I couldn't go about in my old things any longer—particularly here.

So far, dear Minna, I have been able to attend to almost nothing but my health ; it needed the more con-sideration, as I had severely overtaxed my strength afresh through my journey and first few days in Paris. I am growing more and more convinced that my complaint is nothing but a great overstrain, and subsequent running down, of my nerves : once I have strongly excited myself, the seemingly rheumatic pains set in forthwith,—on the contrary, when I have thoroughly rested, they also cease at once. Unfortunately it wasn't till the night before last that I had a proper sleep again, for even after shifting to this lodging I had disturbing adventures to undergo at first. After retiring to bed the first night, past 11 o'clock I suddenly hear the papers being read close beside me as distinctly as if in my room : it continues till 1, with goodbye to my longed sleep for the night. After my complaining about it next morning, the next night my neighbour—who reads to himself all alone—began mumb-ling quite low, as if trying to check himself ; but it went on more and more *crescendo*, till at last it reached the volume of the night before. The same thing the third

night, when my patience gave way ; in a fury I shouted
at my neighbour, Had he gone out of his mind, with his
ridiculous habit ? I should leave on his account next
morning ! He held his tongue—and the fourth night I
heard nothing more of him, and consequently for the first
time got a quiet sleep. You see, good Wife, how things
are faring with your poor sick husband in Paris !

——I have been with Kietz and Anders several times,
and have already made my promenade across the Seine
three times to dine (i.e. evenings) at Truffaut's—where
Anders has fed for 20 years. In fact I shall do it as often
as possible, for cheapness' sake, as in my quarter I can't
get dinner under 2 *fr.*, whilst a *demi-tasse* after costs
another 10 sous each time. I have my morning coffee
in the house : I always keep back half the *flûte* for second
breakfast, and have laid in some cheese and sausage, also
a few bottles of wine, not to be compelled to go out
for it.

Herr Vieweg also has given me a joy : he told me
quite naively I still owed him some 30 *fr.*, and kept
snorting around it so long, that I gave him the cash in
disgust. Franck is behaving very well and kindly to me;
I like looking him up every day at his bookshop, and as I
always light on Vieweg there, it was very awkward for me
not to be able to polish him off handsomely.

Ah, to see these people and their traffic here, is
something dreadful ! Heartlessness and the most un-
blushing egoism, without the smallest disguise, encounter
one at every step.—Yesterday I was at the Garcia's—I do
not think much of her, either.—

My overtures have been in practice for some time, and
are already announced ; the concerts [Union musicale] are
said to be having a great success, and not a ticket is left.

I'm expecting Belloni within the next few days ; I hope to be quite well by then ; also I think of resuming work on Monday.

I sent your letter off from here the 4th all right.

I have nothing more to tell you of myself to-day, but am firmly reckoning on speedy news from you, good Minna, and hope with all my heart that you've been feeling better than myself.   I don't want to appear senti-mental, yet may tell you this : When I pack my traps again, to return to yourself, to my friends and our little pets in cosy Zurich—were I ever so ill, I shall recover my health like a shot.   I hope the Holy Alliance won't oust us from Zurich ; don't let people make you afraid, and simply ask Sulzer.   Hearty remembrances to our dear friends ; Sulzer and Baumgartner's farewell at the station did me a power of good.   They shall have letters from me soon.—

Now write me, my Minel, poor sorely-tried wife with your excellent housekeeping !   Let me know how you are and you feel.   Never mind about Nette, and give her my love.   How's Peps ?   What's Papo learning ?   I must hear of all that, for those are things of importance—as you quite understand.   I shall write again soon.   Fare-well, my good old woman ; think kindly of me, and keep a loving corner for

Thy
RICHARD.

(Address :

Monsieur Wagner
59, *rue de Provence*
à
Paris)

31.

PARIS, 13. *February* 1850.
(59, *rue de Provence*)

DEAR MINNA,

I have just received your letter, and hasten to reply to it at once.

I'm heartily sorry to have left such an exertion to your solitary neck, and you may judge how greatly I deplore it, when I assure you I now perceive that I have come to Paris a whole month too soon, can be of no use whatever to myself for the present, and simply am leading a far more expensive life here than I might have done with you at home. How right I was, when I wished to await a letter from Belloni first ; it was your own impatience that drove me forth : remember that last Saturday. But there, don't let us tax each other with it now : 'twould lead to naught,—moreover, much of the blame is certainly due to Liszt, whose letter virtually hurried me off to Paris, though he must have known that Belloni [would be] still with him at Weimar, not a syllable of which did he mention to me.—Then I have had to write to Meser at Dresden for the parts of the Tannhäuser overture, and before they arrive—as I learn—nothing whatever can be begun.—Now for the matter oppressing you :

My hopes of a really comfortable summer at Zurich have by all means ranked among my fondest hitherto. You know what radical objections we had to remaining in our present abode : nevertheless, not to cause you any extra disturbance now, and to spare you as you feel you need, I will come round to your wish to retain the same lodgings for another half year. I advise you, however, to have a look at the empty suite in the front Escherhäuser first : these suites seem to be self-included, and in any case we should have the advantage of not living on the ground-floor, which, as we have learnt from experience, is a great nuisance. Don't be too timid about the price, dear wife, though you are entirely right not to think of consenting to any exorbitance. The main consideration for us, and particularly for a stay-at-home man full of work, like myself, at any rate consists in one's having to live day after day in one's dwelling, which one therefore finds a daily nuisance if it isn't to one's liking. I have recently been much gladdened and reassured by a letter from Bordeaux : our friend (for she is yours no less) frankly counsels me to stay perfectly true to myself in my art and all else, to undertake nothing that sets me at variance with myself, and to act in all respects solely according to my inner promptings, as she and her friends consider it their bounden duty to relieve me of all anxiety about my outward circumstances. I fancy I shall soon be able to tell you something more precise on this head. At the same time I shall not remain completely without earnings of my own : so—don't alarm yourself too much about the rent ; an agreeable dwelling is the vital point for our residence at Zurich—for my brain-work also in particular.

However, if you do not share my hopes, and at the same time abandon all hope of still finding a really pleasant and convenient dwelling,—why—rest assured, I gladly yield to our remaining in our old abode, especially if I know that at once anxiety and trouble are thereby taken from yourself. To see you as free from care as possible, and above all in good spirits and health,—this, dear Minna, is what carries chief weight in the end with me.—

Karl Ritter will probably come to us this summer ; it would have been well if we had had a room for him.

I can tell you nothing more from here at present,

excepting that only to-day have I been able to begin my work again. I've a capital cold in the head now, which I hope will carry off the slackness of my nerves. The turn my ancient winter-trouble has taken this time has really given me food for thought : let us spend next summer as quietly and strengtheningly as we can. I should have liked to be quite in the country.

I expect Belloni back within the next few days, when you shall hear more from here. —

I'm also writing Sulzer a few lines. Remember me to N., and remain as fond as possible of

Thy

RICHARD.

Of Paris riots—as you know—one hears in Paris least of all.

32.

I have just received your second letter, dear Minna, which reached me through Belloni's again, this time somewhat late. To get an answer off by to-day's post, I will be as brief as the subject itself demands.

By all means I prefer your taking the proposed new abode at Herr Müller's, to your remaining in our old parterre ; also I agree with you that to take the second would suit us better, than the first étage : as the rent is so moderate, we would rather be able to spend a few louis d'or on having it quite comfortably fitted and neatly done up, especially on a warmable bedroom. For that matter, dear wife, you see things are not half so bad ; no doubt indisposition and bad weather contributed much to your despairing so soon in this dwelling affair. Perhaps you may find it possible to defer acceptance a little while, so as to wait and see what information Sulzer brings you, to whom I also wrote yesterday ; but if you must decide at once, take the lodgings you speak of : I shall be perfectly satisfied, were it only for the knowledge that it sets my harassed wife at ease.

I've no further news for you to-day, beyond my general flabbiness and dumps. Belloni, I believe, is to arrive here tomorrow. Anders and Kietz, in whose company I often feed, send hearty greetings ; Anders in particular has you firm in his heart, clinks his glass to no one else, and tells me of a poem he has made in your honour :

> *O, herzgeliebte Minna !*
> *Du, die stets meinem Sinn nah !*

I countersign it, and wish you the best of luck ! Farewell and think fondly of

Thy

RICHARD.

rue de Provence, 59.

33.

PARIS, 2. March 1850.
59, rue de Provence.

MY GOOD MINNA,

I received your letter toward noon : at once I drew up the answer for you, and as that must catch the post by five—for which reason too, I cannot frank it— it leaves me very little time to enclose a few lines for yourself. It is impossible for any person to behave more nobly and delicately than our friend Mme Laussot ! I should have thought, dear wife, it would really have uplifted you to see what a deep impression your husband's works are able to produce on healthy, undistorted, noble hearts ; to see that he is in a position to arouse such sacrificial resolutions of sincerest sympathy ! Can you prevail on your soul to think meanly of such a result of my art—*for that alone* has brought this forth—to say nothing of rating it lower than those so-called "brilliant" successes which nowadays are reaped by speculation and chicanery from the silly, sluttish, heartless rabble of our theatre-goers ? You see what those cowardly sluggards whose favour I also once seemed to have captured now are, and how pitifully they behave to me. Are we to despise them and simply think of money ? Good : here is money, as much as we need for a tranquil, nay, a comfortable life,—and that not juggled from the pockets of the crowd, but most delicately proffered me from a noble heart's delight in works I fashion after my true inner nature ! What would you more ?—For sure, my poor good wife, I've understood you ; I know not only you, but what is actually at bottom of all your variance with me : in the answer to Mme Laussot I have hopes I've quite correctly hit your inner sense !——

Nothing is so unwelcome to me, as to hear you are unwell ; for unfortunately I could not act as a good nurse at present—even in thought—as I'm poorly enough myself. It is 4 weeks yesterday, since I arrived in Paris tired and ill : what has happened in those 4 weeks ? what have I bought with all this sacrificing of my health and precious money ? Listen ! *Belloni hasn't* **yet** *returned !* He is not to get here till next week. Good ! *without* him there was nothing else for me to take in hand, so I just stuck to the projected performance of my overtures. Belloni had written me, the parts would be copied out here at the expense of the musical society :

after long fruitless searching, I find the conductor at last, and he discloses to me that the society is still too young and poor to afford the cost of copying : *so there had been no preparations at all!* Then I wrote off to Liszt, to send me at least the printed parts of the Tannhäuser overture [he had borrowed] from Dresden at once. Only *yesterday* evening did I at last receive those parts.—

How I'm feeling under such vexation, trouble and annoyance—especially with my wearing and worrying bodily state—you may picture if you add my natural loathing of the whole of this cold, shallow, heartless Paris music-mongering. Here I literally seem as in a long, long night, in which I cannot sleep, dream half awake, turn first on this side, then on that, just to be—able to rest at last, i.e. to know no more of anything—and least of all, of Paris ! O you foolish friends, who have nothing in your heads for me but speculation and a big to-do, how little you know me and what I need to make me happy.—Deliverance from this hell is all I wish for. My dear Wife—we'll spend next summer on ourselves, on health and Nature ; that's my sole hope, my only comfort ! Farewell ; greet all ; hold me dear.

Thy
R. W.

34.
PARIS, 13. March 1850.

MY DEAR MIENEL,

If these lines obey my fondest wish, they'll find you in good health ! Will you be cross with me if I acquaint you that I have formed a swift decision, finally accepted the most cordial and pressing invitation of my friends in Bordeaux—as they even sent my travelling-expenses—and am starting for Bordeaux tomorrow morning ? Remember, I'm completely useless here, simply consuming myself with worry and fruitless endeavours. *Belloni has not yet arrived ! ! !* Even of my wretched overture no rehearsals can be held yet ; only for the end of this month have I been given a prospect of rehearsals. Just imagine my position here, dear wife ! If it weren't for this Bordeaux family, and had they not cared so well for us meanwhile,—I believe I should not be alive ! Now they have urgently begged me to break my stay here and refresh myself by a visit to them, I confess I gladly gave my consent to these benefactors, most of whom I do not even know by sight. And if I meant to visit them, this was the very best time : if my overture still comes to performance, it will be next Sunday fortnight : I can be back here by then, and in the first week of April be back at last with my dear wife, whom I then can help with the removal also, not to leave everything on her one pair of shoulders. That will be the thing, Minnako, won't it ? and you're satisfied with my decision ? I hope so !—

My nervous exhaustion has vanished, only the weakness on the chest and the pains round the heart still remain with me. I hope for full recovery as soon as I've got clean away from this useless desert of a Paris life ! No matter, though : I *had* to make this fresh experience before finally clearing up my mind about this place ; spare me the need of dilating, just now, on the impossibility of my having anything to do with it. Merely thus much : it is precisely to prevent my undertaking *anything* against my nature and inmost inclination, to save me from all—entirely useless and fruitless— annoyance here, that the Laussot has acted toward me as she has ; and—think of this—she and Frau Ritter are offering us the yearly income *all alone*, nobody else has a hand in it, no middleman, no banker !—You should but know this lady's happiness, after receipt of your letter, at being able to hope she has quite reassured yourself as well, and won you to my future plan of life ! Her husband also speaks and writes German quite fluently, so that we all—for her mother is at Bordeaux too—shall be able to converse without impediment.   I confess it rejoices me greatly, to think that I shall be bringing into the life of this remarkably amiable family so rare a diversion—as far as my powers permit—as the playing and singing them something from Lohengrin.—

So, dear wife, write your next letter to me to Bordeaux, at the address you know.   May Sulzer only have succeeded in finding you a suitable dwelling by now, so that you may be free of that care !   Then I hope to be able in any case to assist you in the moving.

Farewell, dear Minna ; best wishes all round !   Nette must pin her hopes on nothing here,—I'm sorry, since she seems intent on leaving :   I have done my best. Greet Peps and Papo, and tell them it will be a *long* time before I forsake them again ;   that's *certain*, the parting is too insupportable.   Farewell and stay fond of

Thy RICHARD.

35.

BORDEAUX, 17. [19 ?] *March* 1850.

MY GOOD MINNA,

Here I am in Bordeaux, waiting eagerly for a letter from you, which is at the same time to tell me if you aren't a little cross at this trip of mine ?   Put yourself in my place, however, when I inform you that just after taking my last letter to you to the Paris post I finally learnt that my overture cannot be given *at all* this winter, as sufficient rehearsals to get up this "difficult" work could not be held in time for the last concert, end of March.   I must confess I burst out laughing—really, I hadn't believed things so dowdy as that!   Not a trace have I had of Belloni yet ; just as little of Liszt!   In such circumstances any other than I—who all along had simply forced myself—would have lost all inclination. I was truly joyful when I turned my back on this Paris I detest so, and only wish I had no need whatever to visit it again.   Still, I'll just see if Belloni writes to me— when he does gets back to Paris—and in any case I must return viâ Paris, as I've still a few things to attend to there.—

Here in Bordeaux, where I arrived last Saturday [16th], I am bound to feel almost in Heaven, compared with Paris ; you can form no idea of the kindness and devotion of this family !   It consists of the young married couple and the wife's mother, an Englishwoman who— equally with the husband, who was educated at the Plochmann institute in Dresden—speaks German as well as ourselves.   Moreover, there is a whole colony of Germans here, rich families all, and all of them honour me highly.   What else shall I say to you, than that it certainly is very good for me to have become personally acquainted in this fashion with the dear souls who have no higher ambition now than to make myself and my good, sore-tried, and faithful wife as happy as ever they're able ?   It is a rare and unheard-of good fortune, that has come my way.   The young husband, a most charmingly sociable fellow, shewed a quite indescribable delight when he saw me arrive ; my works are known here to their last note, and all are aware what the question is, and proud to be of such assistance to me.—On one point, however, I've much ado : as soon as my hosts heard that nothing had come of my overture for the end of March, they naturally importuned me to stay here longer. But I explained to them that I should have to help you in the moving, and —honestly—in spite of all the joy I'm tasting now, my whole heart is yearning to be back at home with you ! Believe me, I know no other happiness, than to be able to live contentedly and tranquilly beside you in our own little domicile ; that I now may hope to see your cares allayed, and fortitude and cheerfulness re-entering your heart—ay, body—'tis that which makes me well again myself and happy. Moreover, Bordeaux is a wilderness which no one of our temperament can stand for long ; even my friends feel themselves out of the world here, and in spite of this excellent family, at no price would I exchange our Switzerland for Bordeaux, I've such a Swiss home-sickness. Ah, Nature ! that is something to your partner, after all ! To lead a happy unmolested life with you, dear Minna, in that glorious fresh Alpine world, is the highest bliss I can desire !

Perhaps my joy will have a bitter taste to you, for this letter may possibly find you in the thick of great cares— especially about the dwelling. Please set my mind at rest on this soon, and tell me if Sulzer has succeeded in keeping the promise he wrote me to Paris, to find us a pleasant abode ? Then write me whether you are well yourself, and if the removal isn't troubling you ? Müller once told me, at Zurich they don't hurry one out, and one can arrange it fairly at one's own convenience ; there- fore I am convinced that Escher—if you beg him—will allow you a long limit for getting our things out, or obtain it us from our successors : just say I can't return yet. Then write me, dear wife, until what date the moving-out can be put off, that I may arrange my return accordingly. I don't know whether Belloni has arrived in Paris, but in any case he'll soon be getting there, and it perhaps would be as well if I still could spend a little time with him discussing and arranging something ; I don't want to leave a single stone unturned. So write me the *latest* limit. And now, good Minel, you must also· write me whether you have been able to procure yourself at Zurich that black dress you wanted : if not—that I may get it for you here, or else in Paris. Bobin of the Palais royal no longer exists, but you shall have shoes notwithstanding ; so write me the exact number again, or— better—put a *thread* of the right length in your letter.

Dear child, if you only are well and in a good disposition ! That is my sole concern,—for everything else is ordered well now :—I tell you, they are caring for us as loving parents for their children. Only one thing is accounted a fault in me by the Laussots : if I keep silence to them on anything of weight, any real anxiety. You have no notion of these people's heavenly kindness and affection ! Perhaps the wife, at least, will visit us in Switzerland some day, to convince herself that we are satisfied and lacking nothing.

So farewell for to-day, my dear Wife. Be of good cheer, forget all sorrows, and rejoice in the affection we enjoy ! Keep well, and write me *soon !* A thousand salutes and kisses from

Thy

R.W.

Mr. Eugène Laussot
   26, *cours du* 30 *Juillet*
         à
      Bordeaux.

36.

PARIS, 17. *April* 1850.

DEAR MINNA,

I still call you so despite the signature of that last letter I received from you, in which you prayed me to address you next time with your " Sie." * " Dear Minna ! " so I call you in the heavy hour wherein I turn my face to you to-day ; — so I called you e'er the worst and most irreparable dissonance had come between our souls ; and so—if you will grant it me—shall you live for ever in my memory !——

Your letters to Bordeaux came as a violent shock to me, the wrench from a fair last—illusion about us.   I believed I had won you at last, I dreamed I saw you yielding to the might of true affection,—and terrible was the grief wherewith I realised more infallibly than ever that we belong to each other no more.   Thenceforth I could bear it no longer : I could talk with no one any more, —I wished to get away at once—to you ; I left my friends in haste and sped to Paris, from thence to hurry back to Zurich.   Well, I have been here a fortnight again : my old nerve-trouble overcame me ; like an incubus it lies upon me, —I must shake it off,—I must, for my—for thy sake. —

Hear me out !   The absolute discrepancy at bottom of our natures has shewn itself now milder, now more glaringly, the whole time we have known each other, to my distress—and in particular to yours.   It is not *I* who need remind you of the countless scenes that have occurred between us from the earliest times,—for probably they

---

* It may here be necessary to remind the reader that in this, as in all his other letters to her, past and future, Wagner retains the familiar " Du." The affront involved in a *withdrawal* of that intimate pronoun is hardly realisable by the Anglo-Saxon mind.—Tr.

live more vivid in your memory than in my own. What bound me to you then so irresistibly, however, was love ; a love that looked beyond all difference, —but a love you did not share : certainly not, at least, to the degree in which it governed me. To my entreaties for our union you strictly yielded under nothing but compulsion [1836] : perhaps you felt towards me all that lay in you to feel,— only, the true root of the matter, that unquestioning Love which makes one bear all troubles with a smile, that Love with which we love another precisely as and for the thing he *is*,—that Love you could not feel ; for even then you did not understand me, as you ever deemed I should be other than I am in truth. Since the reunion after that first breach in our wedlock [1837] you have strictly been guided by nothing save duty towards me,— it was duty bade you bear with me the hardships we endured in Paris, and even in your last letter but one you name nothing save duty regarding that period—not love. Had your heart then harboured genuine love towards me, you would never be boasting of endurance of those suffer-ings, but, in your firm belief in me and what I am, you would have recognised in them a necessity to which one submits for the sake of something higher ; when one's mind is set on nothing but that Higher, is happy in the consciousness thereof, all lower sorrows one forgets. But you—of your very nature—at any rate have found no recompense,—you still see nothing save the sorrows !

After my appointment at Dresden, your growing opposition to me appeared exactly at the epoch, and in degree as-—forgetting my personal profit—I no longer was able to bow to the atrocious managerial relations of that art-establishment, and rebelled against them in the interest of my art and independence both as man and artist.

Anyone who observed me closely and sought to understand me in that decisive period of my life, will be forced to admit that all I did was an inevitably direct consequence of my artistic nature, with which I kept faith notwithstanding all personal risks. That at last I revolted not only as artist, but also as *man*, against all those vicious conditions which none could regard as worse torture than I—with my passionate nature,—to anyone who watched me proceed step by step (not at a bound) to the standpoint I now occupy as artist and man, this must appear extremely explicable, and therefore also worthy of no blame. He would have had to acknowledge that in this I did not behave arbitrarily nor out of vanity, for he would have observed how I *suffered* under it ; consequently he would have spoken me words of comfort and encouragement : and my wife would have done so, if she had chosen to take the pains to understand me ; for which she by no means needed book-learning, but simply *love !*

When I came home profoundly vexed and agitated by some new annoyance, a fresh mortification, another failure, what did my Wife bestow on me in lieu of comfort and uplifting sympathy ? Reproaches, fresh reproaches, nothing save reproaches ! Home-keeping by nature, I remained in the house for it all ; but at last no longer to express myself, convey my thoughts and receive invigoration, but to hold my tongue, let my trouble eat into my soul, and be—*alone !* This eternal restraint under which I had lived so long already, and which never allowed me to let myself quite go, on one side, without occasioning the fiercest scenes, weighed me down and wore away my health. What is the bodily tending, you by all means lavished on me, against the *mental* needed for a man of my inner excitableness ! Does my wife remember, perhaps, how coldly she once prevailed upon herself to nurse me on a bed of sickness a whole week without affection, because she could not forgive me a hasty expression before my illness ?

Enough ! The fateful hour had struck : I had to flee [from Dresden] and leave everything behind me. One wish alone had I, ere altogether quitting Germany : to see my wife once more ! All else was indifferent to me, even the chance of my capture,—but without that one solace I would not depart. Neither to give me that solace, nor to receive consolation herself from a final embrace, did my wife at last determine to concede my plea,—but simply to humour an obstinate person into making off at last— admittedly, for his own safety. I shall never forget the night I was awoken in my place of refuge to welcome my wife : chill and reproachful she stood before me, and spake these words, "Well, as you insisted, I've come ; now perhaps you'll be satisfied ! So get on with your journey ; I must be starting back myself to-night." At Jena at last I succeeded in moving you to a hearty warm farewell : that farewell was my comfort when afar. I had only one thought : prompt, instant reunion ; with the full heat of my soul did I beg you for it in my letters. Then at last, in the country near Paris, I received that deplorable letter whose heartless unlovingness froze me to ice : you declared you had no mind to rejoin me till I could support you abroad by my *earnings ;* you further expressed to me plainly, that you had lost all love for me.—All that happened afterwards will be still fresh in your memory. You wrote me again, announcing your decision to come to me at Zurich : I therefore might hope anew. Eh, I nursed the hope of being able to win you wholly to myself at last, convince you of [the truth of] my ideas,

make you more familiar with me in the end. Unremitting
were my efforts to smooth your outer path.   You came,—
how happy I was ! And yet—unhappy me !—not to
myself had you come, to cast in your lot with me just as I
was,—but to *that Wagner* who, as you supposed, would
soon be composing an opera for Paris! In Dresden you
had been ashamed to say you were joining me in Switzerland, but gave out you were going to Paris, and your husband—as you apparently believed yourself—had a contract
all signed in his pocket.   O, the huge mistake between us
two was bound to reveal itself more every day ! All my
sentiments and views remained a horror to you,—my writ-
ings you abominated, though I tried to explain to you that
they were more needful to me for the present than any
bootless opera-writing.   Every person with whose opinions
I did *not* agree, you championed ; all those of like opinion
with myself you condemned,—I durst not so much as
excuse them to you.   For our former conditions you ever
repined ; the only light in which you viewed the future,
was a reconciliation with them, or—a Paris success.   My
whole being was an object of aversion to you ; at every
instant, ah ! almost with every movement, I was bound
to do something you did not approve.—In short, I realised
at length my *boundless solitude* with you, since I saw how
impossible it was to win you to me.   Just to procure
myself peace with you, I resumed my Paris plans more
seriously.   The inner constraint of it, the odious battling
with my own conviction, the impossibility of making
myself understood by my nearest surroundings, there to
find solace, help and counsel,—all this engendered in me
states of soul which could but sorely aggravate my bodily
ill-health through adding sickness of the mind.   I was
still debating if I really meant to go to Paris in *such* a

state ; weak and tottering as I was, the last Sunday I approached you and said, " Minna, oughtn't I to wait for another letter from Belloni first ? " But you were weary of the long delay—for with you it had never been a question of anything save *Paris ;* also you wanted to have the parlour scoured at last and the whole apartment cleaned. In short—*this time again you didn't understand poorest me,* and answered my enquiry in a huff; so that, feeble and ill, I braved wind and weather, booked my place there and then, and at all events had made my mind up, for I knew what a life I should lead if I tried to remain.—

Here in Paris, amid torments of all kinds, at the sight of this shameful huckstering with art I firmly resolved to renounce once for all what to me was impossible, and irrevocably turn my back on the whole bag of tricks. I had only *one* care—not for myself, but for you—the care about our livelihood. And lo ! a bond of friendship of the rarest and most exalting kind had forged itself,— that care was suddenly removed from me : you yourself had been the first to hear it. Then I wrote you from Bordeaux, how I knew but *one* remaining happiness, to go on living quietly with you at Zurich for the health of both of us, and so be able to create after my own heart.

Your letter tore it all to shreds : you stand before me unappeasable—seeking honour where I almost see disgrace, and feeling shame at what I deem most welcome. As said, *not to me* did you come to Zurich, but to the composer of a new opera on order for Paris. Yes, now I understand all !

You refer me to a previous letter,—I know it : it's that letter of last year ! You are true to yourself !—In

every line it stands clear and distinct that you do not
love me, for you mock at every single thing I'm fond of,
even at the *Du* which—following my inner bent—I like
best to call whoever isn't to remain a stranger to me.—
So, what can *my* love be now?   Only the wish, in
reward for the youth you passed in vain with me, for
the hardships you've surmounted with me, to make you
happy.   Can I so much as hope to attain that by *living
with you ?*—Impossible !

37.

Saturday, 4. May 1850.

DEAR MINNA,

          I cannot help writing to you once more, ere
going far away.—It has remained unknown to me, as
indeed I could but wish, how you received the decisive
step I announced from my side in my last letter to you.
As you have so often entertained the thought of living
apart from me and so recovering your independence, I
presume and also hope that, though surprised perhaps,
you were not alarmed at my decision.   For my part I
live in hopes that in separation the mutual recollection
of our past life will take a more benign, even a more
consoling aspect, than would have been the case had we
gone on living together,—when the constant friction of
our radically different and opposing natures might have
only given rise to strife and rancour.

          It was the news I have to impart to-day, however,
that formed my very special reason for writing you again,
since I have a feeling as if it must soften for you all the
possible bitters of our separation.   I am on the point of
starting for Marseilles, to wit, whence I shall take an
English boat to Malta, and thence go on to Greece and

Asia Minor. I have always felt, and the most strongly in these latter days, the need of issuing from this narrow life of books and thoughts, which so consumes me, to look a little round me in the world for once. The modern world is closed behind me for the present, since I detest it and want to have nothing more to do with either it or what its creatures nowadays call " art." Germany can never become a field of interest to me again until all its conditions are totally changed ; any endeavour to set myself in tune with them could only make me boundlessly unhappy, and more and more sick of my life. So my longing of late had again been directed much farther afield, to a complete withdrawal for a time from our modern conditions, and the restoration of my body and mind by change of scene, sight and hearing, in other climes. In this last crisis, then, I conceived the plan [of a journey] to Greece and the East, and am lucky enough to see the means of executing it now placed at my disposal from London. For in London I have gained a new protector, one of the most eminent English lawyers, who knows my works, and in return for a certain obligation—the assignment to him of the original manuscript of everything I write in the future—will accord me his support.*

---

* The "mir seine Unterstützung zu theil werden lässt" appears to imply the future, though this "new protector"—certainly not the Mr. Ellerton we shall meet in London 1855—strongly resembles a myth. But the letter itself is the strangest in the whole collection, with its transitory signs of slight mental unhingement, e.g. the curious reference to Germany in the next paragraph. Neither have we been afforded any clue as to whether it was sent from Paris or Bordeaux ; to which latter city, as we learn from no. 173, Wagner returned awhile ere leaving France about the middle of the month—to join *the Ritters* on the Lake of Geneva, and at length regain his fortitude and equilibrium through their fostering aid. —Tr.

I believed this news must bring some reassurance to
yourself, dear Minna, in case you need it ; under any
circumstances I hope you will not grudge me the execution of my project, and—providing you do not believe
you must sever yourself from me completely—here you
obtain a good screen against any public remark.   You
can tell all the world that, after the abandonment of my
Paris plans, I had found there was nothing suitable or
of profit for me to do at present either in Germany or
France, consequently I had gladly seized a sudden opportunity of carrying out an old pet wish, namely of
spending some time on a visit to Greece and the East ;
and that, alike for reason of the urgency of the opportunity, and to spare myself the pain of a personal leave-
taking—I had started on my travels without seeing you
first.   That would be telling no untruth, particularly as
regards the last point : it would have been quite impossible for me—in all the circumstances—to visit you
again at Zurich, to see yourself, take leave of dog and
bird ; much as I have suffered already, that personal
goodbye would probably have ruined all my future.
Believe me, it had to be so ; it is better *for yourself* so—
equally with me.

So let us be parted now !   If we retain our health,
if times and circumstances alter, we shall always have
the hope of meeting later.   But separation for the present
will do us good.—

From London you will soon receive the needful for
your maintenance.   If you would rejoice my heart exceedingly, you will arrange your life as pleasantly as
possible ; lay out a tiny garden somewhere for yourself,
cherish dog and bird, and—hope for the future.

I could almost wish you not to write to me once

more ; for, in whatever sense you do write, it is certain to affect me painfully. But should you have a kind farewell to bid me for the present, then write *poste restante* to Marseilles. To tell the truth, I don't think I can wait for the letter there, as, according to my information just received, the boat will be leaving May 7, so that I shall have the greatest hurry ; but I'll leave word behind to send my letters after me.

Farewell, then, dear Minna ! sore-tried Wife to whom I can make no recompense, alas, and whom—perhaps for her own healing—I even must forsake. Farewell, and—if you can—remember me with kindness ! Tidings you shall have from me,—and—surely we may still hope for a Wiedersehen !

Salute your parents, salute our friends ! Do not be angry with me for having to part from you all !—

Farewell ! Farewell, dear good Minna ! Farewell,

Thy

RICHARD W.

[*Wagner did not go to Greece—see last footnote—and his friends seem to have brought round Minna also in the end, for he rejoins her at Zurich toward the beginning of July, if not a little earlier. But we possess no further letter to her anterior to autumn of the next year, that numbered " 38 " in the current German edition manifestly winding up the Albisbrunn group, to the rear of which I shall therefore transfer it. Not to dislocate the original numbering of the others, no. " 38 " will therefore drop out in appearance, though not in reality.—Tr.*]

39.

ALBISBRUNN, *Sunday noon.*
28. *Septbr.* 1851.

Ah, you good Wife, what a wonderfully fine letter you've written me ! The only pity is, I have to reply to it this way, and cannot thank you for it verbally to-day,

as you supposed.   Your letter, my dear Mietz,* has only
this moment reached me, namely Sunday noon, 11.30 ; so
you've been hopelessly out with your post time : it leaves
Zurich at 8 in the morning, and there is none after ;
therefore, if you want a letter to reach me the same day,
it must be at the post by 7 A.M. at latest, or else it will
remain there all day and not go off until next morning.
So look a little sharper, next time you want your dear
good husband with you on a Sunday !—

The weather is too atrocious ! As it was fine on
Friday, I had fully expected it to be so to-day, and consequently never entertained the possibility of *not* seeing
you here. Even with this bad weather, moreover, for a
time I was uncertain whether you wouldn't come after
all ; which I should have regretted, all the same, *for your
sake.* Had I been perfectly sure, probably I should have
set forth myself in spite of it ; quite certainly, if I had
received your letter time enough.—The only thing now
is to console oneself and do better next time : we'll write
that up behind our best ears, won't we ?—

For the rest, I conclude from your letter that you
haven't got poorlier ; though it would have been more of
a satisfaction if you had told me so expressly. Much as I
am looking forward to seeing you in the new apartments,
still I fancied we had settled, that—in case nothing happened—you would be paying *me* a visit here first. Now
let us put that quite straight for next Sunday, and this
way : if the weather is fine, you will come out to me
unconditionally—with friends or without ; only if it's bad
weather, shall I come in to you.—

---

* One might render it " Kitten " or " Puss," but as *Mietz*, *Mutz*, and
their various diminutives will frequently recur, this note must do duty
for all.—Tr.

How glad I am that you are seeing " human animals " again, and are pleased with the new abode in general. It's very tedious here ; of an evening I play whist with [Hermann] Müller and Karl [Ritter]. I'm contented with the cure, however ; to-day in particular I am feeling quite brisk, and of a morning I can scarcely wait for my cold bath. Only I have to be very strict about a thing I never knew before : no matter my appetite, I'm not to eat too much ; this large appetite—which is certainly better than none at all—has really become morbid, since I suffer from indigestion as a rule, and on that ground have to moderate it much : if I control myself in this respect, I always feel better afterwards. But on that another time.—

Now one thing more, dear Minna. Please get your-self a pretty bird-cage made (a wicker stand with flowers &c.) just like the one you had in Dresden. I am buying a pair of canaries—male and female—which I should like you to have. It was a singular chance, in a certain sense a lucky chance (I'll tell you all about it by mouth), my meeting the man with the dicky-birds on my stroll down the road ; I thought of you at once, and how it would delight you if I took them off him for you. So write me what you think—for I can still cancel the purchase if need be—and should you care for it, then order the bower at once.—

Time's up : I mustn't write more at one sitting. I have no further news from anywhere as yet, not even the money from Schwerin, but already have written about that. I shall have enough for this Monday, and expect to get that money before the Monday after.—Has Peps made himself at home in the new dwelling ?—Now fare-well, dear good Wife ; be sure that your letter delighted

me greatly to-day.   Accept my thanks for it, and keep
fond of

Your good
WATERMAN.

40.

ALBISBRUNN
Sunday, 5. *October* 1851.
Noon.

DEAR MINNA,

I arranged with you that you should come out to
me to-day *in any case*, and in any case I wouldn't come
in, to avoid our crossing through any uncertainty about
the weather,*—and you haven't come.   I can't blame
you for it ; but please don't let us settle anything again.
When one has fine weather almost all the week, I find it
too absurd to make Sunday one's only day for undertaking
things, when of course the weather always turns out bad.
Yesterday, when it was so superb, I really believed you'd
be sensible and get on the road ;—whoever of the others
cared to visit me, could very well have followed you
to-day.—To speak candidly, I'm much put out: if you
had wanted to visit me, you would have soon discovered
how and when ; but all you seem to care for, is a general
excursion with the rest.   It's different with me : I think
very small beer of the others—for here at least.   A
meeting with X of itself never yields me good humour,
for I always have to curb myself : which greatly flusters
me, particularly during a cure ; therefore, as it really
isn't good for me, I shall not come to town again so soon.
Consequently, if you want to see me, you must make up
your mind for a seat in the diligence, stay the night here,

---

* Either a billet is missing here, or Wagner must have run over to
Zurich himself between this and the preceding letter.—Tr.

and see how you can amuse yourself with me.—But I shan't expect you any more ; for, I confess, this fruitless waiting upsets me very disagreeably just now.

I don't even get my letters !—

Farewell, and entertain yourself well : the hearty wish of

Thy
RICHARD.

So you are not in need of money either, as you told me ?

41.

ALBISBRUNN, *Monday,* 6. *Octbr.* 1851.

DEAR MINNA,

Though I didn't strictly mean to *expect* you any more, since you never come, just now I felt drawn to the Post notwithstanding, to see if you *would* come.   Of course you have not, once again, but in your place a letter of yesterday telling me you no doubt would come to-day. I don't know what to make of it.   For that matter, even if you didn't come yourself, you surely might have forwarded the big letter that lies in your rooms for me ; I am much annoyed at receiving no more letters.—

(Apropos, I must assure you again, that (after my making you the expensive birthday-present) your having gone to *Sulzer* for money has been particularly distasteful to me this time.   You might have said a word to *me* about it first ; it would have been quite easy for me to get money from Karl—and so on.)—

We shall have very fine weather again to-day ; but presumably you'll wait once more until it's bad, and then not come, of course, because of it.   I have been here 3 weeks, and you haven't called on me a single time yet.

VOL. I   7

All the other guests here, who have relatives in the neighbourhood, have been visited by them repeatedly. I'm quite ashamed of myself, and keep saying : My wife will come tomorrow, or, She'll come the first fine day.—But there, remain where you're better off ; I shall just give it up entirely, not to set myself in this eternal flurry of waiting in vain.

—From all which, dear Minna, you will perceive the good humour you put me in. May it soon grow better, or the cure will certainly not take much effect on me.

Farewell, and write soon again to

Thy

RICHARD.

[*To judge by our next, she either came that afternoon by private conveyance, or within a day or two.*—*Tr.*]

42.

ALBISBRUNN, 12. *Octbr.* 1851.

Ach ! Ach ! Ach !—You quite prodigiously good Wife !—Ach ! Oh ! Oh ! how shall I thank you ?—My, what lovely nuts they are ! I've been so busy nut-eating, that I couldn't get to letter-writing until this instant. Ach, and the stockings ! and the cigars ! and the brush ! and the knife into the bargain ! No : it's really too much for a poor waterman.—Ach ! you immensely good Wife !— Ach ! Ach ! Ach !—what *am* I to say to it all ?—

As to-day's weather is lovely beyond any conception, I was just thinking, If the whole lot of them don't come out to-day from Zurich, they've all gone crazy ! Now your letter clears up the enigma. If Sulzer only would come here right out ! It would be the best thing for him.—

Since you people haven't come, I must candidly admit

that I almost prefer it, as I should have been unable to do much gadding about with you : a crisis has set in with me, which I hope will do me a heap of good. Though I have had a couple of days' fever and been very shaky on my legs, my head is clear, my humour fairly good, and appetite excellent ; so you see it's not a case of Heaven-wards yet. On the contrary, I think of making a thorough good cure ; my spots are beginning to shew stronger and stronger. Only, I need quiet for the present.

—Uhlig has written : nothing of importance, and no danger for *him !*—Bülow's letter from Weimar was a real delight : he is doing very well there. But Liszt isn't back yet !—

Halt ! I must stop : it's a quarter to 1. We've *crème* again to-day, because we thought you all were coming.— Now, my good, dear—bad, wicked—Wife, be sensible and visit me again with Pepsel very soon. That—be sure of it—is the *greatest* pleasure you can give me.—

Greet the Zurich clan ; the Albisbrunn brood sends greetings likewise.

Entirely

Thine own

R.

43.

ALBISBRUNN, 17. *October* 1851.

DEAR MINNA,

As I am obliged to answer you at once—on account of the tax business—I can only do it very briefly, since the time between arrival and departure of letters here is very short. I don't at all know *what* I'm to fill up in the form, or what to declare ; moreover, I never clapped eyes on such a form last year, and this is the very first time. Therefore—not to do anything stupid—I shall simply *sign* it, and you must be so good as to beg Sulzer, in my name, to fill up the rubrics for me as he may think fit. What is there for me to declare? I have no property, and can earn as good as nothing, at least nothing settled, and least of all in Switzerland and Zurich. All I could say, then, would be: What I need to maintain me, I receive from abroad. But Sulzer will soon find out the proper wording, and write it in for me.

—I have received the Schwerin honorarium, but with a deduction of 2 louis d'or for the Berlin Jews, of course; therefore only 18 louis, 3 of which were assigned to Hug of Zurich [bookseller etc.]. 10 louis d'or I at once repaid to Müller.—But you can pull along for the present, can't you? The beginning of November—if you will—there'll be money again.

Otherwise I'm doing better; it was a kind of nerve-crisis that had set in, making me feel extraordinarily weak, and at length excited; but it did not alarm me, as I had a splendid appetite all the time.—Since it was too noisy for me down below, though, Brunner has given me a very nice room on the first floor, where it is quieter. To-day I've recommenced the cold ablutions, which suit me; I'm feeling brisk. My digestion will soon get into order, too, I hope.—

So—your excursioning is still a long way off? I expect you people have given up wanting it now; for we have had our fine weather, and it will not return. What id— you all are!

I have nothing more to write to you, dearest of wives, for of course nothing ever happens here. Merely, I have won 1 franc off Karl at billiards; but I shall have to do a lot of sharping before I cover your gaming losses here.—

Now, for God and the Holy Trinity's sake, have you not been to the Prophet ? Do write me what you're doing, and whether Boom [Baumgartner] is in full finger-power to play the grand into trim ? Please ask him to dinner, and give him a thumping beafsteak.—

Farewell now ; give Peps my blessing. Write and come ; and—hold me dear, too.

Thy

first-rate HUSBAND.

[*To Uhlig, Oct.* 30, '51 : "*My wife has been paying me a visit of* 4 *days ; she left again only this morning.*"—*With the following playful scrap of doggrel it naturally is impossible to find equivalents for all the original rhymes,* "*Strümpfe . . Sümpfe . . Klümpfe . . Trümpfe . . Strümpfe . . Fünpfe.*"—*Tr.*]

44.

ALBISBRUNN, 3. *Nov.* 1851.

Minna, send me stockings soon ;
Our swamps are fit for divers :
The mud just sticks to me in lumps.
At whist I also lack the trumps :
So set me on my feet again,
And send a pair of fivers !

45.

ALBISBRUNN, 7. *November* 1851.

BEST MUTZIGEN,

We *are* making vairses—!

Your verses were decidedly the best, though ; there was a swing about them that made a deep impression on me ! They leave me nothing but to thank you in prose ; and that I'm doing.—

But how about your dress ? Is it being worked at ?—

As the elastic doesn't appear on your account, have you by any chance been borrowing money off Sulzer? Fie on you! But I suppose you will pay him back now? If only he'll accept it !—

My longing for home and the pretty abode is growing stronger and stronger, and I really am looking forward very much to my return ; but the wet packings are still too imperative, since my eruption is coming out over a great part of my body now, in fact very painfully. The rest of the cure I can easily pursue at home ; if necessary, indeed, you can—in fact, must—wet-pack me yourself now and then : only, I can't undertake a regular course of these packings at home with you, as certain things will not comport with them at all ; so I must get finished with that part of it here. Nevertheless I'll fix a latest limit, that you may not jump out of your skin for impatience : I shall leave here *Sunday morning the* 23*rd of November ;* that day I'll pass alone with you at Zurich, and Monday the 24th we will celebrate our wedding-day. So long— you'll *have* to wait—there's no help for it ; but between this and then I expect to have got my skin quite clear as well, and consequently to regard my cure as finished and complete. So—that is settled. Muzius, do make a reasonable face at it !—

Karl suddenly drove off to town the other day—after 3 o'clock—to buy himself a very handsome dressing-gown ; in which he succeeded : only, it had become too late for him to call on you as well.—Couldn't you send Nette to the music-shop, to remind them to send me off the old musical journals ? I suppose *you* have returned those I gave you last time.—

But why do you send me no night-shirts ? Oh !—

Now, good Minel, a fond farewell ! Don't flirt too

much ; it might do you harm. Get on with the dress, and hold me dear.

Thy

✠ ✠ ✠

(in Christo !)

46.

ALBISBRUNN, 9. *Novenber* 1851.

DEAR MIENEL,

To-day I have entered the last week but one of my cure here ; eleven more packs (on Sundays I have none) and I shall be finished. My shingles on the thighs and calves are out in fine form, and have pained and irritated me exactly as they did last spring ; as for the rest, the sweating and strong perspirations have chased away the worst of them, particularly on the chest and arms. What a disgraceful thing that sulphur-cure was ! The whole first month here I sweated nothing but sulphur, and then came the bad humours the sulphur had simply driven inwards. I was sure there was something festering in my blood.—I am getting it pretty stiff now, but standing it well, and coming to feel as if in a new body.

That "'Pardon story" I heard on Friday evening, when the postmaster at Hausen, having just read it in the Friday paper, brought both it and himself all hot to my room. Since then, I have read nothing more about it anywhere ; most probably there's nothing in it, or an official intimation would have already been made to the Swiss authorities. Should it be confirmed, all it would mean to me now, would be the urgent necessity for becoming a Swiss citizen, as the refugee protection would be at end. In any event it will be well for me to get naturalised here before long ; the Ritters will supply me the means,—Karl wants to be naturalised himself.—

So you would like to see Lohengrin performed at Zurich ?—Not bad either !—

You say I've started something odd each year, and your only worry is what I'm going to hit on for the next ? That I shall tell you at once : next year, I hope, *the two of us* will take a lovely trip to Italy. Would that be so great a calamity ?—

Klärchen Brockhaus has written me a very nice letter : she asks after you most affectionately. When I get home again, we'll write her an answer together.—

Nothing more has come of Lohengrin at Weimar. The singer of Ortrud had been discharged so insultingly —in Liszt's absence—that she could not be persuaded to oblige. In general, a lot of intriguing is going on against Liszt there, and Mr. Genast is said to stand at the head of it. I am also afraid things will not last much longer there, and Liszt will get sick of it. It is impossible to make head against the present vileness anywhere or anyhow.—

If you care to send me another pair of shirts, please do ; I shall have plenty of the other things to last me. I am counting the days already, and tell myself each morning, Tomorrow there'll be so-and-so many days more. Judge by that, how I am looking forward to home and you. But I still keep thinking of poor Papchen : * night after night I have dreamt of him, and always so touchingly and affectingly (he would bite at my finger for love) that I found myself crying aloud when I woke. I shall *never* get over the loss of the dear beastie ; it was too terrible, our having to lose that bet ! !—Ah, I have to tear myself away from the remembrance—else I can't bear up.— — —

---

* Their parrot, died last February ; see Letter 22 to Uhlig.—Tr.

Now, just you keep in as good health as I found you the last times—and we'll soon see how to shape our life as happily as possible. Already we may be without the least anxiety for our subsistence, and to the end of our lives : there will be nothing more of that sort to disquiet us. But you [plural, clearly including Nette] must grant me quiet too ; take me as I am, and let me do what I have joy and pleasure in ; don't tease me into anything I really neither will nor can : rest assured, on the other hand, I shall always be doing something that somehow gives delight to others and satisfies my inner self.—So, if we do not mutually torment each other, we yet may lead the finest life permitted by our circumstances.—

Now farewell, Mutzius !—Be cheerful and retain your good temper. I shall soon be with you altogether again.

Thy

RICHARD.

[*Nov.* 20, ' 51, *Wagner writes alike to Liszt and Uhlig that a "*pro-vidential inheritance in the Ritter family " enables him to live in future "for nothing but artistic creation, untroubled by material cares." Our next letter, accordingly, must be that which the current German edition has ranked as no. "*38," for it manifestly refers to the first quarterly instalment of the Ritters' definite subsidy—continued, in the event, for fully seven years.— Tr.*]

46 a.

[ALBISBRUNN, *Nov.* 19 *or* 20, 1851.]

Dear little one, herewith I send you money ; go nicely to the banker with it and get it changed, so that I may have some of it too. It amounts to 350 gulden in Reich currency, or 750 francs (French). I almost think you had better get it cashed in French money (five-franc pieces), as we are certain to be reckoning in that currency ere long throughout all Switzerland. You must send me 120 *francs* of it, and *promptly*, that

I may have it by Saturday and pay up everything here, otherwise I can't get home on Sunday [Nov. 23].

I received your last letter on Monday, just as I had sealed up the packet with mine ; I couldn't break it open again. To-day, however, I add my best thanks for your declining the hare-supper.—

I am feeling well !—Emilie [Ritter] isn't here yet, and probably will not arrive till after my departure.—

Farewell for to-day, my most *charmante !* Soon to take you by your good cheek,

Thy lord R. W.

47.

MEIRINGEN, 15. *July* 1852.

Oh, what a wicked Wife you are ! Just to snare another letter from you, I've waited a whole day extra here at Meiringen, since I thought you would be sure to send me an answer here to my letter from Interlaken. I have just come from the post, and the person who hasn't written is yourself ! I reached here yesterday afternoon, and certainly found Uhlig's letter with your greeting [on it] ; but when you sent that off, you hadn't received my letter from Interlaken yet, and so I waited till to-day. I was in need of a rest, no doubt, as I had marched hard Monday, Tuesday and Wednesday ; still, I should have been on the road again to-day, had I not hoped for a letter from you. Perhaps, though, you were simply too late to catch the post ; so I shall leave orders to send letters after me.—

My journey has gone off very well until now : fine weather all the time, saving for a couple of brief thunderstorms, which were only interesting. What pleases me most, is that my boots are behaving themselves ; the 12 hours on the last did much good, and my feet are in capital order. On Monday I left Interlaken early for Lauterbrunnen, walked up the Wengernalp (where one can clutch the Jungfrau with one's hands), and from there across the Wengern-Scheideck down to Grindelwald. Tuesday I climbed the Faulhorn (8200 feet high), whence the view is quite terribly sublime : I stayed the night there and came down on Wednesday over the Grand Scheideck, past the Rosenlaui glacier, to Meiringen.

I have nothing to describe to you, as that would really give you no idea, but I have been planning how to shew you the Bernese Oberland next time, from this side or from that.—It will be my first complete joy to conduct you, proud on horseback, through these parts : what eyes you'll make !—Tomorrow morning my road lies along the Haslithal to the Grimsel ; the night will be passed at the Grimsel hospice, and from there next morning viâ the Aar glacier and the Sidelhorn to Obergesseln. Thence on Sunday over the Gries glacier to the Formazza valley, and Monday evening I shall be at Domo d'Ossola in Italy. From there I shall write you again.—

Money runs away fearfully ; this Bernese Oberland is the most shamelessly extortionate hole one can conceive. Each day I have to change another louis d'or, and saving or economy is quite out of the question. It was a good thing you sent me Uhlig's letter : I had to write immediately thereon to *Frankfort*, for they at last have applied for the Tannhäuser score in hot haste, as the opera is to come out there the beginning of autumn. You may imagine how I insisted on the honorarium being sent at once ; I expect you will be receiving it soon.—See, the louis d'ors will be so pouring upon us ere long, we shan't know what to do with them. Only let me know directly money arrives, that I may reel off a plan *where* you're to meet me and share a little of my beautiful trip after all. I'm truly looking forward heartily to being picked up by you somewhere—preferably at Lugano.—

So, if you write or have letters to send me to-day, address

Monsieur

W. R. Wagner

à Lugano

Poste restante.   *(Canton Ticino)*

Farewell, good old Muzius! Salute our friends, and above all Peps, since of all male creatures he is my best friend. Adieu!

Your husband with the blistered

nose.

[*To Uhlig, Aug.* 3, '52 : "*I got Minna to join me at Lugano. Then with her the Lago Maggiore again ; viâ Domo d'Ossola, Wallis, Martigny, Chamounix, Mer de Glace etc., to Geneva. From here we go home by Lausanne."—Tr.*]

48.

CHUR, 15. *July* 1853.

DEAR MINEL,

I am stranded at Chur, since the only diligence to St Moritz was already booked up, and I have 2 nights and a day to winter here. Grey it is, and pouring in torrents!—So I'm writing letters, to Liszt etc., and want to send you my greeting also, to tell you, if you don't feel very cheerful now, I'm no better off myself.—Otherwise I have nothing to report, as nothing else has happened to me. En route I met a good many people who also had witnessed the torch-lighting.*

---

* An elaborate serenade, etc., in front of his windows at Zurich, July 13 ; see *Life of R. Wagner*, iii. 117, 150. The "Grey" in sentence two is an allusion, of course, to Canton *Grau*bünden.—Tr.

Stay, I can also send off from here my letter to the Ollmütz theatre-director. The second letter I obtained from the post, you see, was from the director at Ollmütz (Austria), who wants to have my Tannhäuser, remarkably enough !—Do write me at once to " *St. Moritz, Canton Graubünden,*" how you are getting on, and how the rest is suiting you, what Peps is doing, and everything concerning you. I feel sure you will be all right now, for you badly required a rest ; it is also quite time that you followed R[ahn]'s orders precisely ; please do, and no subterfuge. But Peps must often have a bath ; make good use of the tub yourself, too, and don't go setting about something directly after. Also write me immediately the Wiesbaden money arrives ; if it dawdles much longer, I shall have to remind them in earnest. Let me know, in fact, whenever money comes ; but send on at once to St Moritz all letters enclosed with the money, that I may answer them prettily. So, so, so, so !—

Now, Mietzel, farewell. Be content for to-day with these trumpery lines, for my humour isn't up to much ! We [Herwegh and self] got here yesterday at 9, and had to trot around a whole hour in ghastly rain before we found shelter, the inns were so full ; we were lucky to get quarters at last in the " Steinbock " ; also, I had a fairly good night's sleep. And you ?—Now, write soon, salute our friends, and in particular thank all the torchists !

Adieu, with the whole heart's greetings of thy
frantically faithful
Husband
and father of Peps, the high-betorched famous
Composer, Poet and Star-reader,
R.

49.

St. Moritz, 22. *July* 1853.

Best thanks, dear Minna, for your deliveries.   If you have come by yellow paper, it isn't *my* fault ; with the yellow there also lay pink and white.   Make a note of that, and don't scare me another time.——

Scarcely had I proposed to devote this morning to a gossip with you, when Dr. Obrist came into my room and prevented me ; so I probably shall bring but little off on paper before meal-time.

We have fine clear weather all the time, up here ; only, it is never really warm, and one has to keep to one's winter clothing.   A severe cold is clinging to me, and I do not expect to get rid of it here.   To-day's bath, however, had a very good effect on me again, and I can quite imagine why the Doctor ordered me this cure ; decidedly my nerves are getting stronger.

For yourself, just follow R.'s advice and go to Baden [Canton Aargau] for a week.   If it would afford you amusement, I should much like you to fetch me from here at the end of my cure, and perhaps stay on with me another week ; then I could retrace with you the best excursions in these highlands, which indeed are very interesting.   In no event, however, could I have expected you to stay up here the whole time *without taking the cure yourself,* for it really is an uninviting hovel, with the greatest lack of comfort in every arrangement, and most monotonous.   I shall also have to be somewhat more sparing with excursions now, as during the cure they are very fatiguing, and especially this driving in carts (without springs) on the stony by-roads plays havoc with my nerves ; I believe you couldn't stand it long, either, for the shaking is awful.

All the same, I took a very fine drive with Herwegh yesterday to *Chiavenna*, over the *Maloja* pass, where we were met in the valley for the first time again by a warm southerly breeze, so that it was with difficulty one could determine to return to this cold height. In bad weather it must be dreadful here !—

I have heard nothing of Franck ; but Liszt wrote me from Weimar again yesterday : he had had a talk with Johanna at Frankfort ; she meant to return there in a fortnight for a second starring, and then to sing in Tannhäuser as well ; she further promised Liszt to sing "Ortrud" at Weimar next winter (what do you say to that ?). Liszt seems to have much shamed both herself and her parents. He was unable to see the Lohengrin at Wiesbaden ; a lady singer was ill.—

You certainly must so arrange your trip to Germany as to take the Music-festival at Carlsruhe (the 20th September) on your way back, when you can call on the Devrients also.

When Bauer delivers the music, just put it aside for the present : but tell him to finish off *everything from Lohengrin* at once ; for that part is then to go to Carlsruhe.—

My letter to the new Grand Duke of Weimar was much to Liszt's liking.—

Now write me exactly when you're going to Baden, *from* which day *to* which day, that I may write you thither. As for any money-letters in the meantime, you must arrange for them to remain at the post till you're back again.—

But when is your Mathilde [Schiffner] coming ? Of a sudden one hears nothing more of her whatever !—

Take good care of Peps ; I had a horrible dream the other

night : you brought me Peps all shaven and smothered with flowers, which so disgusted me that I tore them all off. Couldn't you manage to find the good fellow a match one could keep a sharp eye on, and thus get a legitimate heir to the memory of our old companion? Good Lord, when one is growing old, bereavements come harder and harder !—

Now take care of your health, and amuse yourself to the best of your ability. Be thankful, for that matter, you aren't here too ; to tell the truth—without the cure—you'd have had a wretched life of it. But if you care to, as said, come and fetch me ; it would greatly delight me !—

Farewell for to-day, then, old Muzius ! Write nice and precisely [or punctually—*pünktlich*, see next page] and much ; you know how glad I am to get your letters ! Farewell, greet Peps, and think fondly of

Thy
RICHARD.

They're actually hunting a bear now, who had devoured 6 sheep—not at all far from here—only the day before yesterday.

50.

ST. MORITZ
Tuesday, 26. *July* 1853, 5.30 A.M.

I must be at the spring in half an hour ; but since you are such a good woman, I have risen thus early, washed, gargled and hair-dressed already, to present myself to you as charmingly as possible while you doubtless are lapped in soft slumber. For this letter will go off within an hour.—

First of all—you everlastingly mistrustful spouse !—
I must dissipate a few misunderstandings.

1. The landlord of my hotel is named " Biedermann "
—consequently I am both lodging at the " Hotel Faller,"
and at " Biedermann's."

2. The reason I'm so exact or anxious about the
expected money-letters—as I wrote you before from Chur
—is that with every remittance of money I also expect a
letter, which I generally have to answer at once, or on
account of which I must send Fischer an order forthwith.
Understand ? I'm a " miser " ?—O you perverse piece
of goods !—

3. I wished you improvement in *letter-writing :* by
which—after the whole sense of my lines—I meant that
you should *write*, in general, sooner and more *punctually*.
How could I be finding fault with your *style*, when you
had not yet written me at all ?

From the above—and those are merely trifles—you
see how odd a look your vaunted love must wear. You
naughty wife haven't the very smallest scrap of *trust*, but
behind each step, each word, you spy out something
which doesn't exist at all, and consequently keep imbuing
me with the wish that dear God may mend you ! What
you wrote me about Herwegh, too, all reeks of reproof
and distrust,—for which reason also, I shall leave that
stuff entirely unanswered : the only way ! You foolish
women, can't you comprehend, then, that your greatest
pride consists in this : that your husbands, out of fullest
unrestraint and freedom, always return to your side in the
end ? Ah, if you only knew the meaning of true fidelity
in love, i.e. duration !—

But we'll not philosophise so early in the morning,
and to myself the occasion really seems too trifling for

such earnest : regarded closely, it all was surely nothing on your side but chaff.—

Very good : you will have received another letter from me since ; to that I still await an answer, particularly as to your still caring to come and fetch me ? In that letter of mine, to be sure, you will have missed all talk of "huge affection" or "the loveliest flower" ; * but on the other hand you no doubt will have recognised that the wish to have you with me here breathes more true desire and heartfelt love than any mere rhetorical assurance, for which, like every written phrase, I once for all no longer care :—I prefer to *do*, to *deal!*—

Halt ! it is getting too late now, and my half an hour is nearly up. So, merely a few memoranda.—But dear child, if you require the money, just send the Wiesbaden treasure-slip to Hug's at once, and get it cashed ; what the deuce makes you imagine you must pickle money for me when you're needing it yourself? No, please don't fleer : more money is sure to come in soon ; but for the present you'll manage with that.—Is Mathilde going to Baden too ? Give her my kindest regards ; her faithful staunch attachment rejoices me. As I presume you have somewhat postponed your starting now, I address this letter still to Zurich : in any event it will reach you.—

The day before yesterday we walked a distance of 4 miles on one of the Rosetch glaciers : terrible scrambling over crevasses ! Here and there Herwegh often declared he couldn't get across, and I had to return each time and shew him how. (Whatever you do, don't tell his wife !) It was a very fatiguing excursion : 11 hours of constant

---

* Apparently expressions of Herwegh's to *his* wife, who had only recently rejoined him after a very long separation; *cf. Life* iv, 151-3. —Tr.

scrambling and clambering ; but I have never experienced anything so grand, never before had I been in the
very heart of the sublimest World of Ice !——

I thank you heartily for the vegetables, especially
the parsnips, my favourite dish ; it was very nice of you.
Unfortunately I cannot eat the biscuits, they have such
a horrid taste of rank butter as I never had known in
a biscuit before : I must leave them alone.   Of course
you couldn't help it.——

Wesendonck has written me : he starts for America on
the 27th.   His wife is expecting a letter from you.——

A thousand remembrances to Pepsel, the good, altogether good beast !   Na, what is that beside the out-and-
out good Wife ? !   Words utterly fail me ! ! !——

Farewell, dear Minna ; the goblet tinks, I must be
off.   Let's hope it will taste all right ; the first I shall
drink to your health !   Farewell, and let me hear again
soon.

Thy
RICHARD.

51.

ST. MORITZ, 28. *July* 1853.

Dear Mietzel, I cannot write you much to-day, feeling
fairly done up : in the second week of the cure here it's
said to go like that with everybody.   Tomorrow will be
the end of half the cure-time ; Sunday fortnight I travel
back.

Your letter might have made me very sad, had I not
noticed that your unwellness itself makes you strongly
inclined to a melancholy temperament now.   If R. dis-
played anxiety, it certainly was with the good intention
of spurring you—who are a very bad patient—to a strict

observance of his orders.   By all means you need careful handling of your health ; your blood is greatly out of order, and if you do not take care of yourself, you may certainly look out—in your *old* age—for the sufferings of your mother : you know her asthmatic condition.   It also is quite understandable that poor Jette's fate should be haunting you now ; but the bare idea of your having any tendency to consumption is really nothing but a figment of your fancy.   Remember myself and my throat troubles of 18 years back !   No, in that regard my mind is quite at ease about you ; but from this time forth, now that you have grown alarmed yourself, it's clear enough that you must start another mode of life.   You ought to, and must lead a life of ease and comfort now : it must be your entertainment to dress as slowly and nicely as you please of a morning, and you shall presently receive from me a cosy pretty negligée ; let your occupation be a little embroidery, and above all, pleasant reading, receiving callers, dressing at leisure for out-of-doors, paying calls, and so forth.   In time I shall buy a smart little carriage, and leave it at a coachman's with whom I'll strike a bargain for the horse he is to place at my disposal ; then I shall take you for nice afternoon drives.   In short, you must thoroughly lead the life of a fine lady now ; you're not to bother about housekeeping an atom more than may amuse you : it's the only way for you to get on the high road to the manner of living you need.   What money can do towards it, will soon be seen to ; believe me, as things stand now, my future may become extra-ordinarily brilliant, and there is no telling how far it may lead when Germany is run through and London and Paris are laid under tribute, which will then depend on no one but myself.

Even for next winter the prospects are very auspicious. Hamburg has signed for 50 louis d'or ; I am receiving a note for the end of November. Leipzig has written about Lohengrin ; I had grounds for not demanding over 20 louis d'or. Darmstadt, Carlsruhe, Hanover, Brunswick, have all applied already ; Cologne, Magdeburg, Reval, Olmütz, even Ballenstedt, are asking for Tannhäuser. In brief, it's certain that the whole of Germany must walk into our pocket soon. Berlin also (at Kroll's) is a certainty now, and that is sure to bring me in a couple of thousand *francs.*—

So : you must and shall become a fine lady : to please me, you must wear nothing but velvet, silk or satin, yet not so as to interfere with your comfort. For—if *any* woman has such things, you deserve them too : that's what I shall tell *all* who may envy or sniff at you !—

Undoubtedly, Herwegh has a number of coloured cravats ; but for all that, he doesn't seem bent upon conquests. He sticks to his room and his muzzing all day ; when he comes out of it, he barely mumbles. On the contrary, it is *I* who have to keep a sharp look-out here ; for the fair local world is all setting its cap at me, the famous betorched composer. Luckily I know no one, and no one attracts me to do so.—This morning we had rain for the first time ; but it has ceased already. My former room was very noisily placed ; repeatedly I could not sleep. To-day I've removed to a quieter room in the first storey.

Many thanks for the fresh consignment, though you may make a pause until I ask for anything again ; the food here has somewhat improved now. I was the only one to open his mouth ; no Switzer would ever dare to, and Herwegh still less.—Well, 15 days more and there's an end to it !—

You might get Mathilde, please, to tell them at the Post to send my money-letters also here—till further orders ; they may always contain an enquiry I shouldn't like to leave unanswered a whole week, that is to say, for the time you're at Baden.—Upon your return, order the money-letters to be delivered to you as before. Don't misunderstand me !—Apart from business letters, I answer none now ; I really have to save myself during the cure. See, even this letter to yourself has grown too long ; *that* exertion, though, is not to count, I have made it so gladly.—

Now, my good Minna, farewell, hold your head up ; think of the comfortablest life you can possibly conceive, of the little carriage—na ! and—I say no more ! You'll be bound to put up with me a while longer ! Adieu ; greet Peps !

Thy
RICHARD.

Have you written to the Wesendonck yet ? He wrote me that they were going to Wiesbaden on the 21st for Lohengrin : the performance took place, I've received a playbill and a criticism : Frau Moritz sang the Elsa very well.

Saturday, 5 A.M. [30th].

See, Mienel, I have to re-open this and add to it. Quite a pile of letters came last evening with all sorts of tidings, foolish and good. 1., from yourself, with the Wiesbaden Lohengrin snuff-box, which amused me vastly. You good Uetli-ascender, you ! Otherwise I've nothing much to answer you, except that I am doing tolerably. The doctor may well talk of warm douches ; good Lord, they are simple enough with their bath here. and douches don't exist !—2., from *Liszt* an uncommonly cheerful, kind and splendid letter : the Grand Duke thought very highly of my letter to him : Liszt has had to tell the Princess of Prussia a lot about me. The music from Bauer can wait till I return.—3., From *Karl*.—4., The enclosed letter to yourself, the address of which deceived me ; when I saw from whom it was, I read it through. You can scarcely make any other reply to the crazy young lady, than that the Carlsruhe Music-festival is the 20th Sept., and at it things from Tannh. and Lohengrin will be performed ; beyond that you know nothing.—Now I must be off to the spring. Farewell, bathe prettily, and get quite well. Adieu, Mienel !

Thy

R.

52.

5th August 1853.

Dear Mietz, I leave here *Tuesday* the 9th, and—as I see you cannot come half-way—I shall be with you at Zurich *Wednesday* evening.—

Nobody takes a cure here for more than 3 weeks, and all were astonished at my having been ordered 4. The water is extraordinarily powerful ; I've been stopped up for several days, and my stomach feels bad. Moreover, the place itself is beginning to be unendurable to me, the arrangements are too disgraceful ; for want of convenience, etc., a deal of what the Doctor ordered me I cannot follow out at all. In short, it's high time I thought of turning home. The usual 3 weeks' cure expires tomorrow ; I am throwing in a couple of days, but Tuesday I depart—as said—and hope to find you better on Wednesday evening than you write me you unfortunately are at present. My last letter I addressed to Zurich ; I hope it was sent after you. So nothing is to come of the rendezvous at Chur etc. proposed therein ; perhaps R. is right. We'll soon replace it by some pleasant excursion or other, that Mathilde also may still get a little to see.

What more should I write you, seeing that I soon shall be able to talk with you ? Besides, I've had no more news at all of late ; I know just nothing, excepting that it's odious here when one makes no excursions, and those refuse to agree with the cure.

Write me another once, that you have received this letter, and address to *Chur, poste restante ;* thus I shall find it waiting Tuesday evening. Farewell, old Mietzel ! Give me a good welcome. Adieu ; shake Peps's paw.— Adieu, auf Wiedersehen Wednesday !—

Thy
RRRrrrr !

I don't require money.

[*A fortnight after his return to Zurich, Wagner starts on a long-pro- jected trip to Northern Italy, in quest of inspiration for the music of his " Ring."—Tr.*]

53.

TURIN, 30. *August* 1853.

DEAR MIENEL,

Alack, I found no letter from you here to-day ; but the evening post comes in at 7, when something perhaps will turn up.—Since I wrote and telegraphed you last, I have arrived here, under many difficulties. Poor thanks I owe the Herweghs for offering to book me a seat from Geneva to Turin, which ended in smoke : the best time being lost, at Geneva I could only get a (*villainous*) seat as far as Chambery, a third of the distance ; whereas at Chambery there came a sudden stop to all things, every place in every diligence and other coach being already taken till the 4th of September. So nothing remained but to hire a hackney flyman for 3 days, or take extra-post with strangers. I chose the latter, because two other travellers were in the same predicament : a very dear carriage had to be taken for the whole distance to Turin ; but unluckily there was such a mass of gentry's private coaches also going extra-post, that the supply of horses gave out, and at last our only way of getting forward was by bribing the postilions.—It was a venturesome journey on the *Mont Cenis* by night ; yet everything went right, and, with fine weather the whole time, I reached *Turin* yesterday afternoon.

This is a handsome, big, and elegant new city, quite *à la Paris ;* but naturally that isn't what I'm seeking, and I shall not remain here long ; I merely want to rest a bit, and make an excursion to the environs, which must be very beautiful. Last evening I made straight for a small theatre (there are *a number* of theatres here), where I heard a silly comic opera, which—wretched as it was— was quite excellently sung and acted by the company. Not until 12 did I get to bed after it, but slept very well (in a bed again at last) and did not arise till 9 this morning.—

I should not have written you as yet, before having a letter from you to answer, if I hadn't wanted to tell you *not* to address to *Turin* any moie, but to

Mr. R. W.

à Gênes

poste restante :   (*Royaume de Sardaigne*).

(*Gênes*, you see, is the French for *Genua*—which in Italian, again, is called *Genova ;* but I'm afraid *Genova* might be read *Genève* (Genf), which would cause confusion.)

Yes, it is the Mediterranean to which I'm chiefly looking forward, and hope to reach the 1st September (Thursday).

Good God, I can write you next to nothing about yourself, as it's so long since I've had any news from you; and then the post for Switzerland goes out at 5, and—even if I do get a letter from you to-day—that will not be till 7. So I must save any further remarks for tomorrow, when I hope to have something quite friendly and good to reply to.

So farewell for to-day, good old Minna. Be quite cheerful and calm—and you'll give me the greatest of pleasure. If Mathilde is with you still, my kind regards to her!

Adieu, shake Peps by the paw,

Thy
wholly good
RICHARD.

Turin,
at the Hôtel de l'Europe, on a splendid
square, opposite the Royal Palace.

54.

GENOA, *1st September* 1853.

Ah, Mienel, Mienel, never have I seen anything like this *Genoa!* It is something indescribably lovely, majestic and original; Paris and London shrink into dreary, formless heaps of streets and houses, beside this godlike city!—Naturally I shouldn't know where or how to begin, to describe the impression all this has made upon me, and goes on making; I have laughed like a

child, and could scarcely conceal my delight !—Instead of
attempting an impossible and useless description, I will
merely give you an account of my journey.—

After sight-seeing enough in Turin and its outskirts
the day before yesterday—when I couldn't help admiring
the city's fine position—I determined to quit that otherwise most wearisome den of a capital and get to Genoa
a day the sooner. I had already received your nice kind
money-letter ; it gave me great joy, and I thank you for
it most heartily—especially for your being so " lazy " as
you write me.—At Turin I had further seen the " Barber
of Seville," which amused me much. So I came on
yesterday to Genoa (the longest stretch by rail), where I
arrived after 6 in the afternoon and promptly took a room
at an hotel, from which I have the harbour and sea
directly in front of me. The hotel itself really consists
of two palaces, the *Grimaldi* and *Fiesco*, which have been
turned into an inn now. I am lodging about 6 storeys
high, because one has the finest view there ; flights of
marble stairs the whole way up ; all the floors of mosaic,
etc., unheard of antique splendour everywhere ! Last
evening I got myself led round a bit by Signor Raphael
(that's the name of my guide) ; Lord, how astounded I
was at these palaces, often touching each other, all beautiful, lofty, superb. Their former owners, the proud,
brave patricians of Genoa, of course are all extinct or poor
now, and the palaces are mostly let or sold for vulgar use.
Thus, on the first floor of the Palais *Brignole* there was
a silk-warehouse ; in the parterre and courtyard (with
garden), on the other hand, a café. There I ate an ice,
drank coffee, and smoked a cigar ; a divine night, under
oleander trees tall as a house :—I could almost have expired
for bliss—I confess—and to make you the choicest gift

that *I* can think of for your birthday, this day I promise you to take a trip to *Genoa* with you next spring : a treat, good creature, you will *have* to share ! !—A heavenly slumbrousness came over me at last in this divine air which laps one's limbs so soothingly, and almost seems to waft one.   I threw the shutters open this morning : there lay the harbour, city, and the sea again, all steeped in sunshine ; the sea as blue for leagues as our Swiss lakes, all swarming with ships, masts and sails.   With my famous double spy-glasses I have just followed a big ship from farthest distance right into the harbour, and watched her pick up the pilot.   Na, *you* should be *spying* here ! !

Not a drop of rain has fallen anywhere around for a couple of months : terrible dust on the country roads. For all that, the air is by no means too hot—it has nothing stabbing or oppressive ; one goes about half undressed, but feels uncommonly well and comfortably brisk with it all.   It's a proper human breed here : one might give the Stumme von Portici straight off with the men in the harbour ; almost naked, tall and slender, brown as Africans, and all with very fine dark, passionate and sentimental eyes.   The feminine type loses in comparison ; they all go about with white veils over the head and at the side.   Perhaps I shall present letters [of introduction] tomorrow ; I didn't at Turin.   I have had some strange adventures : at Turin I met *Thalberg ;* in the train yesterday I got into close acquaintance with the Russian Ambassador at Rome, and his wife, whom I very proudly informed I was a political outlaw and couldn't go to Rome.   At last they found out who I was, however, and adhered to their invitation to Rome.

Now, I almost think this letter ought to reach you exactly on your birthday ; besides the other congratulations I'm sending you, I therefore also wish you health and happiness from my whole full heart herewith. For sure, the whole fifth of September shall be devoted by me to your memory ; to your health alone will I eat, drink, walk, look, and taste the air. I expect to keep it in Genoa, which I shall make my head-quarters, in fact, for the next fortnight ; my chief excursion, certainly, will be to Spezia, where I may stay awhile perhaps, but I want all letters sent me here. So please continue, dear Mienel, to send to the address last given you :

> *à Gênes*
>> (*Royaume de Sardaigne*)

I left orders in Turin to have letters sent after me hither.

—Just you be quite well and cheerful for your birth-day, and console yourself with the thought of your wicked husband, who also is served badly enough ! Tell good Pepsel he should only see Genoa too ! Everyone must come and see Genoa !—

I think of bathing in the sea to-day ; whatever occurs to me after, you shall hear when I write again, occasion for which I'm hoping to receive tomorrow through a letter from yourself. Farewell, dear Mienel.

Take a hearty kiss from

Thy
RICHARD.

55.

GENOA, 3. September 1853.

MY GOOD, GOOD MIENEL,

I was seized with such woeful home-sickness to-day, that I couldn't write to you, and gave it up. Already I had closed my trunk, when I found no peace before I sent you off another greeting ; so I have unpacked the writing-gear again, just to tell you briefly that I'm starting in an hour for Spezia by the steamer, which only goes on Saturdays. That will not prevent my getting your letters safely, though ; yesterday I received your second addressed to Turin. So have no fear, but continue addressing to Genoa ("*Gênes*") ; for I am bound to return here, and simply do not know how long I shall remain at Spezia. From Spezia—where I arrive tomorrow morning— I shall write you again at once, also enclosing the lines for *Wyss* to Liszt. For to-day I will merely add, that I haven't been feeling quite well—presumably owing to the great change of diet ; but I fancy the sea-voyage will cure me, even the sea-sickness perhaps. So don't be anxious about me ; rather, take good care of *yourself—do you hear ?*

My God, if a poodle hadn't eaten with me yesterday, I should have been all alone again ; to-day I nearly broke down with home-sickness—my God ! Oh yes— I'm certain to return soon, heavenly beautiful tho' it is here !

Adieu, dear good Mienel ! Many, many kisses from
Thy
HUSBAND.

56.

GENOA, 6. *September* 1853.

DEAR MIENEL,

Ridicule me as much as you will, I'm *turning tail !* I have taken my place for the homeward journey viâ the *Lago maggiore* already ; a telegram has also just gone off, which—as I couldn't get it through in German— I have despatched to Sulzer, that he may bring it you nicely translated, and so no confusion arise. If you follow that despatch's invitation, to be sure, this letter will not reach your hands until after our joint return ; but in case your health should not permit you to come as far as Flüelen to meet me, you'll receive this letter just before my own return, presumably Saturday morning [10th], whereas I hope to be with you by Saturday evening.—

My decision to turn back was unavoidable after my thoroughly convincing myself how things stood with me. At Spezia yesterday, so soon as I conceived the thought of turning home, my whole state of health promptly grew better ; and with a certain cheerfulness I mounted the mail which has brought me to Genoa, where I meant to determine in fine. Hardly had my improvement betrayed me into resuming my former plan of travel and deciding on the tour to Nice, however, than the old discomfort instantly recurred, and I could only dislodge it by a prompt and firm conclusion for return, when I got better at once.

I should have started this very evening, if I hadn't to wait until tomorrow morning for a letter that has gone to Spezia by my previous orders, and therefore crossed me. So don't you write me any more, nor forward any letters. Next Saturday (! ! !) you shall hear 100,000 things by mouth from your good ice-bird and loving husband

RICHARD.

To *a merry meeting !*

Should you have to go to Baden now, why, go of course ; I can come to you there, and be at home just the same.

Adieu, good Mienel and Pepsel.

[*Soon after comes a rendezvous at Basle with Liszt, on the latter's way back from the Carlsruhe festival.—Tr.*]

57.

BASLE, 7. *Octbr.* 1853.

MY DEAR MIENEL,

The pace is awful here : I'm going crazy ; hardly can I bring off two lines to yourself.

Just think of it ! Liszt came with : 1, Bülow ; 2, Joachim ; 3, R. Pohl from Dresden ; 4, Cornelius from Berlin ; 5, Pruckner from Munich ; 6, Remenyi from Hungary. On their entry into the hotel, all bellowed the trombone passage from Lohengrin. *Early* this morning there also came the *Fürstin* [Carolyne Sayn-Wittgenstein] with her daughter, and a relative of Prince Wittgenstein's. —I hadn't slept last night, and you may imagine how I've been bombarded to-day ! So the merest needful on the rush !—

Tomorrow afternoon, Saturday, I go with Liszt to Strassburg, and on Sunday to Paris. All the others turn back.—

For Paris, Liszt has invited me to stay with him at the *Hôtel de Paris* (*Rue Richelieu*). So address me in future :

(*Mr. R. W.*

  Rue Richelieu Hôtel de Paris

       à

        Paris.)

For the rest, these people give me great delight ; the Fürstin proposed *your* health at dinner. All send you greetings.

Farewell, old treasure ; hold me dear, don't let Peps sleep too much, and bring up *Jacquot* well.

    Thy altogether glorious

        HUSBANDDDDD !

I shall write you full particulars of *your journey :* Liszt will remain in Paris till about the 16th or 18th.

58.

PARIS, 11. *October* 1853.

O thou who art good Muzius incarnate !—

So 3 whole days have passed without my being able
to write to you ! Yesterday I had set apart a special
time for it, but when I wanted to commence, behold,
that cursed youngster Hermann [Liszt's servant] had gone
off with the key of my trunk, and was nowhere to be
seen or heard ; so that—put out as I was in general—I
never came to writing.—Not that I'm going to write
much to you, even to-day ; we shall have time enough
here soon, on the spot, to entertain ourselves by mouth
with all past happenings. So merely the main headings
to-day, and what you *must* hear.

Saturday (—I'm all at sea about the days)—yes :
Saturday afternoon we left for Strassburg, where the
Fürstin meant to part company with us. Bülow (that
good young man—he really is !) and Joachim also accompanied us thither, but separated from us midday Sunday,
at Strassburg, to return viâ Carlsruhe. The Fürstin, on
the other hand, suddenly made up her mind to come to
Paris too ; so we arrived here Sunday evening, and Liszt
was obliged to descend at the *Hôtel des Princes* (*!!!*) *rue
Richelieu*, whither he naturally invited me too. He
won't hear of my not being his guest, you see ; I never
get a chance of paying. For that matter, I have to
work it duly off ; poor beggar, I must sing, read, talk,
and explain,—you know how people always tap me !
After all, one does it gladly ; only sleep is very poor,
almost absent in fact.

Yesterday morning I went in search of Kietz : he
was in the country, sure enough ; but he has been sent
for, and I expect to see him soon. I've not yet been to

Anders, and to-day I haven't yet been out at all. Last evening we all dined quite domestically with Liszt's 3 children "*en famille*"—Berlioz joined us later.—

The rest of the day—as I hadn't found Kietz—I sauntered through the streets alone, and had to laugh like a child at the beautiful things [in the shops]. Of course I never lost you from my thoughts, and heartily looked forward to a thorough rummaging around with *you* soon ; the elegance here has enormously increased, and everything is so seductive that one would like to have thousands in one's pockets, just to be able to take the stuff home. I am positively afraid lest our money might also give out on our very first outing, such a quantity I should like to buy you ! So just bring *all the money* you possess and can lay hands on ; for instance, change the 50 thaler at Hug's as well. Simply money : we may need it here ; on our return we shall find fresh money waiting, in any case.—

But listen, Mietzel ! Liszt is staying on till the 20th, his Fürstin also ; therefore I candidly advise you not to come before *they've* gone (particularly *she*) ; it's too gênant. Moreover, I shouldn't at all know what to do about the hotel : here I have a tiny room at Liszt's expense—which gênes me—but when *you* come, I of course must move out, so that we may lodge (in comfort) at our own expense. All that I'll soon attend to finely : so I recommend you

To start *at 8 on Wednesday the* 19*th*,—by 4 in the afternoon you'll be at Basle. Should you want anything there, just send to Herr Merian-Köchlin ; he called on me at Basle, and begged me to direct you to him.—

Then *at* 5 *on Thursday morning*, *the* 20*th*, you take the *express* direct to Paris, where you will be received

about 10 in the evening by your good little hubbie.
The journey is quite agreeable, and not fatiguing ; you
will stand it well, I hope. *Then* what an unholy fling
we'll have here ! Adieu, good old Wifie ; salute the
children (good Pepsel !)—you soon shall hear more from
your

dear little

Dick (*Richardchen*).

So address : *Hôtel des Princes*

Rue Richelieu.

(Best thanks for your lllletter
to Basle ! ! !)

On *no* account trim a bonnet before Paris ; you'll be
surprised ! !

59.

PARIS, 12. *October* 1853.
(*Hôtel des Princes
Rue Richelieu*)

Hm ! Hm ! Hm ! Hm !
    No letter again to-day ! ! !—
So ! so ! so ! so !—
Ei ! ei ! ei !—
Very well, dear Mienel, then I shall simply write you
that it abides by what I wrote you yesterday : Wednesday
the 19th you start, and Thursday evening I receive you
here. I know nothing of Kietz as yet.—Yesterday I had
such a violent headache that I had to come away from
the *théâtre français*. To-day it's better—I actually slept
4 hours. —

What I chiefly have to say to you, is this : I've just
written to Sulzer ; if he gives you the *whole* of the
money for the bill of exchange, then take and bring it

all with you to Paris ; we can make good use of it here.
The *rent* you can also leave till I return ; so—come with
an immense amount of money,—then it will be well with
you on earth, i.e. in Paris ! Adieu, Mutz ; love to the
children !

Thy

HANDSOME HUBBIE.

60.

PARIS, 16. *October* 1853.

Best thanks, dear Minna, for your beautiful cream-
laid letter ; it tasted capital !—But, a truce to words and
fiddle-faddle, the arrangement holds good : I expect you at
the station here on Thursday evening. True, Liszt and his
ladies are staying still longer ; he wants to celebrate his
birthday here, the 24th October [really the 22nd]. But that
need make no difference, as—the *Wesendoncks* are here—
and you can be with them, if necessary, should I at any
time have to form suite where you either couldn't, or
wouldn't care to go. Yes, I really had to burst out
laughing yesterday, when in the *rue Richelieu* I suddenly
met the good American [Otto Wk], who pointblank refused
to believe it was I. *Liszt* is going to pay a call with me
on the Wesendoncks to-day, but all our evenings are so
filled up already, that we can't be in their company at
present ; to-day we have to be at Erard's, tomorrow at
the Countess Kalergis', the day after to-morrow at Jules
Janin's ; and so it goes on. Frau Wesendonck was
highly delighted when she learnt that you were coming
too. They intend remaining here a fortnight in all ;
which will be very agreeable for us, only I fancy *we* can't
stay so long, were it only for poor dear Pepsel's sake, who
is making my heart ache already : what do you think
yourself ?—

I have written to Sulzer again to-day : he will give
you—I hope so—whole heaps of money, all of which I
can repay him after our return.   But—*money* we require
here, immensely much money—else it's no good ; and
you then shall come in for a really fine treat !—Na, adieu !
A pleasant journey, and observe my plan of it !—I shall
fetch you Thursday evening, and tickle you to your heart's
content !—Ah, poor Peps !—Adieu !

Thy
RICHEL.

[*After a week spent together in Paris, they return to Zurich toward the
end of the month, and Minna is the next to leave it, for a whey-cure at
Seelisberg.—Tr.*]

61.

ZURICH, 1. *July* 1854.

O you poor ill-used Wife, disgracefully thrust out into
misery ! !

Be assured, I heartily regret my having so insisted on
your starting ; only believe me, it was from the best of
motives in the world, out of true zeal for your health !
But all our hopes of better weather have shamefully been
set at naught ; each morning I awake with horror, and
think of you with deep regret.   In my opinion, if it
becomes too much for you to wait for decent weather,
you should return at once until it quite clears up.—

Indeed you are right, it is too bad that none of our
acquaintances can ever give us proper information ; one
always tells us this, another that !   Your travelling
adventures moved me deeply, you always seem to have
bad luck when riding.   And then, you're all alone as yet
up there !   My God, that really must be dreadful ; do
please turn back, and don't force anything : perhaps

it will be fine in a week, when you can return
again.

No further reply can I make to your letter of lamenta-
tion, than to help you lament, and declare you are right
should you be wanting to hook it !

It's deuced quiet here ; not a soul to be heard or seen.
On the day of your departure the little Major ran into me in
the afternoon : he was meaning to call on the Marschalls ;
I accompanied him, but the Marschalls weren't in.   So I
took Müller [the "Major"?] up home with me ; Nette had
to brew tea and provide tongue, which the Majorkin
greatly enjoyed.   Otherwise no one has shewn his face ;
but I'm invited to dinner at Herwegh's on Sunday—
tomorrow—they are the only people who have bothered
about me.   Nothing has altered in my mode of life,
excepting that I am even more industrious than before.
Besides the forenoon, I also work two hours an evening
now, from 6 to 8, then go and drink a glass of beer—all
alone—and get home again by 9.   In the early morn I now
go out for Carlsbad water ; I have also given up eating
butter : it was a mistake.

Things at home seem otherwise going fairly straight :
I can detect no disorder ; the food is tolerable, only the
soups are wretched ; quiet reigns.   *Jacquot* is in fine
form, prattling and whistling to his heart's content ; often
he has flown into my room ; otherwise I insist on N.'s
remaining in the parlour with him.   Peps seems to have
lost a little of his appetite all at once ; yesterday, as it at
least was dry again, he had to walk with me to Zollikon,
when I was also accompanied by Herr *Wiedu*, who got
nicely taken in, for once, in this way : of a sudden I saw
him watching a spot in the field behind us, and creeping
stealthily towards it ; really, Peps was snuffing around

there, half hidden ; but Wiedu took him for a cat, and
was just about to attack him very gingerly, when—at
close quarters—he precious soon discovered his mistake.
I couldn't help roaring with laughter !—

Hardly a single letter ; I'm waiting anxiously for
money, or I shan't quite know how to get away. I have
had profuse apologies from *Coburg :* the Intendant was
still absent, they wrote, but they had no doubt he would
comply with my request—for prepayment. The same
letter wound up with the brief intimation that Fischer
had had a stroke, but with no preciser statement, which
Fischer or where, so that I'm waiting for a corroboration
from Dresden ; meantime I shall continue to refuse to fear
the worst.—Otherwise only Schmidt of Frankfort has
written : he cannot come ; their *Lohengrin* had much
success again ; Hoffmann will give the *Holländer* also this
autumn. To-day a letter came from *Selisberg*—but you
already know that.—

If it weren't for that cur * * * Music-feast, I shouldn't
stir a foot, but go straight on composing [*Walküre*, act i];
I am quite in the vein again. It annoys me to think I
must interrupt myself ; if anything were to go just half-
way counter to my wish, I should be equal to declaring
myself ill and letting the whole business drop. Well, you
shall hear again if I start.

So ! So ! So !—I have begun attending to your orders.
Herewith you have the Kladderatatsch ; it's a double
number, and will last you out. Cheer up ; as soon as the
weather behaves itself, I am sure you'll feel quite well
up there. I wish it you with all my heart, and am looking
forward gladly to the certain good result.

The animal and human household sends kind love.
Papo [Jacquot] is just hopping about with Peps. Farewell

and write me pretty soon again, that I may know how you're doing.   Adieu, dear Minna.

Thy R.

62.

ZURICH, 3. *July* 1854.

I cannot help congratulating you, dear Minna, on this beautiful weather !—It has removed a mill-stone from my heart.

Nothing else occurred.—I have received a little money, and so can get away.   I shall write you again, tho', first.

Farewell and keep your spirits up !   I merely wanted to congratulate you, and tell you how delighted I am with the weather.

Thy
RICHEL.

63.

SITTEN [SION], 10. *July* 1854.

DEAR MINNA,

I cannot write you much to-day, as I must soon go out, and probably shan't have another opportunity all day.

I received your letter last evening, and thank you for having so stuck to sending me a greeting here !   I can tell you little cheering as regards myself.   I bitterly repent having let myself be lured here ; how I wish I had followed my instinct, and calmly stayed at work in Zurich ! In the first place, they ordered me here much too early ; since the day before yesterday have I been in this tiny hovel to no purpose at all, and mostly in bad weather. The real rehearsal doesn't take place till tomorrow, most of the bandsmen not arriving till to-day.   Next, it isn't

even a genuine Federal music-feast at all, but merely for
the district ; they will be glad to get an *audience of* 500.
A poor orchestra has been run up in a small church : the
whole thing as pitiful as possible. About 35 bandsmen
are coming ; the rest are nondescripts one had best not
let join in at all. In short, this pickle makes me feel as
if at a country fair where I had to masquerade as Kapellmeister, and I have a very good mind to decamp.   I'll
just hear how the church behaves to-day ; if the echo is
too great, and the orchestra, as I much fear, sounds mixed
and indistinct, I shall transfer the whole mess to Herr
Methfessel, who will lick his every finger for it, and get
away.   It is a pure effrontery, to expect me to deal with
such rubbish ; I am greatly put out at not having followed my own inclination and stayed at home.—

The Karls [young Ritter and bride] are very prettily lodged
on the Lake of Geneva ; I spent a day with them—unfortunately in pouring rain. *He* came hither with me ;
she—most sensibly !—remained behind.   For the nonce I
return to them : if the weather turns fine, I shall stay
there ; I've brought my work.   Then I should tranquilly
abide the time for fetching you.   That part I've reckoned
out with Sulzer : on the 25th we mean to reach you
together at Selisberg—*he* coming from Graubünden, I
from the Oberland.   Should the weather favour me, I
shall cross the Gemmi—with Karl—and march through
the Oberland ; should it not, I shall simply come by
Thun : all which will decide itself later.   Then we
should arrive in your exact 4th week of cure, and you
would return with us to Zurich.—

Lord knows, I know of nothing else to tell you ;
beyond my journey, absolutely nothing has occurred to me,
and I'm as put out as a devil at being here.   The *Karls*

have provisionally installed themselves quite daintily ; she hasn't made at all a bad housewife. But the whole thing seems so curious to me !—

From Dresden I have heard nothing at all ; consequently I know nothing definite about Fischer either, whether he has merely had a stroke—or really is dead. Therefore I shall not give way to the worst apprehensions even yet.—Your dream has no significance ; Karl knows all about that. That you otherwise seem in fairly good spirits, as your letter bears witness again, rejoices me heartily ; I am sure I shall find you in very good form.— Peps turned quite lively again, at the last, when he remarked that I was starting. The *bachelors* kept up the farewell *fête* until 3 in the morning ! I had gone home already at 11. The savages ! !—

Na, I must dress now, to take stock of the church.— I'll just wait for my verdict, before closing this letter.— Adieu for the moment.

6 P.M.

I will just conclude by telling you, I shall probably give in and remain after all ; some of the Berne musicians would have been greatly disappointed. For the rest, I have been unable to take anything in hand to-day again ; consequently I shall be sleeping the 3rd night in this hovel for nothing. Catch me doing it another time !—Presumably you will receive my next letter from *Vevey ;* so, if you're writing *at once*, write me there :

	Vevey
Poste restante :	*Canton de Vaud.*

Farewell, old Muzius ; to a speedy, hale and hearty meeting ! In worse humour I can never be, than *here* and now !   Farewell, have your spit at the Grütli house [just below her], and hold dear

Thy faithful spouse

R. W.

64.

VERNEX, 13. *July* 1854.

DEAR MINNA,

I must prepare myself for being severely scolded by you this time !

The evening I wrote you last from Sitten things there became too loathsome for me, and at 10 that night I rapidly made up my mind and took myself off, after transferring the symphony as well to Methfessel. For I learnt that many even of the bandsmen engaged had not turned up, and in fact were not coming at all. That knocked the bottom out of the tub ; I could do no else than give the business up—whereby perhaps, if truth were told, I quite suited the feast-givers' book. Methfessel had never seriously believed that I would come, you see, and already had provided for another, easier symphony. Even on my way here I met Dr. Ziegler of Winterthur, who likewise had heard I wasn't coming, and was quite surprised to see me.   The gentlemen at Sitten too, a lot of clerics, didn't quite know what to do with me, for doubtless they also could read in my face that the thing would not amuse me.   Finally Methfessel had borne all the burdens, rehearsed the choruses with untold pains, and seen to all other arrangements ; in return for all which he would have been thrust back by myself, in a sense, to obscurity. Himself he took a positive delight in directing my attention to every defect, so that I could see he would like to be decently rid of me.—I'm therefore convinced I did the right thing in the end, and that these people were secretly satisfied. The Rordorf, for instance, declared at once, she would have been astonished if I *had* conducted. It was nothing else—as I said before—than a big unmusical village wake : I am certain my inner vexation and shame at the degradingness of my task would have made me turn seriously ill.—I don't imagine much is likely to be said about it : it is to be hoped they'll pull themselves well out—if not, that's their affair ; never in my life will I take part in any " Music-feast," everything has turned out so badly, and worse than I feared.—

So be reasonable yourself, dear Muzius, and don't make me any fuss ! ! !—

At first I was so put out, that I meant to travel home direct. In the end Karl succeeded, however, in tieing me to his house a bit longer ; he has abandoned me a little sitting-room with a lovely view, where I can work undisturbed the whole morning ; which I also intend doing for the present. So it provisionally abides by the latest arrangement I wrote you ; if all goes well, and I remain in the humour, I shall wait here till your 4th week of cure, and then come—by whichever road it be—and fetch you home (with Sulzer). Consequently I have nothing fresh to write you upon that.

Only one letter has been sent after me, a mile-long one from [Gustav] Kietz, from Rome still ; he writes of almost nothing save the *fleas*. He sends you many greetings.—

It is to be hoped N. has sent you my shoes ; I think they will do you good service.—How goes it with the cure ? are you right already in the body ?—How I look forward to finding you perfectly well !—

Above all, don't take the Sitten tale amiss, or make

me any reproaches ! Never again will I stoop to anything so paltry and petty-fogging.——

I hope to have another letter from you soon ; what you write me, rest assured, ever affords me great pleasure, especially when you give rein to your wit, which suits you very well.

The Karlery sends best greetings ; and your poor excellent husband lays himself humbly at the feet of his precious dame as

Her Majesty's

most obedient

MAN.

Direct your next letter

> *à Monsieur R. W.*
> *chez Mr. Rivaz*
> *à Collonges près Montreux*
> *Canton de Vaud.*

65.

COLLONGES, BY MONTREUX
17. *July* 1854.

DEAR MINNA,

Yesterday I informed you by telegraph that I was returning to Zurich. Really I have nothing to add to it, excepting that I go direct tomorrow evening, and consequently shall be at home by Wednesday night. You know how I originally meant to return by the Oberland, and thus fetch you en route ; but it transpires that the Karls have no present relish for an Alpine tour : moreover you know his whimsicality, so that I gladly save that for another time and good company. *Alone*, again, I haven't the smallest desire for a mountain trip ; I should grudge the money. Nothing would therefore remain for me, if I meant to come to you from here, but the journey by Berne and Lucerne. I was pining for home, however, and in the long run one only bores oneself with Karl, whilst I lacked the convenience for work ; also, the weather is frequently bad. So I swiftly resolved to go home for a week, went to Vevey—an hour and a half from here—and telegraphed. On my return I found your letter waiting, for which I thank you very much, as it thoroughly revived me : only, it perplexed me again what to do, since you write that Sulzer meant to meet me up with you as early as the 22nd, instead of the 26th. It would be scarcely worth the trouble now to go to Zurich first, as I should only be able to stay there exactly 2 days if I departed with Sulzer on Saturday. At this moment, after thinking it over, I'm all hesitation again : there, Karl is calling to breakfast ; I'll determine then.—

Now my mind is made up. If I'm to reach you at the same time as Sulzer, I cannot go to Zurich for 2 days first ; I should be sorry for Pepsel, having to leave him behind me so soon again. Therefore I shall come to you from here, so as to arrive the 22nd or at latest the 23rd. By which road, I don't exactly know : if the weather is fine, I probably shall take the *Brünig* after all ; if not, I shall come viâ *Berne* and *Lucerne*. Of course, you can't write me again, as I shouldn't know *where* you ought to write to ; let us hope no mishap may betide you meanwhile.—

But what a marplot Sulzer is !—

Liszt wrote the other day, but nothing of importance. Avenarius also : he is revelling in the remembrance [of his visit] still.

And so you have a fine theatre with such good actors ? Perhaps there'll be a little left of it for me to see !—

God, how gladly I'd have stayed entirely at home this summer ; I positively deplore the grand time when my humour for work was so good ! People should leave me unshorn !—

Now to a speedy reunion ! Your reports on your health rejoice me immensely ! Farewell, and keep gay till our meeting.

Thy

RICHARD.

[*From Seelisberg they both returned to Zurich by the beginning of August ; a month later, Sept. 2, Minna started alone on a two months' visit to sundry relatives and friends in Germany.—Tr.*]

66.

ZURICH, 3. *Sept.* 1854.

DEAR MIENEL,

Accept my hearty congratulations on your birthday ; you may be sure I shall keep it with great devotion ! I confidently hope you arrived safely and are feeling cheerful to-day in the lap of your family. Think of me, as I think of you !

And now my best thanks for the telegram, which I received before going to bed ; I have been with you all the time, and not had much rest !

Once more—be merry on your birthday !

Thy

RICHARD.

67.

ZURICH, 7. *September* 1854.

Thank God, dear Minna, a letter has arrived to-day ! If none had come to-day, I meant to send a telegram to Tröger [her Zwickau brother-in-law]; I had firmly settled that. For I believed that, had you written on the 4th (Monday),

the letter could have got here by Wednesday (the 6th).
But it has taken a day longer, since to-day is the 7th ; so
perhaps you also did not get my birthday wishes duly on
the 5th, but a day too late ! I'm truly sorry ! In every
way your birthday's falling there has been a regular
*teaser.** I had promised my household, the day before,
that a "half" should be cracked in your honour ; but
on the morning of the 5th I unfortunately arose with a
sore throat, brought on through a chill in my bath : I
had a slight touch of fever, and thought needful to diet
myself strictly all day, to prevent the inflammation getting
thorough hold and my labouring under it about a fortnight, like my poor dear wife. Moreover, Nette also
had been seized with the quinsy, which accordingly must
have been smuggled into our house by yourself; she is
barking finer and more expressively than Peps, and—as
one used to say—has got a rouser. Under such circumstances I also refused an evening invitation to Wesendonck's, whither Sulzer had been bidden as well (on
account of your birthday). So the day passed fairly
dismally, but I decreed that if a good letter arrived from
the wife the next morning, the "half" should be drunk
on the 6th. Well, the quinsy had left me by the
morning of the 6th, but—the letter also stayed away ;
which so annoyed me all day, that I worked like a fury,
but thought of no *half.* In fact I became quite alarmed
about you, and tortured myself with the blackest of fears ;
so that I had a wretched night's sleep, got up for 2 hours,
and longed for day to come and bring the chance of
tidings. Now they've—arrived, and at least I see that
the journey passed off without actual mishap, and you

---

* " Eine recht *verzwickte* Sache " ; a pun on Zwickau.—Tr.

have reached the bosom of your family. No wonder, on the other hand, you're feeling so knocked up; looking back, it really was a great stupidity for you to have taken this fatiguing journey so soon; we won't commit it again! And now I beseech you by everything in the world: *take it easy;* be boundlessly lazy, and cosset yourself to your heart's content! Don't think of leaving Zwickau till you are in perfect condition again. What you write me of the amiable brother-in-law [a doctor] has rejoiced me quite: under care such as that, I foresee, you'll succeed in thorough convalescence. Poor woman, you need it! I am very glad about the good old mother, too, and stout Lotte and the old man with all his wits about him have also put me in good humour. In short —the long-deferred shall come to pass to-day, and your birthday be kept by us after the event; in fact with the Wesendoncks, who have had the good idea of inviting me and Nette to dinner to-day. There a *whole* must do duty!—

Otherwise I have nothing—as you may well conceive— to tell you of ourselves; I go on working (a little too hard, I fear), and look neither left nor right. Neither has anything occurred. Merely a Privy Commerce-Councillor Moritz Cohn from Dessau has called on me, filled his mouth with my fame, and finally declared he knew you *very well* from Dessau days: you had had a recommendation to him from Kaskel [banker], and I was simply to remind you of the "Concordia" (Pretty tales! and I, poor beggar, to be asked to pass them on!!)

Wesendoncks want to decoy me into flitting with them for a couple of days; but they haven't caught me yet: I do not feel like flitting. *Peps* has done another good tramp with me; *Jacquot* makes constant progress:

"Donnerwetter" he had already got pat, and to-day, after many rehearsals, he piped the Rienzi correctly.

Else it's very still with me ; no letters at all ! But just you write me all the more, and they shall ever be my dearest letters ! Give my heartiest greetings to all at Zwickau, and tell them I should like to be there too ; but, were I to attempt it, probably I should have to stay in Zwickau rather longer than either they or I might care for.

Now, farewell, dear good Wife ! Tomorrow I expect with great delight a second letter from you ; may it bring me good news of your *being well !* With that wish I mean to drink your health to-day.

Only be thoroughly lazy, and for once seek the Castle of Indolence ! Farewell, and get well !

Thy

RICHARD.

68.

ZURICH, 13. *September* 1854.

MY ENTIRELY GOOD, DEAR MIENEL !

No, the lovely partridges ! That beats everything ! Only to-day, midst the feasting on $1\frac{1}{2}$ partridge, have I arrived at emptying that "half" to your health with the house of Wagner. You were wrong, if you deemed it a thing of the past ; after the birthday had been made such a mess of, I kept waiting for a really good occasion, to be supplied by the first letter in which you wrote me that you were feeling somewhat better again. I was almost glad not to have received your last letter but one when it came, for you really had framed it quite sadly ; at least, I saw you weren't at all the thing yet, despite the lovely morning-music. Last evening at 10 (wicked

person !) I returned from the Wesendonck outing, of
which you no doubt have had tidings by now through my
Seelisberg letter ; but your letter couldn't rightly cheer
me, not so much because of your forebodings, as for
reason of the mood in which such fears still haunted you :
I didn't go to bed till 12, and got no proper sleep. I
awoke with a shocking nervous headache : the first thing
to greet me was the post-slip from Zwickau. Off went
Friederike to the Post forthwith ; the box was opened,
and on my knees I burrowed for the letter. It was the
good letter, at last, I had longed for, in which you had to
admit yourself that you weren't feeling so bad, had an
appetite and slept well. At once I gave orders : all *three*
must be cooked, and Friederike was called in to dinner ;
with myself and Nette she had to pledge a glass to you
twice over, and this time it didn't taste like schnapps to
her. That took away my headache ; now I'm smoking
my cigar over my wee cup of coffee, and writing you
quite cosily to express my joy at your condition. Peps
and Jacquot have meantime been having a good romp
on the floor. Peps can't make the bird out at all now,
for it calls Nette quite plainly by name too, and keeps
declaring "Jacquot wants his food"—so that Peps
begins to take it for a higher being.—

O yes, dear good Minna, you'll soon be right ! Your
relations' uneasiness about your looks the first few days
does not alarm me : it is always the way with nerve-
sufferers, they often get so pulled down that they appear
to have every illness in the world ; once the nerves are
duly soothed, however, it all has vanished, and the
organs fulfil their whole functions according to rule.
Still, with the frequent derangement of your abdominal
nerves, it may be well to supply your stomach with such

an aliment as costs it the minimum of labour for digestion and yet affords the body the needful nutrition ; Tröger is perfectly right.   If your condition had lasted, we should have hit on that ourselves ; you know, in fact, I ordered it myself to Emilie Ritter.

Your remaining quietly at Zwickau still, is very sensible ; you were to make a journey of *recreation*, remember, not a tearing about from place to place. Never should you leave the one before you've quite recovered from the sure fatigue of getting there, and are feeling thoroughly yourself again.   That is the only way, too, for this journey to end in your good ; and I must calmly wait for your return, provided only you return quite strengthened and refreshed.—

I shall also be sending you money very soon, that you may be hampered in nothing ; to Chemnitz, I expect.—

Nothing else has happened here.   All at Seelisberg renew their greetings to you.   I returned alone to Zurich yesterday ; the Wesendoncks proceeded to the Rigi, but in spite of all entreaties they didn't draw me up.   I bade them goodbye at the foot of the hill, and brought the letter for you on to Zurich, where I put it in the letter-box at 10 last evening, as that was quicker than if I had posted it at Brunnen.—Look forward to next summer on the Seelisberg ; it's too lovely there ! !

So farewell for to-day, my good Minna.   Give my best love to your people, and tell the parents they must kindly keep alive that you may visit them every two years.   To good Tröger give a right brotherly kiss from me : that people should go breaking their legs on your birthday, of all days, I set down as impertinent ; the bandsmen did much better, to be in such good wind.

Please give your thanks to the amiable bandmaster in my name also—it really was quite fine of him, and touched me, too, to tears.

Now grant me the great pleasure of your writing again very soon, to say you are feeling as well, and have grown as stout, as [sister] Charlotte !—Farewell, dear old Minna ; be merry, and so rejoice

Thy

R.

I didn't know that your sunshade was loaded with shot ; I got some of it between my teeth here !

69.

ZURICH, 18. *September* 1854.

DEAR MIENEL,

I suppose you are vexed with me about my last excursion ! I really had hoped to receive a letter from you to-day, and therefore postponed an answer to your last as I knew it had crossed my own letters, and you would already have had an explanation of my several days' silence last week. However, I shall flatter myself you only wanted to write me with partridges again, which travel somewhat slower than a simple letter, and therefore wouldn't reach me with one till tomorrow. For to-day, meanwhile, I simply wish to tell you my uneasiness so as to induce you not to repay evil with evil next time.—

I have a piece of news for you as well, though : namely, *Semper* duly arrived here, and stayed here 3 days ; Sulzer drove up with a spanking equipage to fetch us in state. Everybody was delighted with him [Semper] ; he had a conference with Escher and the President of the School Council, all of whom received him most flatteringly. I think he'll probably accept the post [Polytechnic], but stand out for a fixed salary of 6,000 *fr.* The gentlemen seem very glad, for everything depends on their securing a celebrity to start with.

Semper pleased me greatly ; he was in very good spirits, almost jovial, and as delighted as a child with everything. Unfortunately I wasn't quite up to the mark during his stay ; the *Föhn* was blowing, and you know my nerves are always unstrung then. Still, the weather kept fair, and yesterday we took Semper to Horgen, where we gave him a small banquet ; after which he went on from there with Klapperbein to inner Switzerland, to travel home by that détour.—He sends you his kindest regards, also his wife's.—

Otto Kummer also wrote me the other day from Dresden, craving my intervention with Schindelmeisser, as there was a good vacancy at Darmstadt for a violinist, and he would like to have the berth. I have done it, and accordingly the Kummers will transfer themselves to Darmstadt, not to Zurich.

Franziska's wedding has also taken place ; the blushing pair are going to Weimar, where he [Alex. Ritter] has obtained a violinist-berth through Liszt.—I shall write to Liszt soon, by the way, touching an opera-performance [for you] ; I will announce you shortly, too, to Schmidt of Frankfort. To the Frommann I wrote the very day of your departure.—

Within the next few days I must also be receiving money, when I'll send you another 10 louis at once.

What gladdens me most, is that your reports on your health are turning out so well : they give me fixed hope that the whole journey will do you a world of good ; and then you shall have it with me here as in Heaven, nothing but bliss and delight!—What do you say to that?

(Sulzer dragged us up the Uetli also; moreover, we dined with him once—I and Semper—at Bellevue!)

I haven't set eyes on the Wesendoncks again since the outing; but of course they would send you their greetings. Tomorrow I shall tell them I've taken it upon myself.—

The house is going on quite well. I am sorry on the whole for *Nette*, as she really hasn't one acquaintance to keep her company.—

Now, send another good account soon, greet Wolframs and the old folk from all my heart, and remain faithful to

Thy

quite good again

HUBBIE.

70.

ZURICH, *? September* 1854.

YOU GOOD PARTRIDGE WIFE,

I really must be sending you another keeper's-tip at last!—Hearty thanks for your letter and presents; they delight and reassure me greatly, especially the news of your health. It was quite right of *Cläre* to disabuse you at once of your hallucination about your looks; I was also very glad to learn that *she* remains the same old girl— or young one, as you will—in everything; thus you perhaps may inveigle her into a visit to ourselves in Switzerland some day. Ply her hard with it in my name; I really should be very, very glad to have *her* here for once, of all our family.

Things still go tranquilly at home. I'm overtaxing myself with my work, I am sorry to say, as I do so want to get the fair copy of the score [*Rheingold*] quite finished, to have one thing wholly off my hands.   So I write for another couple of hours after dinner each day now, and again when I come in of an evening.   I can stand it, however, if I only get passable sleep at night.   Practically all my life is spent with our animals, and most of my talking too.   In return they have repeatedly given me trouble of late.   Several times has Peps had the misfortune to get out of his basket the wrong side and lose himself between the beds, where I've heard him pitifully whining till I pulled him out by the tail ; he passed half the night like that once, before I discovered what was up. The other day, tho', he gave me a regular fright on our walk : he was dawdling behind and seemed suddenly seized with fierce cramps, for he wriggled round and round and couldn't keep on his legs : then I see him choking terribly, and thrown into convulsions again and again by it ; at last he vomits up a bone—as large as my fist—which the glutton had swallowed !   It was a long time before he came quite to himself again.   However, he is frisky enough now, and as soon as it is getting on for $\frac{1}{2}$ past 1 nothing will pacify him till he drives me to table.

Jacquot, too, has given me a great shock !   Manifestly the good bird misses *you* very much, and so it may have occurred to him that you were still lying abed : at one swoop he flies through all the rooms into the bedroom, precisely in which the windows stood wide open ; you may imagine how I rushed after him, and what a scream I uttered !   Luckily he alighted on the chair in front of your bed, giving me time to close the windows.   That, also, shall not occur again !

There you have pretty well my whole budget of news ; I hear very little from without.   The other day Liszt sent me an enormous medallion of himself, by Rietschel ; but where am I to bestow all the Liszts ? There are 4 of him now ! I have still to hear some sense from Germany ; God knows what will come of that business with Berlin !—

I am delighted to be able to send you another 10 louis d'or now ; you receive them piping hot, just as I had them from Mainz for the Tannhäuser. Only don't go buying too many cashmere waistcoats, but amuse yourself some other way ! If you return quite fresh and well, and in good spirits, I'd rather have that than anything.—

I suppose you'll be unable to tell me about your return-journey by Weimar and Frankfort till later ; in my turn, I will then address myself to those concerned.

Boom is nowhere to be seen ; he is composing a grand sonata now, and probably won't reappear before it's finished. Sulzer and I shall doubtless meet at Wesendoncks' tomorrow—Sunday—for dinner. They send very kind regards ; I have to keep them well-informed about you.

Your last letter from Zwickau is still being aired ; the partridges had become rather piquant, and strongly perfumed the beautiful paper. Nevertheless they—the partridges—tasted excellent, and effected most agreeable digestion.

Hitherto our weather had been extraordinarily fine and warm, so that I was able to do plenty of bathing still ; but autumn has appeared the last 2 days : together with it an account for firing from Pastor Schweizer. So winter is stealing on ; we will pass it right comfortably and workfully. The birthday shall be held on our wedding-day.

I think it highly wrong of them, to have given you no serenade at Chemnitz ; report it to the musical authorities there.

What you told me of Wolfram's appearance and home has delighted me much ; Lord, one's little mite of household comfort, after all, is everything one has. That also is why *I* furnished 34 rooms, as of course you're aware !

Apropos, did you receive my last letter to *Chemnitz ?* I have my qualms about its address. *Nette* thought the post-office people would be making remarks on the number of gentlemen my wife was keeping company with, first a Herr Dr. Tröger, then a Herr Wolfram.

Now, only keep well and in good humour ; everything else is going quite well. Give a thousand hearty greetings to *Wolfram* and all his family, with my good old faithful *Cläre* at the top ! ! !

Farewell, and greet the parents too. Get hale and hearty ! Adieu.

Thy

R.

71.

ZURICH, 30. *September* 1854.

O you hasty, unjust, mistrustful, in a word—bad woman !

It is quite in the order of things that you should write me very often, since you are reaping experiences and—even if unimportant—they give you something fresh to relate, were it no more than how you fare upon your wanderings. But if I bring it off seldomer, it is purely since I'm reaping no experience at all, everything continues in the same old groove, and with the best will

I've nothing to report to you, consequently the utmost I can do is to attest my satisfaction if I learn from you that you are feeling well. In my very last letter I could really tell you almost nothing but about the dog and bird : nothing else occurs to me. My life is running on completely inwardly, you see ; and with me that finds its fittest record in my works. I am purely a worker; if I don't or cannot work, I feel unwell, and my thoughts keep hankering after work again.

For that matter, I haven't had much mood for composition all this month ; I have finished the fair copy of the *Rheingold* score instead, to get that altogether off my hands at last : Liszt will receive the whole of it shortly. Only now have I resumed the second act of Walküre ; yesterday when I got your somewhat mistrustful letter, I was on the point of composing Fricka's entry ; it wasn't at all a bad match. You consider, though, that I'm working all this out for no one but myself : it may turn out so, too—and yet I'd rather cease to live, than not be working at a thing like this. So you must grant me just this sort of work ; for the Leipzig market and so forth, once and for all, I shall compose nothing more. Others enough are attending to that.—

So—*what* am I really to write to you of ? I have absolutely nothing to tell you of myself, saving that late in the afternoon I take my lonely walk, and then come home again, or look in for a moment at Wesendonck's first. There you have all. The household otherwise is going on quite regularly ; I have nothing to complain of.

Believe me, the only thing to interest me, is how you are entertaining yourself (in place of me). I can easily understand the Chemnitz visit having put you somewhat out of humour on the whole. The whole first part of your holiday has been spent in none but small surroundings, and perhaps you're wondering why? The more sensible of you to have gone straight to Berlin now; from our Switzerland one should only go to a *very big* city, as that affords the sole true contrast, whereas everything else is bound to appear very tame. But you are sure to be in clover now, with the good Frommann; I am firmly convinced she'll devise all manner of ways of distracting you. Besides, she's on the most intimate footing with every princess in the world; so I take it for granted she'll make you acquainted with some of them, and once you're at Court, probably you will soon forget our Switzerland and Zeltweg. I also have written to *Liszt* and *Schmidt* in your behalf; they are to let you know *direct*, if a performance [of one of my works] is taking place with them, that you may arrange your return journey accordingly. They're to write you to Leipzig (c/o Avenarius); that will be quickest, as the information would have gone too roundabout a road if it had come through me. Doubtless you won't be staying long in Berlin, as you want to be at Leipzig again the beginning of October for Röschen's début; consequently I have told Schmidt you might get to Frankfort about the middle of October.— Schindelmeisser has written me a deal again about the representation of *Lohengrin at Darmstadt:* now, that lies on the straight road from Frankfort to Basle; so, if it might interest you to see the Lohengrin there (perhaps for a comparison with Frankfort), you would have to write me to that effect forthwith, and maybe I could arrange for you to witness that as well. Schindelmeisser would be highly delighted, of course.—

Now, dear Muzius, under Alwine's lead make it your

foremost care to feel quite happy. A thorough refreshing of yourself for once is the main object of your journey ; therefore, wherever you do not feel comfortable, you must leave at a moment's notice, and preferably return to the Zeltweg and your good husband.—All send best love ; on your side, give the good Frommann my cordial greetings, be merry and—calm : you *can* be—and return in sound health !—

Farewell, good old Wife—and—na, you know all that.

Thy
R.

72.

DEAR MINNA,

Merely a couple of lines to-day at random : I presume you are at Leipzig.—So soon as you know anything certain about *Frankfort*, please write at once to *Louis Schindelmeisser, grossherzogl. Hofkapellmeister in Darmstadt* (nice and distinctly), telling him *when* you can get to Darmstadt. Then he'll answer you to Frankfort, whether and when he can give you a Lohengrin performance. Tell him to address " beim Herrn Kapellmeister G. Schmidt,"—that will be the best plan. I have provisionally told him you would be at Frankfort toward the 24th.—

Liszt has written me somewhat touchily : You were actually in Germany now ; were you going to leave Weimar in the lurch ?—His letter crossed my own, however, in which I had already acquainted him. Probably you will have had word from him by now ; but in any case you must visit him.—

Schmidt has written you also, has he not ?—

Your being troubled with a complaint of the eyes has greatly distressed me ; it gave me quite a shock when I received a letter in Alwine's hand.   It is to be hoped you have recovered by now.——

My God, I had no desire to make you heavy-hearted, or debar you from anything :—but —— when you are back here at last—let me out with it !—it will be just what I like.——

However—for that sake miss nothing which affords you pleasure—do you hear ? ?—

I hope you'll have also recovered from the petty impressions by now.   I am very eager for your next letter from Berlin.—You will have seen the Kladderatatsch in person, won't you ?

I have nothing at all to announce you from *here ;* nothing ever happens.   Herr Dir. Walther passed on a long letter from Julius [a brother of Wagner's] ; when you see the latter, simply tell him that nothing would come of it.——

Best love to the Leipzig brood—hold me dear—and above all, come back in *perfect health !*

This the chief wish of

Thy

R.

73.

Zurich, 6. October 1854.

Poor dear Wife,

One really may call that bad luck ! !   Whereas I thought I might assume that the aim of your journey was fulfilling itself better and better, that you were diverting yourself, enlivening yourself, and so reacting beneficially upon your jangled nerves, you are actually met by quite special misfortunes !—Going by Alwine's letter, I truly did not take so serious a view ; in fact I wrote to Leipzig yesterday, because you said before that you intended being there this week. Those lines you'll find at Avenarius's ; they consisted chiefly of directions as to Darmstadt : but there's time enough for that when you arrive at Leipzig. It quite turned my head to-day, when I received your letter ; naturally, work could no longer be thought of. Still, no doubt I may believe you have recovered from your wound : otherwise you would have been unable to write me so much ; accept many thanks for it ! Dear Heaven, when ever is *good* luck to hap ? Really nothing, nothing but adversities ; and anything agreeable—so it seems !—is never to encounter us again. So, nothing remains but to be glad if the *mischances* pass over one's head—like the fox and his skin !

But why on earth didn't you let Alwine write at once that you had lost your *money ?* Even in your own letter you don't yet put it as if you really needed more. You silly woman, how could I think of leaving you in such a fix ? To-day I'm sending you forthwith at least whatever I find possible : Alwine must surely have had to help you ; so please return it her at once.—

Ah, my God, how gladly I would have you back again soon, and yet I keep on wishing you might not return before you've had some slight enjoyment from your journey, before you have refreshed yourself to some extent and had enough ; but already arrived in Berlin, you have to make a fresh start, and begin picking yourself up all over again ! O you poor child of misfortune, *do have good luck for once ! You deserve it in truth.* Whether you will have obtained it from precisely Herr Hülsen, I strongly doubt ; your question as to the *reasons why*

Tannh. hasn't been given yet must strike him as very naive, since he knows well enough that it all resides in our demanding a summons for Liszt. Certainly I'm being urged on all sides to abandon *this* demand at last, as the success of Tannh. is now assured, even for Berlin, and I am losing a certain yearly revenue of 1,000 thalers by the delay. That may be all quite true ; only, there was a time when people just as strongly warned me off, and considered the success of Tannh. as not assured : at that time it was decided to set up the condition about Liszt ; he entered into it, and now I cannot so offend him as to thrust him aside and disavow him all at once. If of his own spontaneous motion *he* does not advise me to depart from the old stipulation, I cannot possibly place him in the false position of looking like a man who had imposed himself upon me.—That, dear Minna, you surely will see for yourself, and I therefore assume that you will undertake and utter nothing that stands in contradiction with my friendship. It would be another matter, if you—or better still, *Alwine*—could represent the actual state of things to Liszt in such a fashion that he felt bound to withdraw of his own accord : but even *that* can't be done without offence to him, and it would still be the most rational course if Liszt were really summoned.—

He wrote me rather touchily, that you were positively now in Germany : would you not be coming, then, to Weimar? However, I had written him already. You must visit him, whatever you do.—Schmidt, I expect, will only be able to give you the Tannh. ; the more reason for your working in *Lohengrin* at Darmstadt : simply write to Schindelmeisser from Weimar.—

Your having visited your supposed arch-enemy at Waldheim doesn't at all astonish me in you ; for I know you, you see ! Your heart is broader and more comprehensive than your insight into the essence of characters which by all means must strike you as strange and repugnant, because one cannot expect you women to take in the things of this world with so far-reaching and assimilative a gaze as belongs for certain to the man—the poet. That your magnanimous heart (which you think fit to call stupid and weak !) finally raises just yourself above many ordinary women, I have experienced often enough before not to be surprised in this instance. But on the other hand, that you do not supplement this noble feature of your heart by greater insight, for example to provide you with a more benignant verdict on sundry matters in my past—it is just *this* I must often deplore, and for your own sake also, I believe, since you rob yourself of far too much peace of mind through so much opposition.—However, your visiting Röckel was gallant and fine of you. Your accounts of him do not surprise me ; he has a nature firm as iron.—

Now afford me the great delight of telling me right soon you're feeling well and happy ; if my wishes can assist you to it, be assured they issue from the fulness of my heart sincere and warm !—

Salute dear good Alwine quite alarmingly from me ; I hope to see her here next year !—Farewell, dear good Minna ; be of good cheer !

Thy

RICHEL.

You are receiving 50 thalers to-day ; write me *by return* whether you can manage with them, that I might send on more. *Deny yourself nothing*, simply *ask ! !*

74.

[*Circa Oct.* 20, 1854.]

O YOU GAD-ABOUT ! !

Best thanks for your letter from Weimar to hand
to-day. Your accounts of the Flying Dutchman [Oct. 15]
and singer Milde delighted me much, but also increased
my longing to make music again in my own way for
once ! My residence for such a length of time in Zurich
really is a calamity which at last becomes too appreciable
to be fought down and repressed by nothing but proud
resignation. I confess that, if the Grand Duke of Weimar
were this day to obtain me permission to live in his small
country unmolested, probably I should not reflect long
before availing myself of that permission to choose the
neighbourhood of Weimar, where a little music really
could be plied from time to time. Yourself, too, you
have often expressed to me the wish to settle in Thur-
ingia ; perhaps it would be the only migration you would
care to join in now, though I should have to admit the
justice of your otherwise wishing to remain where we are.
—If you agree with me in this, and should you likewise
think it wishful for us to settle in some place where I to
some extent could have the artistic means for my endeavours near me, then I would give you full authority to
discuss exhaustively with Liszt the *measures* for obtaining
that permission. In my opinion there would be nothing
else to do, than for the Grand Duke to beg *permission for
me* to reside undeterred in his country direct from the
present King of Saxony, whilst *I* in turn should pledge
myself not to quit his country without the Grand Duke's
consent. At the same time I'm prepared to give a solemn
promise never to engage in politics again ; only, they
would have to dispense me from any humiliating and

easily misrepresentable declaration anent the past. If Liszt deemed it right, you might even seek an audience of the Grand Duke yourself, or at least the Grand Duchess, with this intent.—In any case I lay stress on this subject.—

Do not wonder at my stepping forth with such a thing so suddenly, and do not believe that it's only to-day it has passed through my head. It is a feeling I long have harboured, that *without any stimulus whatever for my art* I should be unable in time to go on here. You know how of late years I had kept nursing the hope that something might be done for music after all here : upon my side, in truth, I've spared no efforts for it. The result, however, shews there's nothing to be attempted with these people here ; I shall even be unable to conduct another symphony this winter ! * As long as I wrote books here, and then poetry, it could be put up with ; but for the past twelvemonth, ever since I began composing again, this utter lack of stimulus was bound to end by thoroughly depressing me. I feel that plainly with my present work,—I remark that zest for it is constantly harder to come by, and am afraid lest, if things are to go on much longer like this, I shall be giving up music again. It's too severe on me !—

Well, the only thing against such a removal would be its running counter to *your* wish, and your preferring to remain here ; for you have gone through so much with me, I confess, that in such things now I leave the casting vote with you. Wherefore I want you not to bring me

---

* Nevertheless in the early part of 1855, before leaving for London, he conducted five orchestral concerts of the Zurich musical society, giving his *Faust* overture at two of them, also a stage-performance of *Tannhäuser ;* see *Life*, vol. v.—Tr.

any sacrifice *against* your feeling ; for, if I knew that you would *rather* stay here, rest assured it would be the definitive reason for my continuing to make this place endurable to me. So, only in case you entirely and gladly concur with me. Should that be so, I beg you to regard yourself as my plenipotentiary, and go at any rate to the Grand Duchess.*—Be assured that on this point I implicitly confide in your understanding and *insight !*

Regarding the Berlin production of Tannhäuser, too, you have done perfectly right ; none but *you*, for sure, could have taken the matter in hand : not I. Doubtless *Liszt* feels sore about it : if he retreats [he thinks], he'll really be ashamed ; the decision to do so must therefore come as altogether from himself. Certainly the necessity of looking out for revenue compels me to want to see that production hastened ; why should I seek to conceal it ? The delay with Berlin brings all the other block about ; just as, on the contrary, Berlin's example will quickly draw the others after. Now all are dawdling : Munich, Hanover, Stuttgart, and so on. If *Liszt* could only find another remedy, I'd gladly go on waiting.—Let this affair as well, however, be committed entirely to *you*.—

For the rest, it's very wrong of you to try and make your poor old husband so conceited, with your fairy-tales that homage done to me as *artist* should also be taken as intended for my person. It isn't at all right of you to stuff me up like that, for it hadn't entered my head until now ; I considered my beautiful person quite out of the

---

* Minna had in fact forestalled her husband's wish to some extent already, since at this moment she was really in Dresden as bearer of a letter from the Weimar Grand Duke to the new King of Saxony ; for which endeavour, as also for her efforts at intermediation between Berlin and Weimar *re* the Berlin *Tannhäuser*, see her long letter to Hülsen of a fortnight later, from Zurich, reproduced in *Life* iv.—Tr.

game, and sufficient for no one but you. But I fancy, best Muzius, you are mistaken this time ! Never mind, I must indulge you in that.—

For to-day my very best farewell ! All send you their greetings, though for long I've seen no one. Most cordial greetings to Liszt and his house. You don't say a word as to whether Liszt received the score of " Rheingold " ? Please ask him at once. I'm anxious about it, you know ; neither has Bülow announced its receipt.— Greet Milde too, the Kapellmeisterin and the Child [Psses Wittgenstein]. Many hearty kisses from Thy

HUSBAND.

75.

PARIS, *Thursday the 1st March* 1855.

O YOU POOR GOOD WIFE,

Ah, and your poor stupid husband ! Even at Baden I wished to turn back ; then at Basle,—and most of all here in Paris ! My home-sickness is scarce to be conquered, and it's probably *that* which is making me quite ill.—Not till 11 o'clock on Tuesday night did I get to my hotel ; I took a back bedroom in the *Hôtel Montmorency* for sake of the *quiet* boulevard : sleep wasn't to be thought of that night (any more than in the coach on the preceding one) ! Yesterday I felt so bad, in consequence, that a resumption of my journey on Thursday was quite out of the question ; and as I durst not go to London on a *Friday*, I suppose it will be Saturday before I reach my destination. I passed the whole day yesterday trying to sleep ; I didn't go out till late, didn't find Kietz in, and mean to look him up to-day. Last night was rather better. Ah, if only I were at least back at my work, from which I've been withheld so long ! Really, all I care about in London is the hope of getting back to work there very soon. —

I feel as in a dream ; not a thought can I grasp, except the thought that my going to London is in fact an awful sacrifice !—

And you, poor woman, are left alone again ! Hold me tight another time, that I don't get carried off again ! Yes, I'm sorry for you as well : you will have to do your best with Beaky ["*Knackerchen*" = Jacquot] ; Peps will hardly be of much assistance. Ach, Ach, Ach ! !—

Now I'll go and hunt up my Parisians ; perhaps I shall write you more sensibly tomorrow. To-day I'm still quite sleep-starved and upset ; you know that nasty feeling !—

Farewell, dear good Wife ! Be tranquil, and reflect : " God knows the good it may lead to ! " That's what I mean to think myself, and see how far I get with it !

Heartiest greetings to our friends ; I hadn't time to telegraph at Basle, or I should have sent you another Adieu.

Adieu, console yourself as well as you're able, and— wish me better humour too !

Lord, if I had to conduct to-day ! I'm only glad I've hardly promised anything as yet, and particularly nothing from Tannhäuser !

Farewell, and hold me thoroughly dear for once ! !

Thy

RICHEL.

76.

LONDON, *Tuesday,* 6. *March* 1855.
22. *Portland Terrace. Regents Park.*

Well, I've shaken down, dear Mietzel. The first morning that I can pass in peace—for many days—I mean to devote forthwith to writing you a bit more rationally than hitherto could be the case. I'm full of tales to tell you, even if nothing at all extraordinary.

You know I didn't mean to travel on Friday, but not to leave Paris till Saturday ; neither did I catch sight of our old friends till very late. Kietz doesn't seem to be on very good terms with his *concierge :* even the next day he hadn't shewn her his face, and hadn't had my note at all ; not finding him in again, I left stricter orders. At last I got sight of the foolish young man and his friend Linde-mann the evening of the second day. He was in the thick of a money-lending trouble with his tailor again— of course—but he and Lindemann refused to hear of not treating me and Anders at their restaurant the last even-ing. ˙ *Anders* has become incredibly childish ; he can't trust himself to cross a boulevard now, but waits for an omnibus to arrive and take him over ; he had fallen down in the Bibliothèque a few days previously, smashed his glasses, etc., a regular to-do.

This time I saw the Rachel also, in *Cinna :* it was really instructive to get such a notion of that kind of virtuosity ; she pained me greatly. With her acting, even if the lady sang like a goddess, I couldn't use her for any of my operas. More by mouth on that another time, when I get back.—

The journey to London went off quite safely. The passage from Calais to Dover lasted only two hours, with good weather ; though I felt a little bad, and was obliged to lie down. At Dover, stupidly enough, we had to wait $2\frac{1}{2}$ hours before the train moved off.

It is singular that I should have bad weather all the time in Paris, whereas I arrived in ill-reputed London with a beautiful clear sky. The cabman took a whole hour driving me from the station to Praeger's, and that at a sharp trot ; I might equally have driven all the way from Zurich to Dr. Wille's at Mariafeld.   It's a horribly big city, and so far as size goes, Paris is a mere hamlet in comparison !—As I wrote you yesterday [a missing letter]. Praeger has been very friendly and obliging ; but he at once explained to me that, if I wanted peace, I must pay my visits quickly to begin with.   I complied, and we drove about London as if it would never end ; Praeger accompanied me, and consequently made a sacrifice of his precious lesson-hours.   By dinner-time yesterday we got finished at last ; then we hunted for lodgings, and found one I like very much, where I hope to work quite quietly and undisturbed—which is still the main affair with me, whereas the concerts are really the secondary.   So I am living on the skirt of one of the most beautiful parts of Regentspark, not at all far from the Animal-garden : in front of the house a little garden down to the street, and across the road the fine trees of the park ; so that I may look joyfully forward to Spring, when it all will grow nice and green.   God knows it needs such hopes, too, for me to tolerate the prospect of spending four whole months here on a task so wholly foreign to me.   If I can only get done with my work [*Walküre*], so as to be able to begin the Young Siegfried at once on the dear Seelisberg, I shan't so much mind.

But my lodging naturally isn't cheap ; it costs *two pounds* a week.   Still, an agreeable abode is really my principal aim, else I couldn't hold out here ; I mean to save in other ways.   For the present I still go to Praeger for my meals, as he lives only a quarter of an hour off—a cat's jump here ; how to arrange it later we shall see.   Mr. Anderson promptly invited me to a big

banquet of the Queen's Band on Thursday ; which I
declined with due thanks.   In general I mean to abide
by it : I conduct my concerts, but there's an end !
These people shall see that I'm even more of an Englishman than themselves.   I am in much dread of the
concerts themselves, however ; the orchestra, though very
good, is said to be completely unable to play *piano;*
nothing but *forte*, without any nuance.   It is also correct,
that they have only one rehearsal, and at that *two*
symphonies, *two* overtures, and the other concerted pieces
are played through every time.   How am I to do anything with it ?—When I enquired after the programme
for the first concert, the first joy they gave me was their
having chosen Lachner's " Prize Symphony " as novelty !
No, I struck that off at once, and told the gentlemen they
mustn't expect me to handle such rubbish.   Of course the
foolish devils recognised their error immediately, and
begged me to attend a committee to-day, when they would
dispose the repertoire entirely according to my wish.   So
I fancy we shall give a symphony of Haydn's and the
Eroica or C minor symphony of Beethoven ; for the overtures they had already selected the Magic Flute (to have
something by Mozart) and Fingal's Cave (to have something by Mendelssohn) : I have nothing against it.   *Ernst*
plays a concerto by Spohr ; I don't yet know who sings.
If nothing happens in particular, I shall write you after
the rehearsal (on Saturday) ; I am waiting with impatience
for a letter from yourself by then.   Ah God, if you could
only give me quite good news, especially about your health
and feelings ; it really is too bad that I should have to
leave you by yourself again !

Believe me, dear Minna, even if we don't quite think
alike in some respects, and express ourselves differently

about this and that from time to time, yet neither of us can survey our life without seeing how near we stand to one another through what great proofs of love and staunchness in the most difficult and often the most appalling situations.   Only think of the memories thronging to my mind as I re-tread this London where we roamed in such distress and fearing 16 years ago !   What you have had to pass through with me, has really been hard !   And truly, if I could make things altogether smooth and smiling for you now, it certainly would gratify my inmost soul.   But my not quite understanding how to do so, and actually continuing to cause you worry and distress, has come to be my singular fate, which I often heartily lament for your sake.   It touched me very much, how hard this parting came to you again ; what I can do to make the time of separation pleasant from afar, be sure it shall be done.   Good news from me, I know it, will be the liefest to you : that I can only give you if I feel quite free and easy at my work, which has become in fact my solitary life-task worth the while.   It rejoices me that you yourself expect no more from hence than honour and a good success to my artistic efforts, however restricted the latter.   *Rich* my art will never make me, and nothing save the consciousness of finding a few devoted souls can constitute my riches ; for them alone can I go on labouring in this world.   In *this sense* I hope to be able to give you none but good accounts of myself ; but even *that* will depend on my having to keep an eye on nothing else.   I am heartily glad to know that you *now* think entirely the same with me on this point !   So—await nothing but good, and thus abridge the time of severance, just as I propose to by my darling work !

Now, heartiest greetings to our valiant, precious friends.

Give Uncle and Aunt Wesendonck, dear creatures, my best of thanks for their attachment. To the ferocious Sulzer, the melancholy Boom, etc., convey my respects. Greet Nette also, whom I somewhat forgot at parting ; which has remained a grief to my remembrance. I often see Peps before me of a sudden, but always as he looked when young ; really the old scamp is hardly to be recognised. Teach *Knackerchen* the loveliest things, that I may also have my joy in him when I return.—And so farewell, all you who love me ; I'm ever thinking of you here ! Farewell, dear good, much-tried Wife ; take the full amount of joy in me you can ; no one needs it so much as yourself ! Farewell, and hold quite dear

Thy

RICHARD.

Only now have I learnt the exact truth, that the affair with my Tannhäuser overture did not occur at *my*, but at the *new* Philharmonic ; the conductor was Herr *Lindpaintner*.

77.

LONDON, 13. *March* 1855.

Now I've only 7 more concerts to conduct and I shall be on my way back ! And that's the cream of it all—is it not, dear Minna ?

There you have my whole sentiments in half-a-dozen words. —

After the rehearsal last Saturday it had become too late to write, so I determined to wait and include the performance of Monday [12th]. As a fact it was the rehearsal that gave me most pleasure ; the orchestra is quite distinguished in its correctness and tone, only it has

been let run to seed in its expression by bad conductors.
When I began taking the Beethoven symphony my way,
it staggered them all : I pulled up frequently, and was
very strict about *piano ;* but I had the gratification of
seeing how quickly my people got used to me : each
succeeding movement went better and better, till at last I
only needed brief hints to get everything in prompt
accordance with my wish. These bandsmen *can* do
anything ; the wind instruments in particular are very
good, and naturally there's no manner of question of such
a plague as I have with the people at Zurich, for even the
bassoons are excellent. So it also came about that I
brought the rehearsal sooner to an end than everyone had
feared. — On my presentation to it, the orchestra received
me with prolonged applause ; I got Sainton, the first
violinist, to return thanks for me. After the symphonies,
and finally after the whole rehearsal, applause broke out
again. —

The Directors of the society swam in bliss, and
assured me the orchestra had *never* played *anything like
so well.* For all my reluctance, I had to consent at
once to pieces of my own being presented at the very
next concert ; I chose the three pieces from Lohengrin
(overture, bridal procession, wedding music and bridal
chant) *with chorus ;* the translation is being made already.
They very much wanted the *Ninth symphony* of
Beethoven to go therewith, and at last I consented
because of our needing a chorus already, and also of my
getting *two* rehearsals this time—on account of my own
things—which I certainly am also very glad of for the
symphony. Everything went to shew that these people's
courage had been screwed up several pegs, and they set
great hopes on me for an unusual success of their whole

season of concerts ; so they mean to strike while the iron is hot.—

At 8 yesterday evening came the performance, for which I was allowed to appear in a *black* cravat ; only when the Queen comes, which simply happens once in all the season, must I be white about the throat as well. At the beginning of the performance the band relapsed into its old habit rather strongly, so that I felt I must work hard at it yet, before transforming it completely. The *Eroica*, however, especially the Funeral march, already went much better,—of course I'm only speaking for myself ; for the others, all that went on was a wonder. I had a long and very hearty welcome from the audience— much better than at Zurich !—the orchestra chimed in with loud applause. Every movement was applauded, and at the close I received such an endlessly long ovation with Bravos, that I didn't know which way to turn with my bows. The band has taken me particularly to heart ; many [of its members] assured me that everything I conducted had been *entirely fresh* to them ; they had not known *that* before, though they knew almost every note by heart ; so they begged me just to have a little patience with them yet.—But it is these relations with the orchestra that also constitute my only pleasure : all the rest leaves me cold, and in particular the audience ; which distin- guished me highly, it is true, but in whose regard my peculiar sense of such a thing distinctly told me that it can't in truth be *moved ;* it all appears to me mere phrase and fashion. At bottom that's perhaps the case with every audience, in the bulk ; and it is always a mere handful of persons more intimate with me, for whom I make music from the depth of my heart. Those— I missed very much here ; and not until I transported myself to Zurich, during the *Eroica*, did I warm up and be quite Richard Wagner. Nevertheless, I appear to have made a great impression ; Praeger has just looked in and assured me that everybody who understands music was in great excitement and had gone quite crazy [over me]. Well, we shall see !——

In my next letter I'll give you details of my other conditions of life here. Unfortunately, I am still suffering from a severe cold ; the climate, with this awful cold damp fog, is very detrimental to me ; I can never get properly warm indoors, the rooms are too badly protected, and the fireplace only gives heat when you're close to it. One has to spend a *terrible* amount of money ! Almost daily 1 schilling for nothing but coals ! The distances are so frightful, that I can't get on without a cab-fare every day. Half a bottle of claret at the worst restaurant 3 schillings, and so on. But, as said, upon that in my next. At present I'm awaiting news from you again ; I was hoping for it yesterday. Your first letter rejoiced and touched me greatly ; I thank you for it heartily, good woman you ! Upon my soul, even here I'm really still at home with you and our dear friends. I also mean to write to each of them in time. For to-day greet all from all my heart ; my homeland's solely with yourselves ! Farewell, dear good Minna ; *soon* more about my living. Farewell, good old Wife !

Thy

RICHARD.

I haven't a wife here, but mother and sister ; for Praeger mothers me, and *Klindworth*—a dear young fellow, just like Uhlich, recommended to me by Liszt— sisters me ; so that between them I am very well looked after !

Semper and *Klindworth* saw me home last evening ; they brought wine and champagne with them, and we sat up till 2 in the night.   I'm very tired to-day.—Forgive !

On Sunday I dined at Mr. Anderson's *en famille ;* your health was drunk, which moved me deeply, so that I took a tremendous gulp.—Liszt has sent me no recommendation to Erard yet ; so I'm still without a piano, and—alas—have not begun to work.

So—farewell once again, dear old girl ! Give me *very good* news of yourself, that my heart may grow lighter when my thoughts fly home.— I'm intending to make use of Wesendonck's introduction one of these days—albeit I *require* nobody.

78.

LONDON, (14 ?) *March* 1855.
22. *Portland Terrace. Regents Park.*

Best thanks for your letters, dear Minna, the second of which I have this moment received.   Your uneasiness troubles me, and I hasten to dispel it, so far as in me lies. Concerning the first concert you are exhaustively informed now ; I have nothing to add, excepting that yesterday's newspapers already devoted much space to it.   The reporter to the "*Times,*" an intimate friend of Mendelssohn's, and a man whom every artist arriving here must pay tribute to, if he isn't to tear him to pieces, is furious with me ; blind opposition presumably will go on that way for a time.   Others on the contrary, for instance in the "*Morning Post,*" have dilated on my performance with surprising clearness, and paid it the greatest recognition. You know how indifferent I am to all of this ; so not another word about it !   The orchestra is enthusiastic for me ; I have been assured I could do what I liked with it, down to the very last man. That remains to be seen at the next concert, for which I've *two* rehearsals. —

I promised to be rather more circumstantial this time about my mode of life ; gladly would I have done it in a more cheerful temper than has been made possible to me now by your news. Friend Wesendonck's fear of extravagances, on my part, I do not altogether relish. In the first place, I'm bound to judge from his remarks that he doesn't know London quite well enough, at least as regards the conditions under which it's possible for *me* to live here for a length of time. The statements of Frau Wille and his own wife, that 200 pounds would only just enable me to live decently in London for four months, in his eyes may rank as exaggerations by those who understand nothing about it ; but it is curious that I haven't met a single person here who wouldn't have confirmed *their* view at once, or didn't smile when I spoke of intended savings. For myself, too, with my present experiences I find I should get through the 200 pounds quite certainly if I meant to live without some sort of stint ; but *I mean to stint myself in truth*, and save in any case. In every other way I can and mean to do it, only in that of *abode* it would be a sacrifice which would render my *endurance here* downright *impossible*. A thoroughly agreeable dwelling-place, cheerfully situated and with a little convenience, to me is indispensable, as I shall be indoors and working nearly all day long. There's not a hint of luxury about the lodging I have taken, and if I were to draw you up a list of the conveniences I miss here, as compared with home, it would become a long one ; still, it attracted me, and I have now installed myself as comfortably as I was able. As regards the

price, out of some 20 lodgings I looked at in this neighbourhood with Praeger, I found none under $1\frac{1}{2}$ pound,
and they lacked too much to make them acceptable to me
for a period of 4 months.   Praeger has been in London
over 20 years, and knows it *very* minutely, according to
the testimony of everyone ; he told me I should find
no lodging suitable for me under $1\frac{1}{2}$ pound, 1 p. 15 sch.,
and so on.   It pains me to have to excuse myself at such
length upon this point !

It would be far worse if I had to go on dining at
a restaurant ; I should never get away under 6 schillings,
as I can neither drink beer nor the fiery English wine
[sherry ?], and have always had to pay 3 sch. for half a
bottle of French red wine.   I have tried it repeatedly,
and found that it can't be done cheaper.   On the contrary, I have hit on the expedient of laying wine in (at 3
sch. the bottle), and mostly getting my dinner also cooked
at home ; which comes fairly cheap, since they only
charge me with the actual outlay.   My dinner then
consists of soup (the most expensive item), a rostbeaf, and
Chester cheese.   For my lunch (at 1) I generally send out
for a dozen oysters.   I fancy I shall manage cheapest
that way.   I am often invited out, too (as yesterday to
Sainton's, to-day to Semper's, Sunday to Praeger's).   I
couldn't go on feeding at the latter's (regularly) since he
only dines at home 3 times a week himself, and even
then just scampers through it, as a rule, at 2 o'clock ;
which doesn't suit me.   So the chief remaining things
are firing (very dear—but necessary !) and transport.   As
regards the firing, I have hopes of seeing that item vanish
with the coming of Spring ; I shall probably retrench
in transport also by degrees, as soon as I get to know the
omnibuses and their usage better.—So—set your mind at

rest about my extravagances ; I shall *save in any case*—only, don't begrudge me my *apartment !*

I'm going to write to Sulzer, too, to-day : [that] I shall try and make it possible to have money shortly sent him for yourself; meanwhile he will know how to assist you for a few weeks, so that you may fall into no difficulty and also be able to procure yourself some *fresh* vegetables and meat.*—

To Alwine I likewise am writing to-day, as also to Liszt : [that] this matter must come to an end, and Hülsen is to have the Tannhäuser.—

(I cannot spare another score for private use ; tell *Hug's* that.)

Last night I dreamt most vividly of Peps ; he didn't seem young, though, but quite old and deformed, completely blind, and so deplorable that I started out of sleep with the cry, "O you poor creature !"—In general I'm feeling rather tender ; please send me right good tidings, to help me hold out. The *new* has little charm for me, almost nothing but disgust now ; my heart cleaves to rest, ay, to the accustomed, because I have to keep experiencing the more that I'm to experience nothing joyful any more. I feel much bitterness ; everything here leaves me monstrous cold ; unfortunately I see through the empty and hollow too fast now, and all illusion comes harder and harder to me. If it weren't for my relations with this orchestra, its affection and the hope of thereby turning out fine work, *nothing*, nothing could retain me here ; not even the—so envied *lodging !*—Farewell for to-day, dear good Wife. Be merrier than I,

---

* After certain comments already made in a French review, I fear it is not quite unnecessary to emphasise the obvious irony of this last clause.—Tr.

and perhaps it will make me so myself again ! Farewell, and kind regards to all.—

I had to pay 1 pound 12 schl. for the box of music ! If Hr. Hoffmann had only addressed it to his *brother* here, it would have come far cheaper.—I have also had to buy a feather-bed for my feet.*

Tomorrow I am to be driven to Benecke's, to whom Wesendonck had recommended me ; my *next* letter I shall therefore write to Wesendonck.—I still have no piano !—(Don't take such thick paper again, as the last time ; I had to pay double postage for it.) You see how thrifty I'm becoming, and let us hope you'll rejoice with W. about it.

79.

22. PORTLAND TERRACE. REGENTS-PARK.
Thursday, the 22nd March 1855.

MOST EXCELLENT OF ALL WIVES,

Since you will it, you shall also have a letter from me to-day, though it wasn't until yesterday I wrote to Wesendonck—as you wished—and therewith conveyed to you pretty well all that there was to report—even if not precisely much to rejoice at. Consequently I have little to add about my sojourn here to-day, excepting— that you may think yourself lucky not to be sharing it. Indeed I should be unspeakably sorry for you, if you were here with me now ; I'm in nothing better than penal servitude, and one pleasant day in my house would be dearer to me than all these indifferent pomps of the world-city. That is a long story, however, and we'll see how I survive it ; but in no case will it lead to anything

---

* Praeger speaks of " an eider-down quilt for his bed," the requirement plainly being warmth, as we shall find in Venice later.—Tr.

remarkable, and I stick to it that my coming hither was a sacrifice. Whether I still shall give pleasure to the gentlemen here, or not, is quite immaterial to me ; but even that will not be much : there are too few rehearsals, the choruses are miserable, and a performance of the Ninth symphony like that at *Dresden* simply isn't to be thought of. So I'm just making the best of it, and have the greatest difficulty not to succumb to a sudden attack of Swiss home-sickness and take to my heels.

My setting up is fairly finished. A splendid Érard grand has arrived ; I have had a standing-desk built for me, and have already picked up again, as well as I can, the threads of my profitless work. With Economy I'm also getting even, by degrees ; already I have hopes of coming out of it with what was settled. If I'm not invited out, I take all my meals at home now, where I get them best and cheapest ; these people only charge me for their outlay and the fire, and all in reason. Generally I eat nothing but rostbeaf, with a dozen oysters first ; for what they understand by soup here invariably is nothing but an enormously dear big tureenful of appallingly thick spiced fluidity, which I can't endure. For that matter, I notice no great mischief from the diet here as yet ; the air is very healthy, always wind and sea-breezes, so that I scarcely can clothe myself warm enough or eat to satiety. I'm wearing double under-hose beneath my black leg-garments now.

For the rest, I haven't had sight again of so much of London as that time with you ; it doesn't attract me at all. Klindworth has been and still is ill ; when he is up again and the weather fine, we mean to have a day on the Thames. Long excursions into the country, on the other hand, I probably shall be unable to make ; I shouldn't know where to find the money, if I mean to save, for you have no idea at all of the expensiveness in England. How much dearer everything is than in Paris, you may judge by my having to give 2 schilling here, i.e. 2½ *fr.*, for the same pastilles *de Vichy* I pay 1 *fr.* for there. An omnibus there costs 6 sous—here 6 pence ; exactly as much again. Yesterday afternoon I paid another call on Semper, who lives an immense distance from me, before his departure : I only went by omnibus, but had to take two different ones each way ; making 2 schilling—for nothing at all. By the by : Semper will not come to Zurich till summer—July ; he has work to do in Paris first, for the exhibition. They have been leading a wretched life here ; when I dined with them, they ruined my stomach with pork. To-day I dine with that delightful fellow, *Sainton ;* tomorrow at Benecke's, to whom I was introduced by Wesendonck. Otherwise I stick indoors, now working, then reading. Beyond an obstinate cold, however, my health is passable.

(I've just been interrupted by a caller, and so have lost the time to get this letter finished before post ; also, I must dress to go out. So you'll have to wait a day longer ; perhaps I may add something sensible tomorrow !)

And *still*, I'd rather try and wind this letter up to-day, that you may not have to wait—Sainton's soup can wait, for choice. Indeed I should have liked to fish up this and that, to tell you plenty—

Halt, there comes somebody else ! I can't help it now ; you will have to wait until tomorrow !—

I have just got home, 10 in the evening, and don't want to go to sleep before ending my letter, which couldn't have gone off to-day in any case, since it's a great English Day of Penitence and Prayer (on account of the Crimea) and on such a day the English are too pious to attend to their post after 11 in the morning. I should be glad to report a great deal more to you, as you set some store by it ; only—God knows—I don't rightly know what. You mustn't fret about the *Times* etc. : to me their yelling is terribly indifferent ; I get a little of it told me, that is all. The whole thing springs from purely personal interests, as to which I'm accurately informed now : other motives, people here—as mostly everywhere, no doubt—never have. There is nothing to be done against it, except to retire if one doesn't feel up to it, which is just what they want ; as I do feel up to it, however, I shan't retire this time, but let them go on bellowing their nonsense : in the end—I am told— they will stop. Moreover, I have really nothing else in mind here, and if I only were earning more money, should be quite content ; for it strictly is indifferent to me whether I'm thought something of here, when I see what charlatans have been thought something of before. Besides, there's nothing to be expected even of the Court ; everything is hollow and rotten there—as I strictly had known long since.

I will write to Henniger of Dresden (my haberdasher) and try to regulate the old debt. My last letter to *Liszt* was a very tough job for me : I know I am not pleasing him with my decision about Berlin ; yet it had to be, and the thing is done. I wrote the Frommann at once, also to Fischer concerning the score. Hülsen is to pay me an advance of 100 louis d'or on the tantième, if possible, and send it to Sulzer forthwith : if he does, you'll be well provided for a long time. How and when I shall get my money here, is very uncertain still, as these fees are not paid till the end, as a rule, unless one asks before.

I must see how to manage it, though I don't quite care
to dun for money.

Tell me a lot about Pepsel and Knackerchen next
time. Odd, but I really couldn't get myself a puppy
here; it would strike me as a hideous disloyalty while
the good old chap is still alive; just you keep him going
and lively—by diet. So soon as the weather turns
warmer, I mean to visit the Zoological Garden with its
animals very often; it's not worth while at present, as
they are all shut up. An overworked horse dropped dead
before my eyes the other day; that is said to be something quite usual here : how glorious !—There, you have
your sheetful now, and it is late; pick out the best of
it, be well and tranquil : I'm holding out ! Farewell,
dear good old Minna, sore-tried Wife, and hold me dear.
Adieu, Adieu !—

From your letter of to-day I see it only cost you
55 cent. : here I have to pay 11 *pence ;* I should almost
be inclined to go on writing unfranked, yet will buy
myself stamps ; only, I cannot do it at this time, and a
post-office for franking will be too far out of my way
tomorrow : so, pay once more.

80.

LONDON, 27. March 1855.

Well, my dear Mienel, I've only 6 more concerts to
conduct !—

From my rosy paper, for that matter, you may judge
that I'm in better humour than last week. Merely, I
am frightfully knocked up and tired to-day, and can
undertake nothing beyond writing to you. True, I'm
hoping for a letter from yourself tomorrow ; but it would
be disgraceful if I kept you waiting, and didn't write

you straight off on the success of our yesterday's concert. Everything went quite well, and particularly the pieces from Lohengrin, which were played by the band with great affection and extraordinarily finely.   But I'll tell you my tale seriatim.

The first part began with the " Freischütz " overture (which *I* hadn't chosen, though).   It made such an impression, that it was demanded " *da capo* " at once ; so, having experienced how ill it was taken of me at Zurich that I didn't promptly respond, I laid the good lesson to heart and let the overture be played a second time : for which I also had the special reason, that I wasn't absolutely satisfied with the first execution, and might look for a still better rendering the second time (which was different at Zurich, where I feared it wouldn't go so well again the second, as the first time).   To wind up the first part came Lohengrin.   Now, you must try and realise what opinion of my compositions had hitherto been foisted on the people here, namely that they were a mass of crazy stuff ; so everybody was on the tiptoe of anticipation as to *what* particular sort of nonsense one was going to get : not a breath was to be heard. Gradually the prelude of the Holy Grail with its softness and sublimity seemed to transport these people to quite another region : it was admirably played—as said —and so really seemed to make a deep impression ; long after the last faint tones had died away, all remained still as a mouse, as if at church, till at last came quite a hearty outburst of applause, which after the bridal procession, and finally after the wedding-music and bridal chant, mounted to a regular storm, so that I had to strew my obeisances between the desks on the platform for a considerable time in no little embarrassment.

Naturally the orchestra joined in with great uproar, and when I reached the conversation-room the Directors received me with the heartiest delight ; whilst my friend Sainton almost burst for joy.—

With the second part, the Ninth symphony, a little reaction almost set in ; as it nearly always happens to my compositions, perhaps for simple reason of their colouring, that they somewhat weigh on what comes next. Still, I kept fresh—by dint of the utmost exertion—and so did the orchestra, and the performance pleased me after all ; the chorus also did its best in the end, and only the soloists were good for nothing. Again the orchestra rendered me its enthusiastic thanks for having laid open this work to it, and many features in the execution convince me that I and my method have already made a great impression on the bandsmen. Friend Publicus did not quite seem to catch the drift, and when the thing was drawing to its close, the glorious custom of quitting the room during the music asserted its right ; so that I was half inclined to think the symphony had failed, if I hadn't at once been assured that this work had never yet appealed here (in spite of belief on Authority !) and had relatively had a great success this time. Be that as it may, at 10 this morning Herr Benecke came driving up, to testify—among other things—that people here had never understood the symphony before, and only through this extraordinary performance had an understanding of it been opened to connoisseurs themselves ; but no one, also, had ever heard it given *that* way. Regarding my own compositions [said B.], they had decidedly had a complete and general success, and everybody was astonished at its being even possible to trump up such nonsense about

such "splendid" music as had been done here in the
newspapers.—

I must tell you a few comical traits, as they are
characteristic of the people here. After the Lohengrin
a local connoisseur, Salomon, expressed himself thus:
"Devil take it, they say the fellow's nothing but a
'Humbug,' yet you can see with half an eye there's
genius here!" During the Freischütz overture two
musical gentlemen were sitting in front of Klindworth;
at first they kept nudging each other: at the Adagio
they shook their heads, "Too slow"; at the Allegro,
"Too fast"—then, "Why slow again?"—at last they
held their peace a long while, till suddenly the one
exclaimed, "By thunder, but it's really capital!" and
finally the pair applauded most enthusiastically and
called "*da capo!*"—Then, an old gentleman had brought
the score of the Ninth symphony with him, and he
and his wife religiously followed the performance in it
without moving a muscle; finally comes the last tempo
of all, he slams the book, and makes straight with his
wife for the door; so that it looked just as if he had
been spelling it all out to know the exact point of time
one must be off to escape the crowd.—

You see, my bad temper has cleared up into *irony:*
I smile more at these people now, than let them vex
me, but hold of course to my opinion that it remains
a hollow business with the public proper; single very
warm and sincere protestations of friendship have to
indemnify me for what I really have faith in no longer.
Before the last rehearsal, however, I had grave fears
about the performance, and on Saturday I made an
awful victim of myself to be rid of those fears. I had
ordered the chorus alone, with piano, for 9 in the

morning: after screaming myself hoarse—with my eternal
sore throat—at 11 began my band rehearsal, which lasted
until half past 3.   Imagine the condition in which I
reached home!   Still, I had won hope in return for
my exertions, and that gave me better humour; which
finally has buoyed me up till now, when, although
fearfully tired, I yet am writing, as you see, with
cheerful calm.

I took Klindworth home with me after yesterday's
concert; we consumed 2 dozen oysters, cold cutlets, and
washed them down with a bottle of wine—till 2 o'clock.
Did I think of home the while??   Dear child, it stays
my solitary hope, that the thing may come to end here
and I return at last to my familiar country; for that
is Zurich to me now, my house, my friends, my animals
—and—yes, I must tell it you—my good old, first-rate,
thorough-bad—I meant to say, dear Wife—more than
ever!   Well, I shall try to keep on end till then, as
I see very well it's a matter of sticking to my post this
time, even if it strictly is not my right post.—

Whatever else I might have had to write to you,
I'll make good tomorrow or the next day if I shall
have received another letter from you; I have plenty
more to report: to-day [it has been] merely the last
concert.   Let me hope my present letter will be agreeable to you; if it contributes a little to cheering you
up, and thus to making your thorny life a wee bit
pleasant, it will heartily rejoice me.

Farewell for to-day, then, dear Muzius, be comforted
and hold dear
                         Thy
                                   very good HUSBAND.

A thousand greetings to all!   I shall shortly send

journals and programme (also of the Last symphony—
in English).

81.

LONDON, 30. *March* 1855.

MY QUITE GOOD MIENEL,

Even to-day I shan't arrive at writing you the
promised letter, yet I mean to bring off a couple of lines
at least to keep you from growing uneasy. For your
last letter I thank you heartily ; I see you're doing
all you can to keep me in good humour. Well, it's
to be hoped that *my* last letter, which you will have
received this morning, has pacified you. Nothing whatever has happened since, neither have the papers come out
with anything yet of importance ; the *Times* has kept
silence till now, though I don't know if it has printed
anything to-day. It is only for you folk I mention this ;
if I seek information about it, it isn't that *I* set any store
by it, but because *you folk* appear to. Uncle and Aunt
[Wesendonck] have written me very amiably to-day :
give them my heartiest thanks to go on with ; anyhow I
mean to set apart a day exclusively for answers soon.
Then I shall also send whatever printed matter I can lay
hands on ; only, don't any of you expect something
decent. Sulzer requests me, if anything "substantial"
appears, to send it on to him :—he may have long to
wait ! Meantime I make him a present of his beautiful
faith in English solidity and humanity : here no one
shares it, and the bottomless hollowness of all *modern*
English relations is an open secret, chirped by the very
sparrows on the roofs. —

Last week I was at a performance of the " *Sacred
Harmonic Society*," where they give religious music,

oratorios etc., 25 to 30 times a year. Really that is the best music one has in England : the *Requiem*, indeed, was quite respectably rendered under Costa. I paid him a call on the strength of it yesterday, which appeared to please him very much.—The day before yesterday, however, I was at the *New* Philharmonic Society, where I heard a mass of music (including the *C minor* symphony) so banged about under Dr. Wylde's direction, that I felt quite ill : the *Times* praises it highly. It was awful !—To-day I dine with Ernst, who has married another Jewess here. Tomorrow I go to Benecke's again, where proceedings are sociably wooden, and rather audaciously wind up with music. On that I'll shortly write the Wesendoncks. —For the rest, never a lord, nor yet a lady, has taken me up ; they all are very wide-awake, and none have lost their senses.—

You haven't a word of praise for my decision to let Berlin have Tannh. without conditions ? As to myself, it cost me a hard struggle ; for, as the matter stands and people are, doubtless I have offended Liszt deeply : he hasn't yet answered me. Still, what does one not do for money's sake ? one can't stand firm for ever, especially as nobody would comprehend one's not wanting to tread on the corns even of a *foible* of a friend so proved in other ways. The Frommann has written me as if gone crazy ; I had two letters on one day from her. Well, Hr. v. Hülsen means *ardently* to back my wish for an advance of 100 L.d'or ; what more can one ask ?—

I've also written to my Dresden draper. Now I'm in London, all the world deems me rolling in riches again. Franck of Paris, too, has politely reminded me of my old debt, which I should really like to pay him from my savings here. So it keeps on, dear Mienel : we shall never alight on a green twig—we must abandon that idea ; neither will there be any extra windfall for me here. God knows what will be the end of it ; the best way is to lose the trick of living, which somehow does not seem given one for joy. I'm always offering all I have, and lavishing the whole of my powers—I feel that in my poor body !— but *towards me* everything is leathern, coy, or common. I suppose that's how it's bound to be ! Only the Jews and scamps can make money as " artists " nowadays ; one sees that here.—

For the rest, I'm leading a very retired life of it : work is going fairly, my sole remaining joy ! but when at it, I daren't think of the fate of my works.—Don't fret about me, though ; I'm still keeping afloat. I slept well last night for once at least ; only, I've caught a fresh cold, and no wonder after the concert.—Please don't frank any more ; it distresses me. The Messieurs Directors have just sent 50 pounds into my house for the first two con- certs, which will carry me a long way ; if they repeat it soon, Wesendonck shall have his 1000 fr. out of it. *For you* we'll wait for Berlin now.—If I feel comfortable in the next few days, I will write you a nice letter. Many thanks again for yours.

Farewell, dear old girl, and distribute kind regards.

Thy

RICHARD.

82.

LONDON. 7. *April* 1855.

(*Do* you have to *pay extra* on my letters ? ?)

Yesterday morning, dearest old woman, I received your pink letter ; then Eschenburg came, and brought me your yellow. Touching this latter, it grieves me that an over-

sight at the Post should have turned you so rusty at once.
Since I had had to write to Wesendonck, as you advised
me yourself in fact, I referred you to him for further news
of me : and you thought that so dreadful !—You were
right to disown the yellow letter in advance. For the
rest, as regards Semper's reports, you know my abode now
through my own description : if Semper saw more rooms,
it must be ascribed to his imaginativeness as architect ;
but perhaps you simply understood him wrong, just as
distrustful people sometimes don't hear rightly. Do you
believe I'd tell you all a story, maybe to feather my nest
here on the sly ?—If Semper said I'm standing champagne
here, it was very modest of him ; for it was *he* who paid
for a bottle of champagne after the first concert, and as
I couldn't afford to revenge myself, I promised him a
champagne-fête at Zurich instead. That—it seems—he
has expressed quite elegantly.—For that matter, I was
only three times in his company : when I went to him
last, he had meant to be just departing, but had been
delayed by a row with a workman ; which had thrown
him into such an awful temper, that he wanted to smash
up his whole house. That amused me, and I began
joking about it in my usual way, which ended by sending
him into fits of laughter ; hence his conveying you the
report of my jocular mood, which seemed to you in such a
contradiction with my letters.—Really, a mite of belief in
those nearest one is a beautiful thing. Belief doesn't
appear to strike very deep with you, and I often have to
give you explanations it were better to omit.—

Your having written to Alwine that Hülsen was to
send the 100 L.d'or to *me* in London, is a fresh confusion
again, and will cost a lot of money. What on earth can
have warranted you in believing I shouldn't eke out with

my money here ?   Have I ever cast a moment's doubt on my
even saving something to bring back to Zurich ?   All I gave
you to understand, was that it is dearer here than Wesendonck wished to impress on me, and that I certainly must
live very simply and make no long excursions, if I meant
to save up ; which, on the other hand, has always been
my aim and intention.   My God, please don't read anything behind my lines that isn't in them !   I shall do
better to keep things to myself in future, and not lament
again about my stay here, as you people really always end
by seeing something beneath it, perhaps even affectation ;
for you yourself, alas, have no notion at all of my
candour !—So—let us drop the subject !—

I have been invited by Eschenburg and Gerber to go
with them to Sydenham to-day, to see the Crystal Palace ;
my first outing from London.   Next time I'll tell you all
about it.—

For the last 2 days Spring weather has also set in ;
mild, balmy—but relaxing air.   I enjoyed it yesterday in
Hydepark ; as soon as the trees turn green, I shall go to
Richmond, and some day to the Isle of Wight as well,
where it is said to be very beautiful.   Otherwise I'm
always suffering from enervation, which after all is better
than excitement, only that I have no true spirit for my
work yet ; I feel as if I had forgotten it all : God knows
if it will return to my memory.   On the whole I'm drag-
ing on from day to day, without the smallest zest for life :
—but there, I won't complain !—

I've nothing more to tell you of the concert business
here.   A letter inviting me to the committee seems to
have recently gone astray, and accordingly they made up
their programme without me.   To-day I learn that the
gentlemen have chosen a symphony of Spohr's and a ditto

of Mendelssohn's (the same which A. Müller regaled us
with at Zurich lately): ah, what bliss for me ! However,
I have written Herr Hogarth at once and lodged a
protest, requesting a symphony by one of those gentlemen to be at least accompanied by one of Beethoven's.
I shall see if I'm in time to alter it.—After all, though,
it's much the same to me ; a Beethoven symphony doesn't
make a hair's breadth more effect here, than any other.
You would laugh if you could only see this audience : what
the men have too long between nose and mouth, the
women all have too short ; not one can close her mouth,
but perpetually displays two naked teeth.   Moreover, the
ladies all wear the most atrocious colours, hardly any but
scarlet burnouses, etc. ; one often sees an enormously lux-
uriant coiffure, with roses and curls, and for frontispiece a
nose with glasses.—

Of my future bearings towards these relations I haven't
a notion, but hope the Philharmonic won't be so stupid as
to want to engage me again at double the fee, as I suppose
one would be obliged to accept for dear money's sake ; and
then *you* would have to come too—and then—you'd
be *very sorry* for me.   I say nothing further !   I have
been to the Beast-garden again, and this time made my
chief call on the lions and tigers, who snarled a good deal
at me over their meal ; two lion cubs are very intimate
with a bull-dog.   The birds are fabulous ; a wonderful
species of ostrich with rose-coloured wings surprised me
much.   But the whole thing is very fine !—The other day
Klindworth played me a sonata of Liszt's too beautifully
for words ; it was in the evening, at my rooms, and both
of us wrote to Liszt at once, which will have given him
great delight.—For the rest, I'm living even lonelier
than at Zurich here, but also do not care a rap for

people.   Things will go of themselves, and the time slip by.

For to-day, dear stern Wife, make the best of these jottings, for which I strictly had no other motive than to give you just a sign of life, that you mayn't be harbouring black thoughts again.   I thank you much for the assurance that you're feeling well ; believe me, I would rather hear that than anything !—And just you be easy about me ; I shall arrive at the end, and not come to grief with it.   Give a thousand greetings, and tell Sulzer all the kind things from me one ever can say.   Farewell, good Muzius, don't be obstinate again, and only think the best of me ; even then you won't be thinking well enough of

Thy
RICHEL.

83.

LONDON, 11. April 1855.

MOST FAITHFUL OF WIVES,

Best thanks for your yesterday's letter.   " *All-right*," says the Englishman.   I am in a trifle better humour, as I have a rehearsal again the day after to-morrow, and thus can realise why I'm in London.   I have bowled the programme over : we shall do the *C minor* symphony of Beethoven—with a trumpery Mendelssohnian symph.—and also the Euryanthe overture.   The gentlemen would be glad to have the Tannhäuser overture at the 4th concert, only we should have to go through it first at the rehearsal for the 3rd, and probably there won't be time for that ; consequently I can't yet say for certain.—

For the rest, I pursue my lonely life with very few acquaintances : no lord yet, and no lady !—I had bad luck that time with Eschenburg. I and Praeger, he and Gerber started off together, each pair of us taking a cab for the station ; after I and Praeger had got there and waited half an hour, we took train for the Crystal Palace, waited and hunted there : in vain ! A few days later Eschenburg explained that they believed we all had meant to go to *Richmond ;* so *they* had gone there, and *we* to the Crystal Palace.—As for this Palace, you were much in my thoughts there : I really believe you would have been greatly surprised and pleased ; it contains absolutely everything one can possibly imagine, and also arranged with much taste. It is indeed a sight to be remembered, and I shall tell you about it by mouth.

Edward Röckel has been here on a few days' visit ; you know what an agreeable man he is. I passed the time with him quite tolerably ; naturally we had a deal to tell each other. He is tremendously busy earning money, and brings it up to 7 or 8 hundred pounds a year, but can't lay any by yet. One evening we were at Sainton's, who played us the violin very beautifully. The second evening we went to a theatre—*my* first visit : it was a very small suburban theatre—the Marylebone—which has attracted the attention of the press for some time past. They played the " Merry Wives of Windsor " (Shake-speare), and—as I thought—quite well ; at least the performance made a thoroughly interesting impression on me. Then came a ballet, in which a dancer *à la Pepita* threw up her petticoats and stared at her calves exactly as you had described to me. Then came a big 5-act tragedy, of which we made a present to the good people. For that matter, alas, the house was empty. The English as a rule do not appear to love the theatre. —Yesterday we dined with Präger close to Londonbridge ;

very good fish and rostbeaf—as much as one liked—for
18 pence, *i.e.* 1½ schilling : for a wretched bottle of
Rhine-wine, on the contrary, we had to pay 8 schilling !
It was interesting, how—ere falling to—a gentleman
rapped on the table and mumbled grace, to polish off that
business also.   On our way out the landlord was standing
on the steps to take toll.—Röckel sends you kind
regards. . . .

For the rest, the season proper is beginning now ;
to-day we have our first Italian opera, with the Ney from
Dresden.   You may imagine how eager I am for it !   I
shall be only too glad when another concert is over ; this
pause of 3 weeks has been a great infliction.

There will not be much more to write to you about
myself ; in return, your tidings always rejoice me greatly :
only write much !   I enjoyed the fine weather here, too ;
but then came strong wind again, which set all my
rheumatism going, so that I have risen quite a cripple
every morning.   But you are doing well ?   That would
be the pick of the market !   By the way, Hülsen hasn't
written me yet ; an advance of this sort must really be a
thing of mighty weight.   In a happy event, of course, I
shall attend to your orders.—Unfortunately I, too, must
spend my birthday by myself this time ; but we'll keep
its memory on the 6th Septb., won't we ?   My next
birthday *in any case* we shall be together.   You ask me,
you good woman, what you shall work for me : a dressing-
gown?   But you surely won't be wanting to embroider
that !   Certainly I shall not bring my old one back with
me, for it is deep on the decline already, and in a couple
of months will absolutely not be worth the carriage.
Still, I shan't be needing a new one in the summer, and
for the autumn you are to make me a regular beauty ; but

I can't saddle you with the expenses for that, as you know what luxurious tastes I have in this regard, though *you* remain my dressing-gown purveyor anyhow.   So think out for yourself what else you could make me ; I really deserve something madly beautiful. —

Tell Sulzer I'll send him a " substantial " newspaper article so soon as one appears ; I have waited in vain till now.   But in any case he shall get a very long London letter from me yet ; I shall have plenty to write to him, once I commence.   Whatever would *Boom* think of himself here ? ! — For lack of nobler beings, I relax myself from time to time with Präger's cat, which is very fond of me.   And Pepsel is really so nimble afoot ? Röckel was quite amazed that he was still alive. — My work is going slowly forward.   Much else, that often passes through my head, I am saving up for word of mouth. I have seen *yourself* a couple of times already ; with the grey cape and lilac bonnet, quite lifelike.   My sleep is passable.   Your franked letters I have always received with my early coffee, the unfranked not till dinner-time, at 2.   I am expecting Klindworth for a promenade to-day ; he will feed with me after, which does not cost much more than if I ate alone.   I have a ham in the house, too, but I assure you, no champagne ; *we* are to be the first to drink that together again.

I'm glad you think sensibly now concerning London ; regarded thus, I shall hold out this time.   As to the future, we shall see. — Now, a thorough good farewell again to-day ; keep thoroughly well, and think thoroughly well of me.   Only believe, too, that I'm heartily fond of you.   After the concert I'll write you again.   Adieu, good Muzius !

Many greetings to Zurich !

84.

LONDON, 17. *April* 1855.

DEAR MIENEL,

Now I still have five more concerts to conduct !
The third went off yesterday as well—as possible : there
is not enough time for rehearsing ; at our one rehearsal a
fearful mass of music must be just played through, and
really it is only owing to my great adroitness and energy
that the principal pieces always go as I want them at last,
even if not with that perfection of finish they would if
there were less music and more rehearsals, so that the
orchestra could get a thorough grasp of everything. What
I do bring to pass, notwithstanding, naturally is something quite fresh to these people, and—whoever knows
how to appreciate it, is beside himself for joy. Thus in
particular with the *C minor* symphony this time and the
Euryanthe overture, which was demanded *da capo :* a
repeat, however, was disagreeable to the orchestra this
time, on account of the great heat in the room and the
exertion this overture costs the violinists in especial ;
wherefore the leaders begged me to quit the platform (as
it was the closing number in the first part) in order that
the applause might cease ; which I gladly did, and so
friend Publicus calmed down at last. For that matter, I
conducted with a touch of malice this time, which highly
amused my closer acquaintances down in the hall and up
on the platform. The first part, you see, began with the
poor Mendelssohn symphony announced to you before
[" Italian "], followed by various boring vocal and concerted pieces. Well, hitherto I had always appeared on
the platform in white gloves, but taken them off to
conduct (which no other conductor does here) ; this time,
however, I kept them on, and conducted Mendelssohn and

the rest most gingerly—precisely as the others do, without letting my equanimity be ruffled in the slightest. But when it came to the Euryanthe overture I pulled off the gloves, laid them aside, and went at it in my way ; I looked round, and observed how Praeger and the others were nearly splitting with laughter.

After the concert I took Praeger and Lüders (who always would like to devour me) to my rooms, to consume 4 dozen oysters with me. At any rate I make these people—and their like—most happy, for they declare point-blank they never knew Beethoven &c. before. Publicus also was fairly animated. I have already told you of the abominable fashion of quitting the room before the end of the concert : this time we wound up with the overture to the " Water-carrier," which I am very fond of, and which also was played very well ; after the pre-ceding vocal number —by Mad. Rudersdorf-Kückenmeister (of Dresden memory)—the exodus commenced ; so I took a chair quite placidly and watched, firmly determined not to begin again till quiet had returned, even if I had to wait for the whole room to empty. For which reason I said to Sainton fairly loud, in French : Only wait ; per-haps we shall not need to play the overture at all ! This seemed to have been caught by a very refined and intelli-gent-looking aristocrat and his wife on the front bench, for he and his lady smiled at me most approvingly, which I reciprocated. The others also seemed to understand my attitude, and soon the greatest quiet reigned ; so that I had much relish at last in conducting this overture for the remainers.

But to-day, poor hack, I feel as tired as a dog again, and all to pieces ; I can't place myself at the desk to write this letter, my legs are cracking under me. Good

God, I always exert myself far too much for this world of scamps ; if I continue doing it another 30 years, no doubt I shall have had enough !—Perhaps people will leave me at rest then ; my only consolation.—To change the subject, we are having wonderful weather now ; it is so warm that I suddenly don't know how to clothe myself lightly enough. Naturally the wadded paletot will not do any longer, and so as to have something lighter to throw on, and not finding anything suitable in stock, I've had to order a Spring cloak *à la Talma*, only with sleeves (similar to my cast-off blue summer paletot) ; which, as it is to be all lined with good silk, will cost $3\frac{1}{2}$ pounds, somewhere about 90 *fr.*, but wouldn't have come much cheaper after all at Zurich. The other day I bought a pair of very fine razors, with which I now remove each morning's beard so easily that I never know what has become of it.—As it's so beautifully warm now, I also treat myself to a hot bath now and then, from which I'm expecting dispersion of the pains in the limbs and heaviness of body that have been regularly plaguing me again here. Beyond that, I go on vegetating lonesomely—from Praeger to Sainton and Lüders, and from them in turn to Sainton [Klindworth ?] : no other acquaintance tempts me in the least to cultivate it. Klindworth (a Hanoverian, by the by) used to come and fetch me for a walk or lounge, which was very agreeable to me ; but the poor devil is constantly ill now, and I call on him daily without being able to take him out. He is the best of the bunch to me here, and reminds me much of Uhlich ; a strikingly handsome young fellow, plays the piano quite extraordinarily, and came here, on Liszt's recommendation, to make his fortune. He appeared in public once, and—as others assure me—played better than anyone else

in England ; but he was so pulled to pieces by the press—
especially the Times—that nobody would let him play
again : such are these valorous English, these free and
independent—scamps !—He has been struggling along ever
since, gives a lesson here and there, and remains on the
whole without prospect.   So I have settled with Praeger—
who is a good-hearted chap—that we shall arrange a
special matinée (with the Ney, it is hoped, who has left
her card on me already) at which Klindworth shall get
himself properly heard for once by a select *invited* audience.
Let us hope that will help him !—

Kietz, crazy creature, has also written me ; like the
rest, of course he imagines I am playing a big rôle here
and can procure him any amount of orders from Englishmen.   Lord, if the asses only knew how I'm simply
marking time here till the 8th concert, to take it out on
the beloved Seelisberg.—

You asked me the other day, altogether good woman
you, what superfine thing you could make me for my
return ; I could think of nothing right, but the new-come
warmth and coming summer-heat inspire me with a very
wanton wish.   For the winter, you see, we have invented
a splendid indoor costume for me, which also is to be
a standing order ; now you must further invent me a
summer suit to match.   My luxurious imagination is
enceinte with the following : a roomy loose jacket, something like my winter house-jacket, of velvet or stout silk,
but *not* wadded, only lined with silk ; to go with it, a
handsome pair of trousers, such as I also got you to consent to in the end, but likewise *not* wadded, merely lined
with foulard : linen I no longer can bear on my body,
even in summer, and cotton I hate like sin.   So have a
good think how to make things nice and heavenly for this

poor devil of yours when I return to you ; which latter is the fondest occupation of my thoughts.   To give you some solid background for these voluptuous ideas of mine, I may tell you that Herr von Hülsen (that divinely handsome man in your eyes) has also written me to-day and announced the bringing off of that advance.   I intend answering him this very day, and assigning the money to Sulzer ; thus the latter, too, will get his disbursements repaid.   I also shall bring some money back from here in any case, and quite goodly orders stand in prospect for this autumn again : *Hanover* will certainly soon order *Lohengrin* (at 50 Ld'or), and so on.   It is sure to be of great service to me, also, that *Berlin* is at last taking the lead ; for Germany still remains my field.   At Hamburg, I hear, the Lohengrin is having greater and greater success. —

Otherwise I here learn strictly nothing of the world ; it is always the way in great cities like Paris and London, where one never arrives at a comfortable dip into the papers, as at home.   Murder and sudden death may occur here, and the foreign newspapers report on it like mad-men : one hears nothing at all of it, at least if one lives as I.   Yesterday, however, the illustrious Emperor of the French arrived here with his consort.   Sainton has named someone to me who, when Louis was loafing around here as adventurer, exclaimed on his announcement to him : By God, that inconvenient person again !   To-day they act as if possessed with him.   O glorious world, proud England !   Perhaps I shall become Emperor of Germany myself one day ! —

Unfortunately I have had many sleepless nights of late again.   Once, upon waking from my troubled half-slumber, I suddenly heard a *nightingale* trilling quite close in the Park. A flood of tears poured from my eyes! I hear the dear thing often now, of an evening and morning. Ah, if it were not for this touching Nature, truly I couldn't hold out any longer among this race of men! How glad I am that you have so much sense thereof yourself, and are so fond of animals; to a feeling heart they really constitute the only comfort in a world where Man displays his higher reason by nothing save dissimulation and all manner of paltry insanities. How charmingly truthful these animals are; and behind all his show, what else than they does the average human being strive for, except that they are frank and never play the hypocrite?—

There—that's enough for to-day from your poor tired-out, battered, over-vigilled husband: he's a rogue who gives more than he has! Your last letter rejoiced me again; I see you are well and looking at my situation here quite sensibly: if everyone would only do that! It is their expecting Lord knows what from me here, that worries me; but if *you* judge my position so calmly and sagaciously, then all is well, and we shall get on with each other quite comfortably. Look you, then I myself gain that sense of tranquillity, and even of humour, needed to carry the thing to its close; but if I have to will a thing I *cannot* will, I become downright insane. Poor thing, you experienced that once [letters 36 and 37]; if you only knew what I suffered *for you* then! I'm sure you don't believe it!—But all's well now, and we shall see how to bring our old age to a blithe and happy ending yet.

Farewell, dear Wife. Kind regards to our friends, and hold me *tremendously* dear!

85.

The very finest Good-morning, and thanks for to-day's letter, which I probably received about the same hour as you my last Tuesday's. I have just shut up work, which is progressing very slowly, to write you a couple of lines before going out. Moreover, I'm medicining to-day ; the London diet has rather interfered with me of late, and I was advised to take a couple of pills reputed to give the lungs free play : [. . ,] which somewhat lowers me. I fancy it will have good results, however, and also restore my night's sleep. Early yesterday, with the first grey of dawn, I was tossing sleepless on my bed and waiting for my nightingale ; she held her peace, but suddenly I heard an awful roar instead from the Zoological Garden. At once I recognised the one uncivil lion, and his wish to take the nightingale's place in entertaining me this time. Indeed I could but laugh at the clownish fellow, who presumably imagined he was roaring as gently as any nightingale, like Bottom (*Zettel*) in the Midsummer Night's Dream, and with all my heart I said, " Roar again, lion " ; which he also did, and goes on doing to this day, so that he has often interrupted my work. But when an atrocious street-band came besides, and played " Guter Mond, Du gehst so stille " in front of the house, at last I thought : You'd better throw it up and write Minna the story instead, who herself can roar and sing " Good moon " quite nicely. Which happens herewith. ——

Yesterday Eschenburg and Gerber fetched me to see the animals, who vastly entertained us again. Among the birds I was particularly attracted this time by a wonderful nightingale from New Zealand (in the South sea) who sang to us quite passionately, and bewailed her love-lorn plight in tones so splendid that they still are ringing in my ears. You see what unexpected musical suggestions I'm gathering here! Then we dined in Picadilly, but had the greatest difficulty in getting home. *Fidelio* (in Italian) was to be given at the Italian Opera in honour of the visit of the Queen and the Emperor of the French, and whatever streets the mighty potentates were to traverse on their way to the opera-house were lined already with an awful mass of people. On boxes and boards stood lofty England, to treat the Chef of the French gensd'armes, Jews and jesuits, to its enthusiasm ; it was an illumination night, and transparencies flared " *Welcome Napoleon* " to put one's eyes out. Well, we had to edge through to cross the road, and of course the people we thrust aside believed we merely wanted to secure the best place in front, which naturally made them most indignant. Among other things, I came by a terrible blow in the back from someone's fist ; when I looked round, it was a highly respectable grey-haired gentleman, and I politely bade him " *Thank you, Sir.*" Eschenburg, on the contrary, found a very handsome tassel off a lady's mantle hanging to a button of his, so that he at least made something by it.—To the selfsame Fidelio and Ney I am invited tomorrow by Hogarth, who gets seats given him as journalist ; yesterday the *orchestral stalls* cost 15 pounds apiece, which would have rather gêned me, as I unfortunately have had a good many expenses of late, for the summer overcoat already mentioned, a dozen pairs of stockings, etc. ; so that I have gone far beyond my rule, which consists in taking 5 pounds a week out of Aunt Wesendonck's big pouch. I usually have to pay about 4 pounds in the house, so that something like a pound is left for out of doors, which just covers my cab-fares and other small expenses. But if I lay in provisions, such as wine, ham, bouillon for soup, to say nothing of buying myself anything, I have to break into another week's money ; which throws me quite out of balance, and often makes me sceptical as to my projected savings. Thus much is certain : if I mean to bring back anything even supportable, I must keep myself damned short of theatres and outings.—

I have heard of nothing in the newspapers about our last concert ; the Times has kept silence again. Should anything rational put in an appearance, from a dis-interested quarter [*i.e.* not Hogarth], Sulzer shall certainly receive it ; only I wonder at his making such account of the rubbish : what will it profit him or me ? For that matter, the last concert met with much favour again, and I have been assured that Publicus was quite enthusiasmed. The room is never very full, although well filled ; it follows its own old groove, and only gets notably full when a very famous virtuoso plays ; if the *Ney* were to sing, for instance, the whole place would be packed. That's the truth.—So—compose yourself, I beg !—By the by, the Tannhäuser overture is to come off next time ; even at our last rehearsal it went tolerably.— To-day I mean to take poor Klindworth for a little drive in the beautiful air ; he's still too weak for walking.—I shall be writing to Sulzer next, even if I can't enclose him any journals. Give him and the other dear friends and people my very best remembrances ; and mind you skim off the best of everything, and keep it for yourself.

Your news rejoiced me much again ; continue feeling well and cheerful, and you will greatly ease my mind and

give me agreeable hopes for our mutual future. So—
farewell, dear Minna ; I shall soon have been the longest
span away from you !—

86.

[LONDON, *April* 26, 1855.—Tr.*]

O MUZIUS ! MUZIUS !

What a dog's life it is ! I really need super-
human patience, to hold out here. Yet I recognise that
I must pay the penalty for my folly in accepting this
absurd invitation to England despite my *knowing* that
it was no place for me. Now there still are two long
months before me to hold out ; what idiocy !—I shall
bring you a fairly good crop of grey hairs ; if you mean
to pull all of them out, I shall get some nice bald
patches ! As regards my true province I have absolutely
nothing to look for here ; the handful of trumpery
concerts cannot blind me to that : they strictly are not
my affair themselves. Ah, what nonsense it is, my being
here ! My head grows more stupid every day, and now
you are beginning to try and make me stupid also : you
make out that you received no letter from me between
[those of] the 7th and 17th ! Please have another good
look, and do me no injustice ; I have written you twice
each week. And then I'm to allow that my last summer
paletot (which I got made 3 years ago, when we were
living at Rinderknecht's) was *green* instead of *blue ?* You
would dispute a thing like that with me !—And your

---

* In the current German edition this and the succeeding letter are
printed in the reverse order, but the date of this is established by its
reference to the New Philharmonic concert, which contemporary journals
prove to have taken place on Wednesday the 25th of April.—Tr.

birthday I know quite well ; it's the 5th Sept.—if I referred to it otherwise, it must have been a mere slip of the pen. And all the other nonsense you want to palm on me, whereas it's really you who keep me waiting, and left my last letter unanswered *two* whole days ; for I waited two days for it in vain. And I'm to be the scapegoat ? That's the last straw ; I am quite in the humour !—My God, those cursed 2 months more, and their trumpery concerts ! !

For the rest, the *Tannhäuser overture* (of which I've fairly had my fill !) doesn't come off till the 5th concert ; presumably we shall have an extra rehearsal then, with the music to Egmont. Our next concert will include a symphony by one of the society's Directors, Lucas ; but he will conduct it *himself*, thank God !—Could I ever have believed I should have to mix in such concert trash again ! It makes me feel quite pitiful ; everybody will set me down as a composer *à la* Hiller and such-like. What bliss for me, to be numbered in that sect at last !—

I have made one solitary choice acquaintance. A rich amateur who also composes quite nicely for his own amusement, a Mr. Ellerton, had himself introduced to me at the last concert ; he said he knew my operas from Germany, where he had often seen them of latter years. He paid me a call, which I returned, when he took me into his study and shewed me *my* portrait hanging under Beethoven and Mozart ; where—so he said—it has hung for 2 years. He assured me I had saved the Philharmonic : had Costa conducted again, he and many others would have dropped their subscription. There was something prepossessingly shy in his manner towards me, and he appears quite enthusiastically devoted to me. He also assured me, many here had made acquaintance

with my operas in Germany ; only, he agreed there was
nothing to be hoped for *me* or my works here, and I must
content myself with the friendship of individuals, who
certainly were much attached to me. On Monday he
took me to a performance of the *Messiah*, at which I
nearly died of ennui. Yesterday [April 25] I finally
declined to go with [him?] to the concert of the New
Philharmonic, where that donkey Dr Wylde also meant
to do the Ninth Symphony after me. At the rehearsal,
I hear, he broke down, and they were compelled to stop :
but that doesn't matter at all, his party has money and
pays for the orchestra ; whether a mess is made or not,
it's all the same to the bandsmen.—O, it's a heavenly
nation !—No, Mietzel, to England I do *not* come again,
even if they paid me 500 pounds !!—I've something
better to do, than threshing chaff here.—

Klindworth has already arranged the first act of the
Walküre ; he played it to me yesterday with prodigious
virtuosity. I shall bring the arrangement with me, when
Boom can learn it up—for hard it is—and you'll all get
something to hear from it one day.—

I've heard Fidelio in Italian, with the Ney from
Dresden ; fairly bad. But on Tuesday I went with
Praeger to a minor theatre (the Adelphi, in the Strand)
where a pantomime (*Zauberposse*), " Mother Goose," was
played, sung, danced and scene-changed quite famously.
That was the first evening's real amusement I've had.
Madame Benoni (from Dresden) was one of the dancers !—

The weather has turned windy and cold again, as in
your part ; I don't feel well, in consequence, and have
taken an aperient again to-day.—For yourself, make a
note of those seidlitz-powders ; I'm glad they took away
your migraine. I am truly sorry for poor Müller ; let us

hope he'll get the better of it, when you must give my best congratulations.—For the rest, I hear and see nothing of the world ; cannot you write me how things are going before Sebastopol ? I hear nothing about it here ; not a creature plays politics, saving those who earn money thereby. Your close friendship with the family Jachmus quite touches me ; it will end by your converting me to the opinion that Herr Jachmus understands my music. For to-day only greet the Wesendoncks most kindly ; it really is they I like best in all the Hôtel Baur. And Sulzer, Boom, Hagenbach—and whatever the others are called : salute all of them duly, and tell them I'm leading the life of a god here, what between taking to my heels and remaining ! And you—you wicked woman ! don't make me worse than I am, and bad as I am, hold me dear : I and the good God, we'll reward you for it ! Fare tremendously well, and don't keep me waiting for letters so long again ; it makes me very uneasy, do you hear ? Ah, good old Peps, take good care of his eyes !—Ah, *two months* more !

Ach ! Ach ! Ach !

There's a *good Richel ! !*

87.

LONDON, 1. *May* 1855.

MY COMPLETELY GOOD MIENEL,

Do not expect much from your dear husband to-day ; he's utterly done up ! I fancied I was in for an attack of grippe at yesterday's concert, the catarrh still plagues me so. The concert itself put me out to the last degree : I can't go into everything that annoyed me at it ; enough to say, the one thing lacking is that I should have to conduct " Martha " again : such a programme came

very near it. While conducting an aria from the
" Huguenots " and a miserable overture by Onslow—
an Englishman—I was seized by such disgust and remorse
at having accepted this absurd engagement, that it got
the better of me and I made up my mind to demand my
definite discharge next day.   After the concert I declared
this aloud to my acquaintances, whereupon Lüders, Praeger
and his wife, accompanied me home to make me change
my intention.   Over oysters, lobster salad and punch,
which Lüders prepared with great art, we kept it up till
past 3 in the morning, and the finale was my giving in ;
towards which—I scarcely need assure you—the thought
of yourself, and your distress at such a step, contributed
the most with me.   So I mean to hold out, hard as it
falls on me to have to ply this wholly useless handicraft
for another 2 months.   I must pay the penalty, however,
for having been so stupid as to pave the way for this
vexation with open eyes ; a thing I still deeply repent.—
So be easy about me ; I shan't have so severe an attack of
the dumps again, I hope ! But it was the most idiotic
concert of them all : a mawkish symphony by one of the
directors ; then a fearfully tedious nonett by Spohr ; a
completely insignificant overture by Weber, which—to
make things worse—had to be given *da capo*, as I had
conducted it far too finely ; to conclude, the trashy overture by Onslow !—All these are purely interests of the
Directors, to which I am forced to conform !—Neither did
the symphony in A go so well as at Zurich by a long
way ; such an English orchestra simply is not to be
worked into ecstasy !—

My God, I'd rather say no more about it !—Next
week we have an extra rehearsal, at which (besides the
Tannhäuser overture for the 5th concert) a symphony by

an Englishman—Potter—then a *new* symphony by Spohr, expressly composed for London, and an overture by another Englishman—Macfarren—are to be got through. What bliss for me ! I have been unable to bring off the Egmont music, as they can give me no more extra rehearsals.—Well, the only motto here is Patience to last out ; but I could turn furious at anybody who looks for profit to me from this London adventure.   As said— I have simply to do penance for a folly committed.—

Eduard Röckel has invited me for Thursday to Bath, whence he will make excursions with me till Sunday ; probably I shall accept, for a little distraction.   It is said to be very beautiful there.   I shall write you thence.— Klindworth isn't allowed to go out, even yet, which robs me of much entertainment.—

My very best thanks for your political news ; I couldn't help laughing ! Yes, my good Muzius, one lives better at Zurich ; Lord, what a treat I mean to take at home ! I can scarcely contain my anticipations of the return to Zurich, to our pretty abode, with our good humans and beasties, and its cheery mistress, Madame Wagner, who is sure to drive away the recollection of this cursed London by her thorough coddling, and so make me feel well again and up to my work, which is in a terrible rut here.—

There, Lüders is knocking, to fetch me for a walk and meal (with him and Sainton).   Even so I could not have written much more, to say nothing of my always saving up for word of mouth.   In my next letter I'll retrieve a little, though, especially about a performance of Romeo and Juliet at the Haymarket Theatre.

Farewell, my dear good old Minna.   Be merrier than I, and reflect that we shall never be parted so stupidly again,

nor for so long ; a thing like this occurs but once.   A
thousand greetings to all friends !

88.

LONDON, 4. *May* 1855.

DEAREST MINNA,

    I mean to pull myself thoroughly together, not to
forget anything—as usual.   Apart from that, my life here
would afford me small occasion to, as it creeps away so
drearily and against my inner grain, that I wish I never
had come into the position to have to report on it !—

    Here goes, then !—Your question about the pastilles I
have already answered at last, with Eschenburg ; I must
renew my thanks, however, for your great attentiveness
and forethought, which I do herewith from all my heart.
It really is a little droll, to see myself assisted on this
single very trifling point, whereas so many other and more
important things have still to be paid for so shockingly
dear.   Precisely now, the imposts for this crazy war make
living and all accessories infinitely dearer than has ever
been the case before ; owing to the enormous taxes, every
single article has tremendously risen in price.—

    That by the way.—One letter, according to your
account, must certainly have gone astray ; luckily there
can have been nothing of very great moment in it.   Did
you get my letter with the lion anecdote the other day ?
With our wind from the North-East I constantly hear the
naughty fellow roar now, which also is a sign that we
shall go on having fair dry weather, but cold and inhospi-
table, so that I have to keep reverting to my wadded coat.
Nevertheless I have ordered a complete Spring-Summer
outfit now : trousers, coat, and two of those stout English
piqué waistcoats.   These things weren't dearer than at

Zurich here, if anything a little cheaper ; consequently I am erecting myself a memorial to England, and at the same time lightening my tailor's bill of next New Year.— Regarding the colour of my cast-off summer paletot we will not quarrel any more ; you mean the one made 5 years since at Zurich, which I took into indoor wear at last, and *I* mean that made 3 years since at Zurich, which I hitherto had worn out of doors.—From London there will fall to yourself some lovely Irish lace, in any case, and maybe something else.   When the end draws near, I must also bear our Zurich friends in mind quite decently, don't you think ?   As I shan't be bringing back much money, it would be the most sensible to bring nice souvenirs ; for—to London I shall not return.   There's time enough for that, however.—

I fancied I should get another 50 pounds from Anderson after the 4th concert, and in that case meant to send the 1000 *fr.* for Wesendonck at once to Sulzer—an occasion I had destined for the long letter I promised him ; but Anderson appears to have forgotten it, and as I still have enough money to live on, I would rather not remind him, but go on waiting.   Please say so to Sulzer, who won't be so afraid of calling on a grass-widow, I hope, as the " uncorrupted " Wesendonck.   Let us hope the last good creature doesn't think that nothing save the presence of her husband holds a woman back from every kind of silly prank she else would necessarily play with others ; I'm sure he has no such dismal notion of his wife, for instance, just as I am happy not to have it of you, whom I therefore heartily permit to receive whatever caller you may find agreeable.

That brings me to your account of the bad odour into which the Wesendonck has fallen with Mesdames M., H.

and B.—If the lady has really become so disagreeable of a
sudden that those individuals can't abide her any longer,
it must indeed be a very bad case ; for the Wesendonck
was universally regarded as a most amiable woman only a
short time since.   If one should " pity him," Wesendonck,
for this bad odour of his wife, it certainly would shew
much charity toward *him*, but not towards the lady whom
one brings into bad odour oneself, and I could not deem
that pity very cordial.   It is to be hoped, however, that
you will set Mad. H. and M. a good example, and shew
yourself more lenient and indulgent toward peculiarities
perchance arising, which at bottom may well be excusable
and not so terribly forbidding.*   Naturally, no constraint
can be put on you either, and if you have a genuine
antipathy towards the Wesendonck, I myself should not
account the thanks supposedly due to her sufficient to
oblige you to keep up an intercourse distasteful to you.
But should your aversion repose on any manner of
mistrust appearing to involve your honour, I believe
I may give you the assurance that such mistrust
is perfectly unjustified and groundless : on the contrary, you may take it for certain that no one more
deserves your confidence and friendship than Mme
Wesendonck ; just as I myself, for all the difference in
characters and parts, have a firm and hearty confidence
in him, a confidence I also hope that he returns me of full
right.—I have so often made no reply to what you say
about the W., that I thought it incumbent upon me to go
into the thing at greater length this time, as I could not

---

* All these good ladies might have remembered a fact evidently
communicated to Wagner by the husband (see next page), viz. that
Frau Wesendonck was then half-way toward her confinement of next
September.—Tr.

help remarking that an utterly erroneous suspicion has put you out, in however natural a fashion, and warped your judgment. You are not cross with me for this, I hope?—As for my grey hairs, why, tell that to the Wesendoncks without any fear of wounding my vanity; for, notwithstanding your calling me a "handsome husband" in your last letter, I have no great conceit of my beauty. —Touching the "Uncle and Aunt," alas, I've no secret to tell you : there's absolutely nothing in it ; you surely ought to know how often I have quizzical flashes with no further meaning whatever. With the best and most honourable will, I must therefore leave your curiosity unsatisfied this time.—

By the way, please tell Wesendonck, to whom I lately sent a few lines for his wife—on a hint from himself—that he has still to expect a thoroughly rational letter from me.—

I have nothing to say to the violin man ; Praeger has passed on his address to an instrument dealer here, who— if he means to go into the matter—will write himself.— But tell me, how ever did you come by the infamous idea that there's a bang on the gong in my Tannhäuser overture? For the life of me I know nothing of it, and therefore with the best of will can't leave it out, which I would otherwise have gladly done to please you ; if I mistake not, that gong is a banger out of Sulzer's head. That's how one gets paid out for leaving one's wife all alone with strange bachelors !—As for the concert anecdotes, I wrote you all that was needful last time. The next programme will somewhat compensate me for the last ; besides my overture and a Beethoven symphony, we're to have a Mozart one I've entirely re-nuanced to my liking, and for the close—the going-out piece—the over-

ture to Preziosa. At the last concert we did quite an
obscure and insignificant—earlier—overture of Weber's to
" The Ruler of the Spirits " ; I was astounded and annoyed
at its being demanded *da capo*, for which I could discover
no reason whatever. It has been explained to me now :
it was a deliberate demonstration by the audience in my
favour, to compensate me, as it were, for Herr Lucas with
his boring symphony having been received before (as
Englishman and director of the society) with more applause
than he was certainly worth. That's how these people
are : the thing itself makes no true impression on them,
and leaves them cold, as I recognised again thereafter
with the effect of the A -major symphony ; but so soon as
they interest themselves in a person, they shew it with a
deliberateness that looks almost like enthusiasm. Consequently, all is design !—

To retrieve another point forgotten, I may tell you
that the *Ney's* Fidelio left me very cold : a fine, equable
soprano voice, but the whole thing drill, and already all
those mannerisms I detest so ; added to which, she is
hideously ugly. The whole representation was bad ; to
particularise, Costa didn't understand the tempi at all,
and dragged everything : only Formes as Rocco was *very*
good ; I could make use of him some day. I also saw
Shakespeare's Romeo and Juliet at the Haymarket Theatre
the other evening, by very indifferent actors who nevertheless had the tradition at their fingers' ends—so it seemed
—which interested me in many ways. I and Lüders had
a droll experience with the impersonator of Romeo himself : an old womanish chap whom we ranged in the
sixties, without any nose, with a mouth all sunk in and
a monstrous big chin which made so disastrous an impression upon us that we couldn't help laughing whenever

he shewed himself in profile.   After the 1st act we con-
sulted the programme for the old boy's name, and found
to our surprise it was a Mistress Cushmann, a woman ! !—
The day before yesterday we were at another theatre, the
Olympic, small, but very elegant and with quite excellent
comedy actors.   The actual chief genius was a Mr. Robsard,
who played, danced and sang in a concluding pantomime,
" The Yellow Dwarf "—for all the actors here must be able
to play, dance and sing.   The man was really admirable—
a mixture of what I need for Mime and Alberich ; I wish I
could have him !—I won't deny that an occasional visit to
the theatre—always very expensive, though—agreeably
distracts and helps me to endure the otherwise abominable
stay here.

Yesterday I also resumed my work, in which I had
been interrupted awhile by hideous ill-humour.   Nothing
came of the excursion to Röckel at Bath—as you perceive—since Praeger couldn't accompany me ; in return,
I'm expecting Eduard here.—Liszt's visit is out of the
question : you read aright ; he is going to Hungary.   Has
Hülsen sent that money yet to Sulzer ?

Your finding nothing more about our concerts in the
Zurich papers is natural enough ; it can't be kept up thus
for ever.   The ordinary reports in the press here are
brief, and disparaging or appreciative according to party.
Moreover, there has been nothing special to discuss ; only
because there was a novelty at the last concert, the symphony by Lucas, has *Dawison* written something in the
Times again : for that matter, I didn't have to conduct
the nonett of Spohr, the execution whereof he found so
poor.   Quite funny tales are told me of this Dawison.   It
is certain that he has been bought by Meyerbeer's agent
(the Jewish music-dealer Brandus) to pull me down, to

prevent my making any way here lest I might have a shot at Paris later. In any case he felt he had lent me more weight by his enormous tirade in the Times than he naturally meant to ; also, his editor may have given him a hint ; so he has confined the venting of his gall on me to his own rag, the " Musical World." To criticise me to the bottom there, he has also instituted in the said rag a literal translation of the text of Lohengrin, which, as I have been assured, isn't at all bad. Now this translation is being generally read with great interest, and arouses the liveliest sensation ; so the stupid fellow simply is playing into my hands again. But I have further been assured that he—Dawison—himself is quite enraptured with this poem and told a friend of Lüders the other day point-blank, The man who wrote this text must be a very demi-god !—Now, what is one to make of it all ? Praeger says, it is just like him : he can be quite transported by a thing one day, and tear it to pieces the next if his position requires. Pretty tales !— I must still wait for anything solid and sane to be written about me, although a fitting opportunity to make my full acquaintance will in no case arise. Meanwhile, however, my hand alights on something in the *Spectator* anent the second concert ; it is appreciative, exactly as far as the man who wrote it [Hogarth] could *know* me. Please give it to Sulzer for his provisional edification.

That will be about enough for you to-day, dear Muzius (why ever do I choose to call you so? mustn't there be something behind that as well ?) Take good care of yourself and keep in thorough good health for me, and all will come right. If Pepsel gets lame again, just give his paw another sound rubbing ; give him and Knackerchen my very best regards. Yesterday I saw a perfectly beautiful

puppy for sale, but—remained faithful and staunch ; as I
am in everything, to sing my own praises for once.—Have
I forgotten anything else ? ?

So—farewell, accept my heartiest kisses ; be thoroughly
sensible, hold me dear, and salute the whole Switzery a
1000 times.

Thy

WILHELM RICHARD WAGNER.

89.

LONDON,—*I fancy the—8th of May* 1855.

DEAREST SPOUSE,

Yesterday completed the 9th week of my dog's-life
in London ; 7 weeks from to-day I put an end for ever to
this joy. It's all calculated out already. Tuesday, 26.
June, I depart in the evening, reach Paris Wednesday
forenoon, and the only question is whether I shall leave
for Basle on Thursday morning, when I should get to
Zurich on a Friday, which you may not like. Write me
whether I shouldn't start from Paris a day later, so that I
might arrive at Zurich on the *Saturday*. You see, I'm
counting nothing but the time for leaving here and reaching you again ; everything between this and then appears
to me a hell !—

When I had closed my last letter, and asked myself if
I hadn't forgotten anything, it finally occurred to me, too
late, that I hadn't answered your question about the
band here. At first I thought of making up for it at
once in a letter to Boom ; then I reflected that Sulzer
might take it amiss, perhaps, if I wrote to *him* before him.
So I shall report on that enquiry *to yourself* to-day. Unfortunately the orchestra of the Philharmonic Society,
which also is that of the Italian Opera, consists of almost

none save—Englishmen : only one trumpeter, a trom-
bonist, and a third, are Germans ; of Frenchmen likewise only 3 ; all the rest are good English.   Not that
there aren't many German and French bandsmen here ;
but Costa, who had the appointment of the bandsmen, in
his time, always engaged English in order to ingratiate
himself.   Now, these gentlemen play quite well, no
doubt, have thoroughly mastered their instruments, and
can take anything that is set before them ; but—like
machines, exactly like Geneva snuffboxes.   For instance,
they strictly have only one volume of sound, and can't well
play softer or louder.   The Paris orchestra is far superior.
These Englishmen are blocks of wood, and I would rather
fan a German dance-musician into fire, than one of
these wearisome fellows.   Moreover, it comes very difficult
to me to make myself intelligible to them ; French, of
course, is no help at all, and whenever I have a minuter
explanation to give, Sainton has to translate it, excepting
a few short phrases which I have picked up, such as
" *Once more, please !* " *i.e.* " noch einmal ! "   However,
I have been rewarded at last for my bassoon long-sufferings
at Zurich : the first bassoon here, a Belgian, is truly
excellent, perhaps the best musician in all the orchestra,
excluding Sainton ; he often has made me quite happy.—
The oboist—albeit an Englishman—is also first-rate, and
especially devoted to me ; on the other hand, the clarinet
—one of the directors—is bad, and I much preferred Ott-
Imhof (you may get him told that).   But Sainton is a long
way preferable to the good Hessian Heisterhagen ; he is
the best leader I have ever had—by no means barring
Dresden.   If I ever produce the Nibelungen, he is to be
with me.   Last Friday he had arranged a quartet at his
rooms in my honour, with—Piatti, the first violoncello-

virtuoso in London ; to anyone who knows the ropes here, and that these gentry are not in the habit of handling their bows under 10 pounds apiece in the season, it was an enormous distinction.—

So much for the orchestra.—These last few days I've had the pleasant occupation of studying the scores of the magnificent works to be extra-rehearsed the day after to-morrow for performance in course of the ensuing concerts. Sterling English compositions ; as unimpeachably correct as an example in arithmetic, but without one trace of fancy or invention : the joy it gives me to be let conduct these tone-poems, you may readily conceive ! My bitterness is awful, and only with the most ferocious irony, which it is lucky that no one understands here, am I able to stand it any longer and hold out. However—I don't intend to start that tale again !—

I have had to submit at length—in the month of May—to putting my skin into an under-vest ; naturally not of flannel, though, but of knitted silk, such as Dr R. recommended me at Zurich before. Everybody here wears such a vest, and declares it impossible to survive here without one. Hitherto I had rebelled ; but my catarrhal state became so serious with the persistent cold wind, and so affected my brain in particular, that I yielded to the advice of my friends here at last. I have worn the under-vest the last 3 days, and at any rate feel somewhat better for it already. I bought them with Eduard Röckel, and luckily found a bargain ; a remnant of exactly 2 vests of a pattern now gone out of fashion, for which reason I got them at 18 schill. apiece after 24 had been asked. As I have been compelled to wear a foulard under-vest at Zurich in the winter, this will be of further service to me there as

well, I hope ; so tell R. that I've followed his former
advice. The trouble given me by this everlasting chill
quite baffles description ; now its seat is in the lower
regions, now in the brain, and I'm so tormented all
the time, that I could often cry aloud at this eternal
obsession by an evil spirit. And you, too, don't appear
to have been quite the thing again of late, since you
speak of having been so hoarse ? I haven't suffered
yet from that here excepting at the concerts, where
I've always had the best occasion for catching cold
thereafter. Well, take the greatest care of yourself ;
if N. tends you nicely, I may bring her something
back as well. Sulzer's indisposition is nothing serious,
I suppose ? I wish him good recovery, and hope my
wish may come too late. Send the Major word he's
to be up and about again soon, and I'll bring him a
superb collection of corns : meanwhile he must be
strengthened with chicken-broth from you—without
eyes.*—

Hülsen's not having sent the money yet is most
provoking ! I'm simply waiting for your answer to
my last enquiry, to write the gentleman at once, to
whom I had to send my receipt in advance.—How
fatal it is to me, good God, I can't possibly tell you !—
Neither has Anderson made me another payment yet ;
he's in a horrible fix himself now—which I'll narrate
to you by mouth.—

All my friends here are taking it into their heads
to visit us in Switzerland ; I shouldn't be surprised if
Praeger came nearly as soon as myself. Ed. Röckel,
who wants to see his father at Wiesbaden at the same

---

* The pun is on "*Hühneraugen*," lit. " hen-eyes."—Tr.

time, will visit us almost for certain. He really is a very decent fellow ; last Sunday he treated me and the Praegers to a famous fish-dinner at Greenwich. To-day I go to Sainton and Lüders, tomorrow to Praeger's ; yesterday Klindworth dined with myself. Liszt has written me in a very friendly tone again ; he will visit us in Switzerland next September. May I only have recovered my voice then ; but I fear the wretched thing will never return.— —

There, I have talked myself dry for once again ; which often is a need to me in this shameful existence. For your Sebastopopopol news I thank you most sincerely ; it's enough to make one laugh, that you should have to supply me from Zurich with that sort of thing. At bottom, however, this Popel is indifferent to me ; the whole affair is arrant nonsense scarcely worth a glance. How happy I shall be, on the contrary, when I breathe the pure delicious air of Seelisberg again ; here I simply grow stupider day by day. Often I stare at my music-paper for half an hour at a stretch without the remotest idea what to write ; as for that, I am assured it's the same with everyone here, the heavy English atmosphere seeming to choke all volatility and freedom of the mind. I hardly think I shall get even my second act finished now, so slowly my work is crawling on. What a folly it was of me, *by God*, to come to London ! ! !—No matter, one must buy one's wisdom.—Fare splendidly well, good old Mienel, hip plenty of baths and think of your poor husband, who well deserves that one should let Brex spinster come again !

Na, that *will* be a joy; I hold my tongue !—Once more, then, be well and of good cheer ; I've already

been here 2 weeks longer than I have to go on being
here.   Salute left and right, and hold him dear

—who

—Virtue

—is

—itself ! ! !

90.

MY DEAR MINNA,

My last letter was merrily worded, not because
I *felt* merry, but simply because I wished to *appear* so
to you.   I had previously given you to understand that
I should already have thrown up my engagement here
if it hadn't been for my regard for *you ;* for I know
it would have greatly distressed you, whereas I don't
care in the least, for my own part, what the newspapers
might have written about my sudden throwing up of
that engagement.   Not to let my resolution to hold out
here for your sake in particular appear too heavy a
reproach to you through my laments, I tried to brighten
myself up in my letter to you as much as possible ;
for I saw that you, too, were in need of good humour,
and I wanted to contribute to it that way.   But unfortunately I now perceive that all my show of mirth
could do, was to embitter you against me, and that
for reason of a money trouble so acute that it even
affects your health anew.   Of course I shouldn't dream
of making that a reproach to you, and I must admit
your perfect right to feel bitter ; only, you do wrong
to lay the blame for the present dilemma on me.   As
I foresaw that no fees would be coming in from theatres
just now, at the very commencement of my being here

I wrote to Sulzer that I meant to try and raise the whole amount of my fee for the concerts on a promissory note—with Praeger's assistance—in order at once to send you out of it the money needed for your keep at Zurich. Thereupon Sulzer wrote and begged me on no account to do so, particularly since it was unnecessary for your sake, as he could assure me he had already prepared himself to supply from his own pocket whatever you needed during my absence. That wouldn't have eased my mind, however, had not the prospect at the same time opened to me of receiving the advance of 100 Ld'or from Berlin, which—as I begged you at once to tell Sulzer—I should direct to be forwarded to the latter. Finally, a month from to-day I received consent to that advance, and the receipt demanded for it went off to Berlin the selfsame day, together with my instructions to despatch the money to S. forthwith. Consequently you will agree with me, I hope, that I was justified in feeling at ease about your situation, and in believing I had done everything needful for your security. That Hülsen should not have sent the money even to this day, I certainly couldn't have anticipated from a gentleman so extolled to me as supremely handsome in his dealings ; your latest information, however, with your assurance that Sulzer has left you in the lurch despite his protestations, sufficed to induce me to get money from Anderson at once so as to send Sulzer a bill of exchange for 1000 *fr.*, which will have reached Zurich as I write these lines to-day, I hope, and thus have put a thorough stop to your dilemma. I am also expecting a reply from Hülsen during the next few days, and if I don't hear that the 100 Ld'or have arrived at Zurich within a fortnight,

I shall ask for money again here after the 6th concert,
to forward to Zurich.

—As for my life here, the worries of your situation
(deeply felt by me, in truth !) inspire you with a bitterness which renders you unjust to me.   It would be
most foolish to want to pay you out in kind, but just
to guide you away from that injustice—for your own
sake—I again must repeat to you that you are under
a mistake about my style of life here.   In that regard
I must confess it needed nothing save a money fix to
do for me completely.   I lead the dreariest, most
melancholy and lonesome life one can conceive, and—
which is the worst of it—with neither aim nor profit.
Moreover, the smallest attempt at distraction always
sets my budget in disorder ; a thing which those alone
can comprehend, however, who are really acquainted
with London and can allow for a heap of expenses
which nobody leading a life like that at Zurich, for
instance, can form the least idea of.   Do not expect
me to go into everything here ; in due season you
shall hear it all by word of mouth.   Only thus much :
whenever I have visited a theatre, e.g., it has cost me
5 schill. each time—not counting omnibus ; when I
have been invited to the Italian Opera—gratis—I have
always had to fetch Mad. Hogarth and daughter (in
whose box I sat) and escort them home, the cab-fare
costing me exactly 5 sch. again.   The transaction for
the remittance to Sulzer cost 5 sch., and the cab-fare
(twice—since everything is shamefully dilatory and
complicated—especially for foreigners) another 5 sch.—
If I buy a fresh supply of stamps—especially for business letters to Germany—I have to put upwards of
$\frac{1}{2}$ a pound down ; 22 cigars cost me 6 sch.   When I

lay in a fresh stock of provisions, ham or wine, it promptly runs into pounds. It is so cold here, that I still consume 4 schillings' worth of coal a week, etc., etc.—In brief, I've given up all thought of more extensive outings, to the country, the sea-side, or such-like, and hereby declare that I shall bring back 1000 *fr.* of *money saved*, but not a penny more : whoever understands it better, let him go to London in my place next time ; a pleasure I accord him with all my heart ! To be sure, I've provided myself with sundry articles, and in particular a whole new suit ; you also are to have your little presents : but this itself only becomes possible through my throwing in a small fee for my Faust overture from Härtels with which I had intended to surprise you—as a gift. As said, whoever understands it better, let him come next time in place of me ; I *cannot* manage otherwise, and there's an end !—

The Tannhäuser overture went quite beautifully at yesterday's concert ; when it was over, the first thing I heard was loud hisses from a single person, but then it was applauded fairly well, although the hissing was kept up by one or two. Besides a Mozart symph., we had the Pastoral symph., which went quite passably, a half-hour pianoforte concerto by Chopin, 4 vocal pieces, and to wind up, the overture to Preziosa. I need say no more about this concert. The Frankfort correspondent in the Zurich Tageblatt might be corrected [to the effect] that the dissatisfaction is not "mutual," but confined to myself ; the Directors have no inkling of it, and the concert audience, on the contrary, is said to set much store upon me, though it certainly might prove it somewhat more adroitly than appears to be good English tone. Thus much is certain : there was a large attendance

yesterday, and the room for the first time was packed :
this was generally attributed to the interest in my compositions ; possibly that is so.   For the rest, these concerts,
with all that comes to light there, are a penance to me,
and I will keep silence to-day on the bitterness that often
fills me to the point of nausea.   Enough—I shall conduct
3 concerts more, and 6 weeks from to-day I depart ; God
grant I may find all well at Zurich, and that your own
atrocious cares don't further undermine your health !   It
only needed that as climax, that one should fret oneself
to death about these cares.   Of a truth, dear Minna,
we've—no luck ! Just as everything always turns out
as badly for us as it possibly can, so with this Berlin
Intendant once more ; who could have foreseen such
remissness !   Instead of my considering you quite well
provided for, at this very moment you are in the most
objectionable straits : I should like—!   But we shall see.—

I have nothing further to communicate to you to-day ;
it isn't worth the while.   Sainton (a Frenchman), Lüders
(a Hamburger), and Herr and Frau Praeger (the latter
French, and far advanced in pregnancy) send you their
kindest regards ; they came to my rooms after yesterday's
concert, and devoted much good will to helping me rectify
my not particularly rosy mood.   All that dissatifies them,
is that every day of my sojourn here should not be turned
into a festival of thanks for the extraordinariness of what
I offer people ; and if things went according to their
mind, I should be carried round in triumph all the while.
This time Herr Ellerton took me to the concert in his
carriage ; you should hear him speak about his fellow-
countrymen !   He also is the first and only Englishman
who thinks nothing of Mendelssohn ; something quite new
to me.—

Give our friends my best regards.   Tell Mad. Stockar [their landlady] I'm very curious to see her new works [water-colours] as to which you write me such extraordinary things.

I hope to learn from your next letter that my bill of exchange has arrived, and—better furnished with money—you are now in better humour also.   What you write me about the bad effect upon your health, worries me more than I can tell you!   At any rate don't trouble on the score of visitors; probably nothing much will come of it, and they shouldn't prove a load to *you* at all.   So farewell, poor good Wife; restore yourself, and make me happy with good tidings of your health!   Greet Nette, too, and rest assured—I am leading no life of pleasure here, but looking forward to home *in every* respect! Farewell,

Thy RICH.

Hearty greetings to Sulzer.   I send him best thanks for his letter: but tell him, as concerns the philosophic part of it, I've racked my brains to find its application to my words; and as for England's décadence, I had simply listened to the song which the birds on the eaves all sing here, the text whereof is most indifferent to me on the whole.

Give *Boom* my greetings too.

91.

> 'Twas in the lovely month of May
> that Richard Wagner burst his shell:
> therein had he prolonged his stay,
> his best friends think it were as well.

Thus I congratulate myself in the name of you all for my birthday!

I've simply nothing to write you to-day, dear Minna, beyond my anxiety lest my letter to Sulzer with the bill of exchange may not have arrived safely, as I haven't yet heard from him, though he easily might have dropped me a couple of lines.   I sent him that letter last Saturday—a week from to-day—consequently he must have received it Tuesday morning.   Your writing me on Tuesday (15. May) without any mention of it, I explained to myself yesterday on the simple assumption that you posted your letter to me in the afternoon, whilst Sulzer did not call on you till evening.   But then you could have written me on Wednesday, to relieve my mind about the bill's arrival ?   However, that's always the way ; what I expect for quite certain, is never punctual in turning up, and so my head is always filled with nothing but unrest.   Neither has Hülsen answered me as yet. On the other hand a young man here, son of a deceased tailor at Riga, has presented a bill for over 34 roubles ; with the best conscience I don't know if I really owe the money still [from 1837–39 !].   In any case it is unpleasant for me to have to refuse the young fellow, who was quite delighted at the prospect of recovering the sum here— where I stand in such glory.   It's a veritable joy.   If this ragamuffin world becomes too mad for me ere long, I shall clothe myself in sackcloth and ashes ; but of a certainty I also shall make no more music then : you may all depend on *that*.—

For the rest, I thank you profusely for your yesterday's pink letter.   I shall have to forgive your repeated enquiry touching my debt to Karl Ritter, together with your singular allusions to " after-pains from Sitten," since I unfortunately have had to accustom myself to seeing things brought on the carpet again and again by you after they had been fully discussed and set right.   Therefore it shall not vex me to explain to you once more that from Zurich in September of last year I borrowed 1000 thaler (3800 *fr.*) from Karl, to pay off pressing debts, which he has refunded to himself by keeping back my year's allowance : 1500 *fr.* last autumn, 1500 *fr.* this April, and 800 *fr.* next autumn.   Accordingly, instead of my having to devote my takings to repaying Karl, they have been employed to fill the place of that withheld allowance ; which comes to the same thing, only that their incoming was not so regular.   Now that is at an end, however, through Berlin and my London savings.—So set your mind at rest on this point also.—But next time you are writing me *to London*, please ask me questions about other things ; I have disagreeables and annoyances enough here already, God knows !—

—I will attend to the cotton stockings with pleasure. I have abandoned all idea of gifts for our acquaintances ; I think you are quite right.   Next time I'll write you all particulars about my advent ; I fancy we had better stay a week at Zurich first, and not go to Seelisberg till after that—as you originally proposed ; but you might as well order our rooms in advance.—I'm very sorry for Baum-gartner's misfortune ; give him my condolence.—

It continues cold and wintry here.   Yesterday I had a call from Dr. Franck, who means to get his son trained in the English marine.   Tomorrow I'm invited by Eller-ton.   Otherwise my life is supremely amusing, glorious and gay, as you indeed will suppose.   Yesterday I took to sweating again.—Reassure me about your health ; it is to be hoped you'll soon be looking out for a good maid. I have a good, handy and willing indoor servant here ;

shall I bring him with me?—I know of absolutely nothing fresh, but am very uneasy about Sulzer's silence concerning the draft; let us hope a letter from him is already on the road.

Best greetings to the house; I shall thoroughly appreciate the week there. The inner affliction I put up with at having to abide by this mortifying engagement here, I can hardly express. Be glad you're unacquainted with that sort of affliction.—Take care of your health :

The most instant request of   Thy

R.—

92.

LONDON, 22 *May* 1855.

MY POOR DEAR MINNA,

You have made me a very mournful birthday-present with the news of your illness! Your last tidings, however, already pointed to your having caught a severe cold, and I almost must deem it as well that the immanent storm is discharging its force in a sound inflammation, which is always better than dragging an uneasy feeling about with one of being inwardly unwell. Thus it was a good thing in the end that you underwent that fever and inflammation before your journey of last year, as you got rid of what was lurking in your system, and then felt so much better at last that I still remember with great joy how well you looked on your return. You will see from these remarks that, to support the bad news, I at once am trying to forecast this case's progress in a favourable light; in which I luckily believe I've hit the mark this time. But I hope you kindly think of sending me oftener than usual a few lines—however few—to keep me posted in your state of health; at any rate do so as

soon as this letter arrives, and continue it each day till
you can write me that you're quite restored again.   To
be sure, that thorough restoration is generally a slow
affair, because fever always pulls you down and leaves
much weakness behind for some time ; yet I may hope
to find you quite well again on my return, and whatever
may still be lacking we shall certainly put to rights
together on the Seelisberg, where I am going to behave
myself as gently as a lamb this time, am I not?—So—
bear up, my dear old Minna !

Unfortunately you have lately received a pair of cross
letters from me, and what particularly grieves me is that
to-day itself, as I'm writing these lines, you will be
getting my last letter, in which I express myself somewhat testily about an enquiry of yours.   Ah, child, if you
only knew how these silly money difficulties on your side
helped to put me out just then ; it seemed to me as if one
were never to experience anything reasonable and cheering
again ; which—with all the rest I have to swallow here—
gave me a regular fit of the blues.   All that has since
come straight, however, and if friend Sulzer had only
fulfilled his own offer a little more punctually, neither
would you have suffered care, perplexity and bother, nor
I have needed to give myself somewhat away with
Anderson here and with Hülsen at Berlin—which was not
exactly to my taste ; for Hülsen wrote me yesterday that
the money had been despatched before receipt of my
reminder, which Sulzer simultaneously confirmed.   Don't
be angry with me, then, if in such circumstances I was
less able to conceal my ill-humour than, out of due regard
for you and your condition, I usually endeavour to.   No
matter, everything's in order now, and I can only wish
your health may also soon be quite restored, as it really

was my concern for it that most disturbed and nettled me on that occasion. Do give me a thorough good account of it soon !—

I haven't much to tell you of the progress of my life here. Unfortunately my own health is not in the very best order ; what plagues me most is weakness of digestion : I greatly miss the tender vegetables you always serve me up so excellently ; here I stuff myself with strictly nothing but meat and potatoes, which suits me very badly. I can hardly ever get to sleep before 1 in the morning, and therefore always rise quite late and very peevish ; then I stare for long into the cold grey atmosphere, and need an effort to constrain myself to do a little work. For some time past I have been taking *cocoa* for breakfast again, with rusks, which I've unearthed here at last. When I feel less of a weight on me, for lunch I take a cup of bouillon with an egg ; otherwise a small bottle of seltzer water, frequently in fact with milk. Then I slink from the house toward 3 o'clock, prowl about in Regents Park, where the beautiful ducks and swans form my chief entertainment ; hunt up Lüders or Klindworth ; and then, if I'm not dining at the former's (with Sainton) or Präger's, return home to my lonely dinner, which usually concludes my day's work.—

Last Sunday I had been invited by Ellerton ; his wife (a Lady) still being ill in the country, he entertained me at a club he is member of, where one is very well served. Sainton, whom he had also invited, was unfortunately detained ; but besides Lüders and Anderson there were present two old gentlemen, subscribers to the Philharmonic, who seemed very satisfied with me. It is certain I'm making quite a singular sensation here, and my friends say that the actual success of my appearance will only shew up later, perhaps after a few years, when I might even get marvellous orders from here. Thus the Tannhäuser overture seems to have really made more impression upon many people than I believed ; Ellerton shewed me, among other things, a letter from a lady of high rank expressing the most rapturous admiration of it. So much, accordingly, seems certain : already I have a small party here that regards me as a heaven-sent wonder, and upon which—as also on the audience in general—the venomous critics, who could almost burst for gall and fury, exert not the smallest influence, or at most an influence in my favour. But alack, I've neither taste nor time to cultivate all this and wait, since I know too well the insufficiency and inappropriateness of my position ; whilst this public's true distinctive feature, incompetence for music, repels me far too much. Get to know a thorough English soul, what a wooden creation of God's it is !—

On the top of it all I have only to inform you that people in America have been casting strong glances my way, and an enquiry has already reached Präger from a Mr. Mason, whether I might be prepared to accept the call and offer of several combined societies in New York to present my things there ; they hope to let me have the formal invitation in a few months' time. Just imagine the bliss of that prospect, immediately after my return from London to have to set sail again for America ! At any rate you would be of the party, would you not ? or should we prefer to remain in the Escherhäuser after all ? I rather think so. For my own part at least, I am *heartily sick* of it, so sick that I swear that nothing shall decoy me from my work again ; indeed I am not made for this farrago, and should precious soon be done for, were I forced into it.—No, my dear Minna, let us quietly keep to our beautiful Switzerland, attending to health and good temper ; and if a contented mind can help toward that, I'll be content in every way henceforward, and gladly not grudge to others their being better off.— Full stop !—

If Klepperbein can make nothing better than such portraits, I should advise him to drop it ; I could do as well myself by smearing a handful of ink over the paper. And yet the stupid photograph has touched me : there always is something direct about it that attracts ; the outline of your form is plainly recognisable, and it suddenly seemed as if you were standing before me. *Peps* surprises me whenever I see him again, and so in this picture ; it always moves me deeply when I think of the old fellow's being still alive and with us. He doesn't appear to have grown very slim, though ; as he lies at your feet there, one remarks his old podgy obesity. I hope you're out of bed again by to-day ; if not, how goes it with Knackerchen ? Hasn't he come flying into the bedroom again to find you ? As soon as you've a little strength again, give Peps a good dig in his fat ribs, in my name, and follow it up with a spank ; that will do him good !—

I shall leave here five weeks from to-day, and get to Zurich and my old Muzius on Saturday the 30th June at latest. All details concerning my arrival we will settle later on ; we've plenty of time for that, alas ! But don't you worry in the slightest as to guests ; probably Präger will be unable to come at all, and Röckel at the outside would only come to Seelisberg for a day. In no case should we put ourselves the least bit out. So—relieve your mind and keep your courage up. The worst is over now, and in general I trust we both have got the worst

part of our life behind us ! A thousand fervent wishes for
your welfare are herewith sent you on his birthday by

Thy

RICHARD.

I have just written a letter to Wesendonck also,—his
(which reached this house, remarkably enough, two hours
earlier than yours) has given me great and hearty joy ; he
wrote me very amiably and nicely.   Poor devil that I am,
though, I couldn't help almost laughing at the purse.—

93.

LONDON, 25. *May* 1855.

Your letter of to-day, dear good Mienel, has conferred
a great boon on me ; the very first glance dispelled my
serious fears about your health ; for I saw that you had
been able to write so much, though it is only 3 days since
you were hardly able to write at all.   Indeed I had been
very anxious, and as I know how long the weakness after
high fever continues, I was almost afraid I should get no
letter from you to-day whatever : the greater, naturally,
was my delight.   But I am sure it was a transgression
of R.'s orders, and all I now fervently wish, is that you
haven't harmed yourself thereby and brought on a fresh
attack of fever.   Still, you appear to be getting over it
better this time than last autumn, on the whole, and I
congratulate you with all my heart.   Your being able to
make such beautiful verses straight off, however, surely
is also a result of the fever ; I should think you must
have been quite exhausted after this poetic effusion.   If
that sort of thing goes on, you'll be writing me opera-
texts in the long run ; Lord, had I known it before, what
a deal of pains you might have saved me !   Who knows
how it may turn out yet ?   If my head remains as dull

and heavy as it is at present, I'm unlikely to write poetry again in all my life. The trouble any working gives me is boundless, and my condition wellnigh insupportable ; I feel each day as if I had been up all night, heavy, limp, a wreck. Of the Walküre I shall bring back nothing finished beyond the first half of the second act, and just this act is such a great exertion because it contains none but situations of atrocious suffering ; the " Young Siegfried " will naturally go much easier and faster, so much depends upon a cheerful subject. I no longer believe I shall begin it this year, though ; my mind is very weary !—

You surely do not doubt my holding out here to the end ; after my supporting the last 3 months, it would be very stupid if I finally lost patience with the remnant. So we won't speak of that again. Tomorrow I have the rehearsal for the 6th concert : a symphony by an Englishman—Potter, a queer old fish who thoroughly amuses me, and has turned my initial anger at his fabrication into laughter ; a symphony by Mendelssohn (which I once gave at Dresden [" Scotch "] and at any rate is better than the earlier) ; an *overture* by Spohr (awful !), singings of sorts, and as recompense for it all, at last the Beethovenian overture to *Leonora !* Moreover, Sainton will play a violin concerto of Beethoven's, which he already has rendered to me at his rooms, and which I am glad to conduct this time.—Whether the Queen will yet come to a concert, is still undecided ; neither does it concern me any more.—Herr Benecke, who may have been offended by my rather cold conducting of a Mendelssohnian symphony (in glacé gloves), has become reconciled to me again through the last concert, and in particular through the Tannhäuser overture ; so I have at last had to accept for next Sunday, when—as I hear—he also has invited all the music-Jews

of London in my honour.   God, how absurd I appear to
myself here !

I feel as grateful to you for your present as if I had
already received it ; but I think it very luxurious of
you to want to spread such a beautiful cover on the
piano-stool at once ;   surely you will put the new embroidery away to save for me.   You had a happy
thought with the camp-stool, for which I thank you
much ;   but   before   you   get   the carpenter to make it,
remark my ensuing description of such a chair, taken
from a pattern one meets in almost every house in
England—in mine as well.   It consists of two portions,
which are joined in the middle of the seat in the following
fashion, and can be shut up flat :

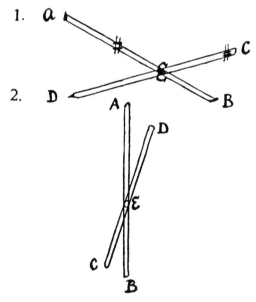

1. The chair when it is set open.   E is the axis with
the screw ; from A to C forms the seat (C the knee, E

the most honourable, A the head) at a most agreeable,
nearly recumbent angle, in which one gets excellent rest.
D and B are the legs.   From A to E, and from E to C,
the space between the two supports is filled with rushes—
or even with plaited straw ; if you liked, you could also
fill it up with your embroidery.   A band can also stretch
from ♯ to ♯, to rest the arms on.

2. The chair when it is shut.   As the part from A
to B is rather longer than the other, one could shorten
it above by means of a hinge, where it would likewise
shut to.

God the Omniscient may know if I have expressed
myself plainly ; but you are so immensely clever that I
believe you will at least have understood me.—

On my birthday I spread out on my bed all the things
I've procured here, and couldn't resist the temptation to put
them all on and display myself to an astonished world ;
you'll be delighted with the suit.   I and Klindworth
spent the evening at Präger's, who devoted half a bottle
of champagne to your health.   Otherwise the day passed
pretty drearily.   But there, such birthdays shan't occur
again ; one learns wisdom in the end, does one not ?

I have had many another look at your photograph, and
at last made out from it the portrait, so that to my delight
I saw you quite lifelike before me ; the notion was therefore quite capital, and I thank you for it much. *Peps*
looks hugely like a sausage ; everyone has had to laugh to
whom I've shewn him.   Now Heaven grant I may soon
receive news of your total recovery ; even your letter of
to-day has quite picked me up, as you doubtless will see
from these lines.   Continue that way, and it will end in
a reunion of the first water, will it not ?   Fare quite
enormously well, so well that you won't be able to

contain yourself; greet R., and thank him on my behalf
as well for his care of you.   Adieu, many, many hearty
kisses from

Thy
Husband.

94.

London, 29. *May* 1855.

Good morning, dear Minna!

In good London fashion I have risen at 10, after
somewhat restoring myself from the racket of yesterday's
concert.   So *that* too is over, and 4 weeks from to-day
I depart, to convince myself at Zurich whether you've
recovered entirely.   Your unexpectedly swift convalescence, or at least your leaving bed again, has been the
solitary good experience, and the fondest, I have had of
late; it has relieved me greatly, and put me in as good
humour as possible.   So I give you the testimonial that
you have behaved very well this time, and you shall be
rewarded for it to the best of my ability at our reunion, especially if I see that you've procured yourself
the needful blood again.   Let me take this opportunity
of assuring you that I can't abide blood-letting;   I am
convinced you haven't too much blood, and also am of
opinion that in inflammatory cases the application of
water—by cold compresses—is more beneficial.   Now
do your very best, as said, to get your blood back;
provide yourself with a good appetite and good spirits:
I hope the riddance of the money trouble will be a help
toward that.   You are perfectly right: harassments of
that sort are most depressing, and injuriously affect the
health;   which also was the reason I was so worried and
put out myself, when—in spite of my provisions against

it—I learnt of your strait. Now I have begged Sulzer—after deducting his last disbursements—to place at your immediate disposal the 1500 *fr.* for the current half-year, together with the 500 *fr.* for last Easter, so that you will receive your full house-keeping money down to October 1, and in addition 150 *fr.* of the 500 *fr.* extra, of which you have already had 350 *fr.* for the rent.—So be of good cheer ; then blood and courage no doubt will return to you also.—

Yesterday's concert went off as usual ; the principal piece was the violin concerto by Beethoven, which Sainton played wonderfully and I got very delicately accompanied for him. For the rest, as regards the applause I have grown accustomed to expecting the opposite of what really ought to be expected. Anything majestic and powerful is always received pretty coldly ; anything natty and trite, on the other hand, always gives these people great delight : it seems to be fashionable never to excite oneself, and for God's sake never let oneself be carried off one's feet—it would be against good tone. Certainly it is the most unimpressionable audience in the world, and nobody has any other aim with it, than—to pocket its money ; as to which Albert Wagner was perfectly right. They practise the proprieties each time, however, toward myself, *i.e.* I'm always fairly well received ; that goes without saying.— Moreover, the Queen will attend the next concert ; which will cost me a white cravat. Prince Albert will draw up the programme himself ; I have been told that at least *four* pieces by Mendelssohn would be played in consequence. Doubtless I shall survive it.—

Last Sunday I had the good fortune to dine with the family Benecke in the company of a number of music-Jews.

That entertainment cost me 8 schilling ; as all the Sunday omnibuses were full, I had to take a cab there and back (8 English miles each way).   Of such are my joys !—

Indeed I shouldn't know what else to write you on my humdrum life here ; I am always in perplexity what to find to tell you.   In return for the wretched 1000 *fr.* I'm saving by it, this expedition has thrown me far, far back : I inwardly feel so disgraced and maltreated, that I've long since almost lost my artistic belief ; it will be a hard job to recover it : with my work—as I've already written you —I am far in arrear.   The worst of it is, I have *only myself* to reproach for it justly ; for I alone know this public world of music as no one else can know it, and *I* alone know *my* position toward it : consequently, even when everybody else was speaking up for it, I ought to have declined this invitation most emphatically.   How free and strong should I then have stood, whereas I now give every vagabond the right to say I never was in earnest with my former views, but simply playing the fox with the grapes.—That will do : what's done, cannot be undone.—

You misunderstood me, if you thought the Riga tailor's son had touched me by his *friendliness ;* on the contrary, it tormented me to find that the fellow had such perfect faith in his claim.   His father died a long time back, and among his papers they found an acceptance of mine, which the young man treasured up as an heir-loom, and, lighting upon me in London, now hoped to cash.   I turned him away, however, as I really cannot remember this debt, though I have a very good memory for everything else.   It was disagreeable to me in any case.—

I must beg you for the contents of Pusinelli's letter,

as I heard from Fischer that Meser was on the eve of going bankrupt, whereon I begged him to urge my business-creditors to make my property secure. As for that, people all behave like muffs, and from nowhere—so it seems—can I ever learn anything pleasant. Did Pusinelli write reassuringly, then ? I should have been glad to learn that, you silly Muzius !—I don't like hearing that you have such confidences with Sulzer that he has told you something with regard to money which you are not to repeat to me ; in that case he would have done better also not to make such an absurd remark to you as this distasteful question whether I hadn't been receiving money from the theatres and sending part to you. You did very right to tell me that, and my giving Sulzer an explanation on the point was quite in order.—In your state of health I should scarcely have expected you to be champagning on my birthday, and when you told me of it I was almost horrified ; as it did you good, however, I naturally was very glad, above all since I saw that your illness had passed off more smoothly this time. Knackerchen's feather gave me great delight ; it was quite an excellent idea of yours and his.

Tell me, you seem to have been wanting to come as far as Paris to meet me ? That surprised me ! Dearest Minna, I am looking forward to home and to Switzerland, and to rejoin you *there* will be the most agreeable to myself ; unfortunately also, I have been unable to earn enough here to afford a stay in Paris with any pleasure ; whilst I dislike the idea of gadding about in Paris again—even with you—just after leaving London. I should much prefer going direct from here to the Seelisberg ; yet I gladly consent to a week of home comforts at Zurich beforehand. But let me get over the journey, and set foot in our home, as quickly as possible ; and what I should like best, would be for you first to receive me in Zurich itself, where I hope to find rest.   To me it has a truly moral meaning, and for God's sake do not seek behind my wish some slight upon yourself, but directly the opposite.   I want to be reminded as little as possible of this whole expedition, and can hope to grow mirthful only when at home and with yourself, our animals, etc., I forget this entire metropolitan joust.

But there, I've time enough to tell you all particulars of my arrival.   In any case I shall travel back as fast as possible, and my only question is where to sleep a night en route, so as not to reach you too exhausted.

So farewell, dear good Minna.   Be sure your letters are always very welcome to me, and contribute whatever is possible to bring me a good day !   So keep your spirits up ; our parting will soon be over now ; let us celebrate a right joyful reunion !   A thousand salutes and kisses from

Thy

R.

95.

LONDON, 1. June 1855.

DEAR GOOD WIFE,

To-day, this 1st of June, I've had a roaring fire lit again ; which will shew you the delicious climate I am living in.   Everything combines to make my sojourn here as charming as possible !   However, I already am thinking almost less of that sojourn, than of the departure ; for I shall be at Zurich 4 weeks from tomorrow !   The day before yesterday I commenced my purchases, Mad. Präger helping me ; for which I had to remember her as well with lace, of course, and presented her with a collar and cuffs—in revenge for *much* that I have enjoyed in her house. Concerning this lace, however, a doubt has now cropped up in me ; for Mad. Präger declared that only collars and cuffs of it are generally worn, as people always have high bodies to their dresses. As to the Wesendonck, it immediately occurred to me that she always wears high bodices, and therefore needs no embroidered chemisette (chest) ; but how about yourself? Of the richest lace I've only bought collar and cuffs for you, as also for the Wesendonck ; in the *less* expensive lace, however—such as Mad. Wolfensperger wears—I have added a chemisette. So, if you think a stomacher of the *richer* lace should also be purchased—both for yourself and the W.—please send exact instructions, that I may buy it yet. Of course the thing is not precisely cheap—for there's a difference in the quality ; but if it is needful, don't hesitate to speak straight out, and the cost must be saved off something else.—I have also got you stockings : $1\frac{1}{2}$ pound the dozen.—

At the French Customs they're very strict, and I have been generally advised to declare the things, especially the lace, and pay duty, which comes to 25 per cent, though.—But there's no hurry about that.—

As to news from here, unfortunately I know of absolutely none to give you, however much I rack my brains ; so that I really am only writing to give you a sign of life and thank you most sincerely for your letters, which have truly rejoiced me by relieving my mind in respect of your health. As for *my own*, I couldn't remain here much longer without becoming downright ill : my lower regions are badly out of order ; the food here is doing me great harm, particularly the lack of soft vegetables and plenty of them; the only way I can remedy it, is to eat as little as possible. However, I don't intend to fall into laments again; you have heard them often enough. If I only had anything pleasant to tell you instead; but I know of nothing good, except that it's drawing to an end here. —

What we shall set before the sovereign Court at our next concert, I haven't heard yet; moreover it is infamously indifferent to me.—At last I have the score of "Rheingold" in my hands again; the Dresden copyist hadn't even yet got through the half of it, so I lost patience and begged Fischer to send the whole bundle to me here, as I meant to get the copy finished at Zurich. (It cost a tidy sum per post.)—Tell me (before I forget it), has Schmidt of Frankfort had the present I intended for him??—

A lady here is plaguing me for my portrait for Berlin, where the last doesn't satisfy and they want a better one of me. For that purpose she wishes me to get photographed again, which I won't; nothing decent will come of it in all my life, and I haven't the least desire for any of that sort of nonsense now.—The day before yesterday I and Präger were at a theatre no farther off from our abodes than 7 Engl. miles; it is called the *City-of-London* theatre. The dearest seat was 1 schilling; Publicus was in its shirt-sleeves etc., and kicked up such a row that it took me a long time to get as accustomed to it as the actors had, who played on quite calmly albeit not a word of theirs was understood. They played Schiller's Robbers, and after it a French piece, the *Corsican Brothers*. In the Robbers it startled me to see Frau v. Marschall as Amalie; please tell her I should never have believed she was playing comedy incognito

in London.   At one point in the last piece there appeared
the ghost of the slain brother, which was represented so
vividly that I've been quite afraid of it at home of nights.
There also was a *duel* in it, carried out so intensely naturally
and excitingly that I rarely remember my interest being
so held at the theatre.   Präger has assured me, moreover,
that the most celebrated English actors do not play a
hair's breadth otherwise or better than those at this out-
of-the-way theatre—which I simply wished to see for
the sake of enlarging my experience.—

There, I have pumped up all my news now, and
it's your turn to tell me Zurich novelties, which will
amount to pretty much the same.   That doubtless arises,
dear child, from our having led so moving and eventful
a life that we no longer take an interest in what strikes
others as still of account.   Neither do we need anything
of the kind, and the beautiful Seelisberg shall narrate
us more news than this whole big political and artistic
Jew-world, to which *I* at least am dead for good.   God
rest its soul !—

Klindworth, who is better again, has just turned up ;
we are dining together at Sainton and Lüders' to-day.
If it were not for these good amiable fellows, and the
Prägers, decidedly I should have been unable to hold
out here.   Within their limited means they give themselves all conceivable pains to make my life agreeable.
What nonsense, that they should need to !

As for that, I did *not* invite them after the last
concert ; to speak candidly—out of economy (you will
laugh at that, but it's the truth).   The disappointment
was general, however, and I shall invite them again
after the next Royal concert in the white cravat.—

Now fare immensely well, good Muzius !   Keep brave

and of good humour. Hearty thanks for your letters
once more. To a speedy, glad, glad Wiedersehen !

Thy

RICHARD.

96.

LONDON, 5. *June* 1855.

DEAR MIENEL,

It is too bad that I should really have nothing
to write you from here ; I do not even know the
programme for our next concert yet, and probably shan't
till this evening at Sainton's. Consequently I am only
writing lest you should come by evil thoughts if a
letter were skipped, though they never do occur to
you (do they ?).—Nevertheless I have a little trip to tell
you of, which I took this last Sunday to Brighton
(pronounce, Breiten), where Präger is spending a few
days with his family, and whither he had invited me.
Unfortunately it was so windy that I caught a fresh
cold on our sea jaunt— the chief amusement there ;
then I tried to rid myself of the results by sweating,
which always makes one still more liable. But the
winter will never end here, and—with the exception of
a few days—I have been wearing winter clothes for
nine full months now—God be praised !—my wadded
overcoat, for instance, is on my body almost all the
time. The only thing wanting, is for this bad weather
to break loose at home when I get back. That prospect
exists, to judge by your accounts of the constant fair
weather at present ; what bliss !—If one could only
throw off the habit of life, since it really is made such
an affliction !—

That you are passably well again, and seem to be
in good spirits, gives me just as much joy as your

illness and bad temper (in consequence of that silly money fix) made me uneasy a little while back. So I'm in a somewhat better frame of mind myself. As for Sulzer, whom you appear to be treating extraordinarily harshly, he told me he had placed the whole 250 *fr.* for April at your disposal ; if he really only gave you 150, no doubt it was because he remembered my having left you an advance of 100 *fr.* before I started. However, that will soon explain itself when I get back, which won't be much longer to wait for. Three weeks from to-day I depart (in the evening) ; already I feel that I ought to be packing, so absolutely am I in London no longer in spirit. To-day, too, I've come to a stop with my work ; I have only reached the end of Wodan's great scene in the 2nd act of the Walküre— horrible to relate !—so that I have instrumented something over 100 pages in all here ! ! I haven't the smallest relish to begin a new scene here, and shall merely pass the remaining time away with the fair copy and preparations for it.—

By all means you might write to Trüttmann [Seelisberg hotel] : I want a small room in the *old* house for my study, and on the Chapel side, that I may have no morning sun ; I also should think it as well if you engaged for our parlour and bed-chamber those rooms in the new house, on the other side of it, which Frau Landamtmännin Reding occupied last year, as they are the least exposed to the sun—which, as you know, is a great consideration.—

It would be dreadful if Peps couldn't go out with us any more. He had that lameness in his fore-paw once before, and yet it left him ; so I still have hope this time : only do not let him eat too much. God,

the thought that one soon must lose the good old chap
entirely, makes me quite doleful !—Give him my kindest
regards.—

As spinster Breck is making such lovely things for
me, I suppose you must give her my regards as well ;
only don't make them quite too cordial ! Apropos of
my domestic luxury, I've been led by chance to an
increase thereof which mustn't make you cross with
me. Präger's wife saw one of my Paris silk shirts,
and declared one could get them still better and cheaper
here, as these materials are more largely made here than
in France. In brief—she has shewn me samples, and
I have bought material for three shirts ; which must be
made up here, however, as I should have to pay duty
otherwise upon the stuff. But set your mind at rest :
you too shall have an extra something nice, especially
if you behave yourself, and I shall still bring back that
1,000 *fr.* intact.

I've also had annoying business matters to attend
to ; Meser, in particular, has cost me a bad day. What
a champion piggery that is ; it is enough to make one's
heart bleed, to see how such a fine and hard-won
property is managed !—Lucky I'm not there, God knows !
If only the world would accord me at least one thing :
my keeping good humour for work ; for indeed that's
the sole thing I *want* in the end.—

I know absolutely nothing further of Berlin ; but
there is ample time for that ! The whole thing is
terribly indifferent to me at bottom.—

Now wheedle Sulzer into supplying good weather
for my return ; a Director of Finance on the English
model can do anything ! As for yourself—be nice and
calm, look after your health, lie down and take things

easy, don't slave about anything : that I may find you
in thorough good condition.   Then we'll do nothing
but fool around the whole first week.   Adieu !   A
thousand heartfelt greetings and kisses from

Thy
R. W.

97.

LONDON, 8. June 1855.

MOST EXCELLENT MUZIUS,

I cannot write you anything definite about the
next concert, even to-day.   Tuesday evening Sainton told
me the programme had already appeared in the newspaper, and my Tannhäuser march was upon it.   Therefore
Prince Albert must have demanded some of my music,
and, without a word to me about it, these stupid devils
of directors blindly set down this march since it chanced
to be still in reserve.   For we had run through it at an
extra rehearsal before the 5th concert, that it perhaps
might be given in course of the concerts as a closing
number.   After the 6th concert, however, when I attended
a committee to arrange the programmes for the remainder,
they shewed me a written sketch of the last two concerts
(before they knew whether the Queen would attend one
of them), and behold you, they hadn't included this march
in it.   At any rate, then, the undecided success of the
Tannhäuser overture had made it advisable to these gentlemen to give nothing more of mine ; whereas *I* in the
meantime had made up my mind, should they still want
the march, that I *wouldn't* consent to it, since I have lost
all desire to produce myself here.   For all that, these
gentlemen behaved very shabbily in vouchsafing me no
word about it, but slinking away like cats from hot broth ;
so I have just taken my revenge.   Immediately I heard

of the programme arranged with Prince Albert, I wrote
the latter: It much rejoiced me to perceive that the
Court wished to make acquaintance with some of my
music, but I regretted that the directors of the society,
without consulting me, had fixed upon a march that
was merely a piece of scenic decoration, and to myself
did not seem qualified to give a sufficient idea of my
music; consequently, if the Court insisted on its wish,
I besought the Prince to command an execution of the
Tannhäuser overture, which had certainly been given
once before, but in any case could only gain through
better understanding by the audience on a second hearing.—Sainton himself delivered this letter next day at
the Palace, where he had to give a lesson.   At the same
time I wrote to the directors, telling them that this
march, which *they* had considered unworthy to set on
the programme of their ordinary concerts, was bound to
strike myself as still less worthy of an extraordinary
concert, if it were a question of giving the Royal Court,
in compliance with its desire, an adequate idea of my
music; consequently I had written to Prince Albert, and
begged him to demand the Tannhäuser overture.—Well,
it appears that the Prince has at any rate fulfilled my
wish and asked the directors for the overture, as I'm
bidden to an extraordinary committee for 5 this afternoon;
whereas if the Prince had *not* entertained it, he would
certainly have told me so direct through his secretary,
for which purpose I had written him my address.   It
would be droll, accordingly, if in this way I arrived at
a minor amende after all; although I could have done
quite well without it, as this whole London expedition
simply strikes me as a sin committed by me, for which
I heartily admit the justice of stern punishment.—For the

rest, we have a thorough good programme, and one that —if it weren't for *too much* music—may give me pleasure : the lovely symphony of Mozart which I conducted once at Zurich ; then the 8th symphony of Beethoven, the second movement whereof we once had to repeat at Zurich (by request !). So we shall see : I'll write you *after* the concert ; meanwhile you may assume with tolerable certainty that the Tannhäuser overture will be given.—

Thank you for your 4-leafed clover, though it will have caused you no very great effort, as you hardly find any but 4-leafed clover ; it shall be a token to me, how-ever, that you are well and in good humour. I am equally glad that you're satisfied with my economy and my purchases : I'm not quite at the end of the latter yet, and you shall get something pretty besides ; neither did you need to give me any orders for lace insertion ; instead of $1\frac{1}{4}$ ell I had already purchased several, which I hope will suit you. The stockings I've bought you will certainly be considerably finer than the previous ones ; they are of the *best* quality.

The other evening I went with Präger and Lüders to the Surrey Gardens, where there are wild beasts in variety (among them many lions), and Sebastopol is so surprisingly represented in the open, that I really didn't know at first where I had got to. When it grew dark, the bombard-ment was copied in fireworks, ending with the final capture of Sebastopol while the band very touchingly played "*God save the Queen.*" The irony of the thing became complete for me when I learnt that the same soldiers were employed for this sham fight who had been in the Crimea and, after fighting in reality, returned here wounded, to go through the thing again with pasteboard, canvas and rockets, but victoriously this time.   The public naturally feels very gratified : what more would one have ?—

Otherwise I have nothing to communicate from here, except that I'm counting the days to my longed-for departure already. Liszt has written me very amiably : at Düsseldorf, where he also was invited to the Music-festival, he likewise heard on all sides that I had left London, at which all the world felt hearty joy (namely, at my having been kicked out) ; a joy Liszt spoilt for them by the assurance that it wasn't true. Ah, this adorable crew of musicianers ; how odious I seem in my own eyes for its having assumed the appearance again as if I were one of themselves !— God preserve me in future even from that appearance !—Farewell, best of all Minnas ; continue so sensible and bright, and you shall be rewarded by having in me the very dearest of husbands, who now presents himself with olden love as

Thy superlatively faithful partner and spouse,

R. W.

98.

LONDON, *Saturday, after the rehearsal.*

DEAREST MINNA,

I must send you just a word, to tell you the Tannhäuser overture will *really* be repeated.

I haven't a postage-stamp left in the house, so you'll have to bleed 55 cent. for this bulletin, which will *amuse* you, however.

Adieu, I'm very tired, and have just ordered a small bottle of stout (porter).

God save the Queen !

Your

very truly

RICH. WAG.

99.

LONDON, 12. *June* 1855.

Good Lord, dear Mienel, I am quite hoarse from so much talking with—the—Queen ! First she asked me how was Peps? Then, if Knackerchen was well-behaved? Then, if I was taking anything back for my wife ?—Finally she asked after Sulzer, and whether Baumgartner had really failed the other day ? And so on, without end. You may imagine what a deal I had to answer ; in short, I can't squeeze out another word to-day.

No, don't you believe that's my fun ; it's all in earnest, and the Queen of England had a very long conversation with me. Further, I can assure you that she *isn't* fat, but very short and not at all pretty, alas with a slightly red nose ; still, she has something uncommonly kind and familiar about her, and even if she isn't precisely imposing, she is pleasing and amiable. She doesn't care for instrumental music, and when she attends a long concert like this—which is by no means the case every year—she does it simply for her husband's sake, who goes in more for music and is fond of German instrumental music. This time, however, she really appears to have received an impression. Sainton, who kept her in eye the whole time from his desk, declared she followed my conducting and the pieces with unwonted and increasing interest, whilst she and Prince Albert quite warmed at the Tannhäuser in particular. So much is certain : when ⊤ faced about at the close of that overture, *both* of them applauded me most heartily, and looked towards me with a friendly smile ; of course the audience did not leave them in the lurch, but honoured me this time with very decided, universal and prolonged applause. That was at the end of the concert's first part, and the Court thereon withdrew to a refreshment room, whither I was summoned forthwith and handed first to the Lord Chamberlain for presentation. That lord I treated much *en bagatelle ;* on the contrary, I must confess I felt touched to the heart by this kind and gracious Queen when she assured me quite cordially that she was delighted to make my acquaintance, for I involuntarily recalled my outward situation toward her, which really could not be more difficult and embarrassing. Pursued by the police in Germany like a highway robber, with passport difficulties made for me in France, I am received by the Queen of England, before the most aristocratic Court in the world, with the friendliest sans gêne : it really is very nice ! Neither did I hesitate to give her to understand this quite frankly ; whereon ensued a lengthy conversation about my operas, in which Prince Albert—a very handsome man !—joined with most gratifying interest. To the Queen's opinion that my things might perhaps be translated into Italian, to be given at the Italian Opera here, the Prince quite intelligently replied that probably my texts would not be suited for it, and certainly Italian singers would not know how to sing them. Upon that said the Queen very naively— " But most of the singers at the Italian Opera now, you see, are Germans ; consequently they would only need to sing in their mother-tongue." We were obliged to laugh, and I then replied that unfortunately the German singers also had much deteriorated, and—if I wanted one day to produce the big work I now was working at—I should seriously have to think of first training my people. No doubt they didn't altogether understand that, but they expressed themselves sympathetically, adding that they had been quite enraptured with the overture ; whereon

I thanked once more for its commanding, and assured them both that they had greatly rejoiced me by this proof of their interest.—And that was the truth ; for, although this evening can bear no further outward fruit, it has given me a most agreeable satisfaction, so that I can depart from London with some sense of reconcilement. At the close of the concert both very kindly applauded me again to my face (they were sitting in front, quite close to the orchestra), and thereby elicited from the audience a longish outburst of applause.—My handful of friends, who assembled at my rooms thereafter, were swimming in bliss. Präger had lent me a white cravat ; he means to hoard it up in memory of a German dema- gogue who struck up " *God save the Queen* " in it before the Queen of England. For the " *God save*" had to be played when the Queen entered, and I had to beat time for it. I should think the German police might let me pass in peace now !—

At bottom this event rejoiced me chiefly for your own sake, since I knew that the account of it would affect you most agreeably. If you are greedy of honour for me, it has been dealt me in full measure this time. It will take the press a long while ere it swallows this revenge vouchsafed me ; the reporters' wrath may pass all bounds.

I hereby make you a present of the whole occurrence ; do with it as you please. If it affords you satisfaction, communicate some of my account to Marschall or Spyri, that they may narrate a portion of it in their journal. Whether the other newspapers will say much about it, I almost doubt.—

So I still shall conduct my last concert (a labour of Hell every time to me, which I shouldn't care to under- take again for all the money in the world)—and then take leave as cheerfully as possible. A fortnight from to-day, at 8 in the evening, I depart from Londonbridge ! ! ! May it be for a right joyful reunion ! Farewell, very best Muzius ; be of good cheer ! Greet all our dear friends heartily from

Thy
Knight of the Order of the Garter.

100.

LONDON, 15. June 1855.

GOOD MORNING, DEAR MINNA !

This morning you'll be getting the letter about the last concert, which is sure to entertain you highly. I'm still quite hoarse from so much talking with—the— Queen ; which appears to have made a great impression here. Of course the principal papers, to whom the affair was a thorn in the eye, mention nothing of the interview ; but the " Globe " has been brought me, wherein it stands that the Queen had had me summoned after my over- ture, and spoken with me for some time. Yesterday I sent this sheet to Sulzer in a wrapper : to-day I learn that he has already left for Winterthur. Please find out at once from the usher whether the sheet has been sent after him ; if not, beg it back, and pass it on to Spyri— or Hagenbuch ; perhaps the latter would be glad of it for the N. Züricher Z.—

As a fact, the kind and distinguishing behaviour of little Victoria has ended by putting me in quite a good humour. You know the only thing I ever care for when I ply my art : a kindled, sympathetic glance affords me satisfaction, whilst other tokens of applause, which I have to share with so much rubbish, mostly leave me in un- certainty. And it came straight from the tiny person's heart ; I marked that well. In any case both she and her husband had been informed of the vulgar campaign of abuse pursued against me by the noble English army of reporters ; consequently they gave me a conscious satisfaction, made easier to them, which delights me most, by the impression they derived from what I offered. Sainton has given another lesson at the Palace to the young Princess Hohenlohe, a relative of the Queen's on the mother's side : the young lady was likewise quite enraptured still, and told Sainton the Queen and Prince Albert had declared that they only regretted being unable to hear the overture once more forthwith—and so on. —

Dear God ! if I could really bring myself to make my footing firm here, so as to play a big rôle, perhaps very soon, and even become a rich man, probably it would stand entirely in my power. Already I'm very famous here, and all are beginning to think me something *quite unusual ;* and this has largely been effected by the fury of the press against me. Among my audience there are many enthusiasts who positively take me for the greatest genius of the century, and people never speak of me otherwise than as of a " great man." So much is certain : the Times critic (Dawison), in particular, has merely been waiting for me to take some kind of step to win him over, which is also said to have been the reason of his temporary silence about me after his first long article in the Times ; people assure me it would have cost me nothing further than the according him some sort of notice. The greater, naturally, has been and is his anger at my doing nothing of the kind. And that is quite in order ; for, once granted that one doesn't need the Press here, the whole fear thereof, and consequently its whole importance, would be lost. They tell me he is keeping the door open even yet, to change front as soon as I took the smallest notice of him.—But nobody, I hope, will expect that of me ; it would be a poltroonery I could never forgive myself ; however, it also is sheer impossible, because I simply—*cannot* do it. Under any circumstances, moreover, I have nothing at all to seek here ; and even if they praised me to the skies, I should never return here—just because I have nothing to seek here, and in particular, such a concert-conductorship is not my affair. —Consequently I am only too glad that the whole dreary time is drawing to its close now, and I shall be regiven to myself : care and suffering are not the worst evil, if one only is *free* in his noblest conscience ; but nothing in the world could delight me, if it made me a dependent on demands that go against my insight and my feeling. So—Tuesday week I travel back. I am pleased, however, to be concluding this distasteful sojourn with a little reconcilement, and I owe that sense of consolation this time to my little Victoria. —

The only difference of opinion is as to *how* I managed to make such a favourable impression on the Queen. Präger declares, I looked so handsome in his white cravat, that she fell in love with me ; others maintain, it was the beautiful Zurich tail-coat. For my own part, I have to reproach myself with having deceived her throughout the whole concert ; she is said to have stubbornly fancied, to wit, I had entirely new gloves on, whereas they were nothing but cleaned. In that you'll recognise my savingness, no doubt, but alas, a lack of candour too.

Yesterday I had a call from Berlioz, who is tramping for his daily bread, and really is hard pushed ; he cannot

earn a sou in France, so has to eke out a scanty subsistence by concerts in England and Germany (which—
as I happen to know—bring him mighty little in).
Here he is invited by the *New* Philharmonic for *two*
concerts. He has made his peace already with the local
press, after being likewise torn to tatters by it to begin
with. Besides his Romeo and Juliet symphony, he also
conducted a symphony by Mozart, which he let them
murder so horribly that I turned tail. But that's quite
English ; they like it that way, and Berlioz, who only
looks to money now, knows how he has to do things.
For that matter, he lacks all *depth*.

So farewell for to-day once again, my very best
Muzius. Congratulate yourself that I still associate with
you ; after my Rendez-vous with the Queen, I've grown
so proud that I speak to strictly no one any more.—
I'm very sorry about Sulzer's illness, though—if the
man would but give up his cursed legislating ! He easily
might leave it to his thick-skulled, phlegmatic fellow-
countrymen ; *they* never ruin their health with it, but
it's different with such a sensitive nature as his. He
seems to have had a severe attack this time, or he would
never have given in. Will he be remaining at Winterthur
awhile for the present ?

Now, the very best farewell ; greet left and right ;
tell people, too, they'll not be rid of me. Adieu, dearest
Wife !

Thy

GOOD HUSBAND.

Prägers send kindest regards. The wife has marked
your stockings, and had them washed ; otherwise I should
have had to pay duty in France for them ; it's *terribly*

strict there, and several people have told me they were searched to the skin.

101.

O YOU WICKED MINNA !

How can you declare that I never mention your letters? Please look mine through, and you'll find that almost every time I thank you for the letter last received. So it shall be this time also, and I will give you the good advice besides to clear out of the house next time you have upholsterers in it, that you may not hear the knocking.—To abide by your news to commence with, I am glad you've had some rain at last ; when *I* return, there'll probably be rain and cold enough, just as I continually enjoy them here. At Sainton's yesterday we had the fire lit to dine by, and I had gone out in my wadded coat. Doubtless I shall have the same thing again on the Seelisberg ; I know its ways. That foreboding, however, shan't hold me back.

Yesterday I had my pass visé by the Swiss and French consuls for the journey home (which cost another half a sovereign !). These gentry live behind the Bank and at London-Bridge : to get there, I *drove ;* back to my lodgings I *walked*, which took me exactly *two* hours at a fairly sharp pace. That teaches one what Time is made for ! And charming rain all the time. It's magnificent !

But there : a week from to-day I depart at 8 P.M. I have the last concert the evening before, and shall therefore approach my night-journey as tired as a dog. The more need of my having a good night's sleep in Paris, which I *hope* to do from Wednesday to Thursday ;

to that end I shall get a first-rate bed engaged for me
by Kietz. From Thursday to Friday I shall already
have less chance of sleep, as I must leave for the station
very early in the morning ; then [the night] from Friday
to Saturday I shall pass on the Basle mail-coach again,
arrive very shaky at Baden [Aargau] at 5 in the morning,
wash and rinse my mouth there, to reach my spouse
a bit presentably at Zurich 6 o'clock. I think it will
be enough for you to do, to get to the station by 6,
when we shall have the whole day before us for a gossip.
If you wanted to meet me at Baden, you would have to
go there the evening before, sleep there till 4, and so
on—which perhaps would be too much for you. So
receive me on the spot where you left me four months
before ; that has the best sense, has it not ?—Certainly
I don't require an evening-party ; it would be different
if Boom etc. were just to look in.—

So I am back in Zurich already, you see, whence
no devil shall lure me so soon again ! Consequently
I'll tell you at once, as to Löbmann, that the good
man has dropped down on me most inconveniently ; in
my conviction he is quite a mediocre musician, and
also violinist. I cannot keep compromising myself by
friendly recommendation of mediocre people ; it is a
hard thing to ask of me, who am otherwise so strict
in my demands, and have so entirely withdrawn from
all that sort of company. And to Spohr, of all men,
with whom I stand in all but no connection ! And
what could *Liszt* do for him ? The whole thing is so
vague and void of prospect, that I'm only too sorry
if Löbmann came away from Riga on this account.
It really is very painful to me, and I cannot decide so
at random to give him a recommendation from here ;

we will go into the thing again at Zurich. What a misfortune that every one insists on taking me for something altogether different from what I am !—

Well, my time is running to its end here, and the Devil may care for the rest of it ! Yet it amuses me to look on at my (so highly disputed) successes here. There exists here, you know, a New Philharmonic Society (which got Lindpaintner over from Stuttgart last year, and had my Tannhäuser overture conducted by him), and it would gladly have *me* for conductor next year. Its present conductor (Dr. Wylde, an execrable musician, but good fellow) puts it to me that I should have a much larger and less starchy audience there, besides all conceivable means, and in particular, as *many rehearsals* as I chose. Of course I've given him an answer in the negative. Yet he will not be denied the repeating of my Tannhäuser overture at their last concert (beginning of July)—when Berlioz conducts and gives things of his own ; he wants me to instruct either him or Berlioz in the tempi most minutely, that I may be sure of its going according to my wish. Perhaps I may consent : for, once I'm out of London, they can do what they like behind my back ; moreover, it would really be another good revenge.—

Fischer also wrote me a few days since, asking if I couldn't give him a little information about my position here, which he might communicate to the editor of the Sächsische Constitutionelle-Zeitung in order to refute false rumours. I since have done so, and told him in particular about my interview with the Queen : that will make a deal of stir in Saxony. You musn't let the heap of detractions and lies in the journals disturb you : in the first place, it is only scamps who write there, to pick up money ; no respectable person ever writes to a newspaper until some lie becomes too shameless and needs disproof.   Präger has now seen to that for several German papers : a New York music-sheet, in which he also writes, ·has already begun a regular campaign against the critics here, and shewn up their mendacity ; since *Dawison* has been so stupid as to take furious notice of it in *his* journal, this American paper has suddenly become widely read in London, and a long war has accordingly commenced, the end whereof is not in sight yet.   To *myself* that end is immaterial, for nobody will lure *me* here again, and some day no doubt I shall find an occasion for letting these people know why.   For the present, however, I stick to it :—it would have been better if I had declined the invitation hither, as even in the *most favourable event* I have—*nothing* to seek here.   I have *other* things to do, than conducting symphonies and concert-arias for asses. Full stop to that !

—So farewell, dear old Minna ! Probably you will get 2 more letters from here ; then *one* from Paris, and finally in supreme person

Thy
magnificent husband R.W.

The evening before last Präger gave me some pills to assist me ; but I couldn't lay hand on the confounded little box, and have been unable to take any of them yet. I've found it again to-day, though ; so it shall do the job !

102.

LONDON, 23. *June* 1855.

YOU ENTIRELY GOOD MIENEL OF MINE,

I really must send you a letter, even if there cannot be much in it.—I have just been slightly resting off the *last rehearsal* I ever am like to have held of a concert, it pulls me so utterly down now. In thought I left England long since, of which I therefore shall have seen but little. I don't believe I shall even get to Richmond still ; but it also is quite immaterial to me. So wretched a life as I have enjoyed here these 4 months can only conclude with sheer disdain.—

Such a cold wind has been blowing the last few days, that my catarrh has become wholly unbearable. By Präger's advice I am taking a daily aperient now. Finally the rheum has invaded my nose, in such force as to make me already fear getting my Face-rose [eruption] again. That flower would be the only one still lacking in the garden of my London joys ! Indeed it is a deuced dog's life I have led here ; I can't look back on it with any other feeling than upon a hell. But this latest lesson no doubt will leave some fruit behind it—I think and hope so !—

Well—what more shall I write you from this loathsome hole ?—I know of nothing better than the assurance that on *Tuesday* (the evening of the day on which you uncover these lines) I shall be clearing out ; whilst a week from to-day I shall have drunk coffee and eaten my dinner already in the arms of my children and on the neck of my spouse :—so—all in fact is well. Now see that that spouse is *thoroughly well* herself, in *good health* and *good humour*, that I may have the whole delight I wish in her ! Be on your best behaviour, take good care of yourself this remaining week, that we poor souls may reunite in thorough gladness.

Tuesday I probably shall write once more, ere starting ; if not, I shall write from Paris.

Fare 1 000000 times well, and hold me 30 000000 times dear !—

Kind greetings to our good friends from Thy

RRR Richard.

Thanks for Schmidt's letter. I expect to write him yet from here.

[*The Paris letter is missing, and husband and wife had no further need of written communications till he was ordered away to attend to his health next summer.—Tr.*]

103.

MORNEX, *Wednesday*, 11 *June*. 1856.

At last, dear good Minna, I breathe again and commence to hope !—I moved in here yesterday afternoon, and now propose pursuing my thorough restoration, without which I should not care to go on living !—But first of all I must narrate to you at length, after my two brief telegrams, how things have gone with me ; for which reason I have taken a large sheet of paper straight off, as a smaller would never hold even the half of what I intended to write to you.—Now for it !—

First the journey ! It was the unluckiest and most miserable I've ever made—unfortunately it came to a Friday while I still was en route !—From Baden in the evening on the diligence to Aarau, in an awful coupé with two stout chaps who naturally would have been choked if they hadn't opened the windows, which compelled me in turn to draw my cloak over my head and sweat like a joint in the oven. At Aarau change of carriage in the night—then the same story till Biel. There—in the morning—I hoped to be released and board the steamer ; but all water-traffic had been suspended owing to the inundations, and consequently the whole

advantage of this route was lost ! So by coach again to
Neuf-Châtel: terrible rain there ; 2½ hours by steamer
to *Yverdon*, in the cabin of course, the whole landscape
veiled in clouds. Then it began in earnest ! The
steamer arrived half an hour late, and instead of taking
the 1 o'clock train—which had left already—I had to
wait for the 5. Good ! When I get to the station, they
declare that my dog must be put in the dog-box ; you
may imagine what a scene ensued ! All my pleas,
entreaties, threats, were of no avail ; at last I took Fips
under my arm, and tried to mount in spite of all denials :
fresh uproar ! Finally it was heard by some ladies who
were seated in a coupé : they declared themselves perfectly
willing to admit myself and puppy to their carriage ; so
the martinets gave way at last, and I got in with Fips
in triumph—but after shameful vexation !—

That is by no means all, though ! At 7 the train
arrived at *Morges* on the Lake of Geneva ; the steamer—
which, if we had left Yverdon by the right train, would
have brought me to Geneva in 2 hours, so that I should
have arrived there by 5—this steamer of course had long
gone, and its missing would have to be remedied by a
fresh journey of 5½ hours in the diligence—i.e. half
another night ! So I decided to stay the night at Morges,
and take the first steamer next morning ; but the station
people had already put my luggage on the diligence,
which I mistook for a mere omnibus to Morges. Ponder-
ing what's to be done, suddenly I am ordered out of the
coupé into which I had mounted ; my coupé ticket does
not hold good here, the passengers from *Lausanne* have
first right. Very well, say I, I shall get out and remain
here ; give me my luggage !—That's stowed away, they
tell me, there's no time left to get it down.—A running

accompaniment of rain and storm ! I was beside myself, used all the bad language I could think of—but in the end was obliged to give in, as I didn't want to be left with no luggage. Which seat ? Inside, the middle place back to the horses ; opposite me two pedlars with big bundles on their laps, beside me a woman with an enormous hump—exactly poking my way—and added to it all, a screaming child ! The best, moreover, was that the incensed conductor wouldn't even let me keep the dog : Not allowed in the intérieur, must be tied to the carriage ! ! I thought I should go mad ! The other passengers naturally intervened, however, all burdened as they were, God knows, and Fips remained without so much as stirring—the good, well-behaved beast ! That journey to Geneva was the crown of all joys, and truly I had not believed I should ever have to go through such a thing again in my life ! At last I arrived, half past twelve ! At 2 o'clock to bed, in hideous agitation and constant terror of another outbreak of the Roses !—There's a *pleasure*-trip for you ! ! Viâ Berne it would have gone almost uninterruptedly smoothly, but I wanted it pleasanter ! However, it was all the inundation's fault—otherwise, and especially with fine weather, everything would have been decidedly better.—So there you have my travelling adventures !—

At Geneva a hurricane from the north raged for two days, which certainly was to bring fair weather, but made it extremely risky for me to go out. On Saturday I sent Dr R.'s letter to M. John Coindet, who had left home, however ; so I followed R.'s counsel, and sent the letter with his card to the brother, *Doctor Coindet:* instead of appointing me an hour to consult him, he was so kind as to call at once himself. He directed me to *Mornex,* as the only place where I should find what I sought, and further gave me good advice about my malady. So I took a carriage on Sunday, and saw to everything ; only I couldn't get consent as yet, for reasons which you shall learn in an instant. In the afternoon I returned to Geneva, and made another excursion that evening, to Cologny, to see Pastor Bourris (whom I know from Albisbrunn) ; but he, too, had gone for a holiday.

Well, my new landlady kept me waiting until Monday evening for her answer, which turned out favourably in the event : yesterday afternoon I finally moved in.—Now let me describe my place of refuge.—*Mornex*—a sort of village—is two leagues from Geneva, already in Savoy ; it lies on the other side of *Mont Salève*, half way up that mountain, which is ascended by tourists from Geneva for the sake of its beautiful view. The air is splendid, since the spot itself stands very high. I'm living at the pension *Latard*, in a summer-house that lies quite isolated, divided from the pension by a garden ; it really is the garden salon intended as a drawing-room for the boarders. There is quite a good *piano* in it ; which was a great consideration to me, as I should otherwise have had to get one from Geneva at huge expense. I had only one condition to agree to, for the immense favour of obtaining this pavilion to myself : every Sunday I must clear out from 9 to 12 in the morning, as the salon is arranged for Divine service then for the Genevans staying here ; the parson comes, and the devil takes flight. I have to accept it with a good grace, as the other advantages are so numerous that I could have attained them nowhere else. Firstly : complete seclusion, private attendance, *warm bath* (enormously important !), meals to my choice ; then a hydropathic institute close by, where I shall be able to have my cold baths later in the greatest comfort; still later I shall have the Arve (the river) fairly near. From my door I step direct into a pretty garden; from the window I step on to a balcony, with the most glorious view of the entire Mont Blanc range and a lovely broad valley between.—Naturally it wasn't to be had very cheap, but I must hit on some means of enjoying it as long as possible; for *I need it*— and it *isn't* to be had any else!—I have bargained for the most complete non-disturbance; except François, the waiter, I never see a soul!—

My malady indeed has made great strides; last winter it used to vanish entirely at times, and I knew no more of it for weeks: now I don't pass an hour without dreading a fresh outbreak, so that I feel myself the wretchedest of men. That must be radically altered, and I am doing everything that promises it. Dr Coindet assured me, the principal thing was the strictest *dieting* and rest: I might have remarked, he said, that the outbreaks were always connected with preceding errors of diet and irregularities, the results whereof I no longer experienced in my abdomen, as before, but precisely in an attack of these Roses. How right he is: I can prove it to have been so, and feel it, moreover, at last. I am therefore to live wholly by rule, never the slightest deviation; *beer* and the like lead direct to attacks. He has also forbidden me *coffee*, and that most strictly, not even half milk. (Just ask Dr R. what he says to that!) Out of doors I must avoid both wind and sun; in the sun I'm to bear an umbrella. He expects much from the air here, great repose without any excitement, and regular diet. Do tell Dr R. that no one here has ever heard of Tavaster water; Coindet recommended *Laxir lemonade* of a morning instead ; meanwhile I stick to Carlsbad salts, *two doses* of which I take each morning.   I'm to begin the sulphur baths to-day—God grant me restoration of my health !   No sacrifice can be too great to me for that ; for in this condition I'm the most unbearable of men, and can give no one any pleasure !—

To write Fips' praises I should need to take another whole sheet, the animal is so touchingly well-behaved, kind, docile and reliable !   Seated on the little table, when the train left Zurich he suddenly began to howl, and kept his eyes fixed on the side from which you vanished ; he took no notice of me at all, talk to him as much as I liked.   When I got into the diligence he reconciled himself, and behaved so well, so quietly and quite unnoticeably throughout the journey, that I can't possibly praise him enough.   But he would neither eat nor drink the first few days, and it was only with the choicest morsels that I could tempt him in the end. Even now he'll hardly take anything else ; though I make him his soup at dinner-time—with tit-bits, be it said—and he's gradually coming round.   He seems very pleased with this place ; when I open the doors for him, he first goes and lies on the balcony, taking stock of the landscape, the people and cattle, then makes his promenade round the garden.   He is watchful beyond all measure : people like him very much.—He sends best greetings !   On our promenade this morning [. . .]. Suddenly a *cuckoo* was heard ; he pricked up his ears and whined : he imagined it was *Jacquot !*—I took *Pepsel's portrait* with me purposely :—I shall observe the death-day of that dear good friend with all my heart !— —This fine weather makes me wish you would go to the Seelisberg quite soon yourself ; I don't like

to think of your being at home with that eternal provocation ! Do go very soon. But you *must* take
Jacquot with you—I stick to that—his big cage too :
please see to it.—

Now I thank you again most kindly for your good
letter ; agreed, we remain the same old pair. If I could
only make life thoroughly agreeable to you, and banish
all provocation, how happy it would make me ! So hold
me dear, as I hold you ; be cheerful, do all you can for
your health—and hope for a right merry reunion, unruffled by the cares of illness ! Farewell, good Muzius,
be heartily greeted and kissed

by Thy   RICHARD.

I've had news from Liszt that the *M. family* thinks
of spending the summer at Zurich and seeing a lot of
me :—I couldn't help laughing when Liszt expressed
regret at it ! Well, I have happily escaped from that,
and its like ! !—How fortunate that I'm away !—

Give my kindest regards to the Wesendoncks ; I
think of writing them tomorrow or the next day.—

No letters can get here direct, because there's no post
here whatever ; so just go on addressing *poste-restante*,
Genève. A *messenger* goes to Geneva every day, taking
letters in, and fetching them out.—

104.

Poste restante No. 111 à Génève.

MORNEX, *Thursday* 19. *June* :856.

I've only just received your telegraphic answer, dear
Minna ! You cannot have written the first sentence quite

plainly; it was pure nonsense till an inspiration came to me that it should run : " Karl seit heut hier " [" Karl reached here to-day "]—instead of which it said, " Nurt seit heut sieger."—Your letter had already reassured me : everything arrives here very late. To-day, however, I merely wanted to retrieve what I couldn't write more fully yesterday.*   So, I have had to move out, and therefore to renounce the lovely solitude of my garden-house ; that sort of joy seems really not appointed me, and all my life I shall have to suffer from disturbance, disquiet and outward commotion : if only I be not made entirely unfit for further work through no prospect ever opening to me of a pleasant, quiet refuge for my home !— already I've highly taxed my nerve-endurance.

In no case should I have removed to where I'm staying now, had I had nothing but commencement of my work in view ; but I have been feeling more and more that the first question could only be the restoration of my health, and in that respect I believe I have done very right.   Even Dr Coindet, to whom R. recommended me, was startled when I shewed him R.'s prescriptions, especially about the sulphur baths, and told me to entrust myself regarding baths to *Dr Vaillant*, who presides over an institute here, and not to do too much.   Well, scarcely had I installed the baths with difficulty—in strict pursuit of R.'s instructions—when I fell into such a fluster again that I didn't know what to do with myself.   Dr Vaillant, to whom I addressed myself anent the ordinary baths, was horrified when he heard of the sulphur baths, and implored me to stop them at once ; with which I very willingly complied.   Under Vaillant's treatment, I feel considerably

---

* A missing letter; see also the opening of No. 105.—Tr.

better since ; he is handling me with uncommon care, extremely cautiously and soothingly, and getting at the mischief's seat so thoroughly that I already have the greatest trust in him—which he seems to have won from others also, for it is he who was summoned to Florence express by Rossini, and owing to whose advice the latter is so much better now than 2 years back. In short, my health is now ensured, and I recognise that R.'s quack-salveries, just as they haven't yet cured me, would never have thoroughly healed me ; consequently the drug-shop, God willing, shall cost me nothing more.—But please tell *Heim*, the *only* thing Vaillant allows me to take internally is *Carlsbad salt.*—As to my life here otherwise, I'll write you more another time ; the situation is splendid, the air wonderful, and the garden walks most agreeable. *Fips* finds much amusement in them, and is making himself quite at home. About him, too, another time. — But now to conclude with something serious !—

Dearest Minna, N. *must go :* there's nothing else for it. Rather put up with anything, than this everlasting provocation, recurring every instant, which not only is hurtful to yourself, but truly sours my life. It is utterly impossible to accustom her to our persons ; it would be a misfortune for *her*, as well as for *us*, if she remained any longer. I cannot tell you how our domestic life is spoilt for me by this eternal irritation, which I partly observe in you, partly also feel myself ; no longer can I tolerate this everlasting scolding, occasion for which never ceases, alas ; and you are ruining your health with it, just as it is completely hardening N. and estranging her from us. God knows what her future is to be, as she is so totally unfit for household duties ; but thus much is certain, in other social relations, such as at Zwickau perhaps, she will get on better, and also lead a more contented life herself. For all that, she shall not be abandoned by us, and I therefore pledge myself for good and all to pay her the 100 fr. quarterly your good parents received before. That shall be an absolute fixture ; consequently I don't think she will prove a burden to anybody, and even the Trögers will be sure to take her willingly into their house on this condition. I beg you, make the settlement of this affair your chiefest care now, and—if possible—get rid of her before I return ; for, I swear it, this disturbance—and vexation—in the house is a terrible strain on me. If my circumstances improve— toward which I shall take steps—we're sure to find a suitable young person soon, to fill the place we intended for N. ; you might even begin to think of it now, and any handy girl may congratulate herself on entering such an agreeable relation as N. might have had if she had possessed but a modicum of the qualifications.—Now you know my opinion !—

So farewell for to-day, dear old woman ; I dreamt of you quite vividly the other night ! Lord, if I could have anything like an agreeable, quiet, semi-rural abode, and kind, congenial household, I am the most domesticated man in the world and never should wish myself anywhere else for a moment : in a strange house like this I'm always very dull and mopish. So adieu !

The best of wishes from   Thy

RICH.

Fips is unceasingly on the watch again.—To-day the weather has also turned fine. I have obtained a piano from Geneva, for diversion at least. Please send me the musical and illustrated journals in wrapper—it won't cost much. Perhaps also the 3 volumes of Beethoven's sonatas, but in a parcel—otherwise I shan't be able to hold out.

105.

MORNEX. *Poste restante No.* 111.

À GENÈVE

22. *June* 1856.

MOST EXCELLENT MINNA,

How cross you get at once, whenever it appears to you I'm lazy ! You will be having *two* letters from me now ; so just consider the impression such reproaches make on me, after I've long since told you everything there was to tell !—But, that apart, the postal arrangements here are absurd enough : I wrote you Wednesday that I should write again on Thursday, assuming that the Thursday letter, which unfortunately doesn't leave Geneva till Friday, would reach you at Zurich on Sunday morning. On Friday comes the messenger, and brings me a letter—it was *mine* to you, which the asses at Geneva had sent me back because it was addressed to " Wagner " : they hadn't regarded the " Frau." Consequently you will have received that letter also a day late, presumably at Seelisberg, whither I shall send to-day's direct.—

Naturally I haven't much to tell you from my solitude, except that the weather has at last turned fine again to-day, and I've already had a glorious walk with Fips on *Mont-Salève*, whence I bring you back this gentian to compare with that on the Seelisberg. It was bad weather almost the whole of last week, cold and damp, so that I couldn't well do much with my cure ; nevertheless I already feel infinitely better than when I left Zurich :

the dread of a relapse of the Roses has already left me ;
I have gambolled outside in the deadliest rain and storm,
got my face cold, and yet had no uneasiness about it.
Who ever would have told me that ten days ago, when
I always went out with my nose muffled if the tiniest
breeze was blowing ?   No doubt I owe it in the first
place to the wholesome, frugal diet, without coffee etc.,
the repose and removal of all effort and vexation ; but
chiefly to the baths I'm taking under excellent Dr.
Vaillant's guidance with the greatest energy and success :
washings and rubbings with a wet clout, first lukewarm—
then colder.   The *cold* foot-baths also do me special good ;
you must try them yourself : only a little walk first, to
get the feet warm, then 20 minutes in cold water, gently
rubbing the feet one on the other, and after that a good
half hour's march.   You will hardly believe what an
excellent effect these foot-baths have !—

I told Vaillant of the infamous water R. had pre-
scribed me through you ; he thought we might just wait
for its arrival, when he would analyse it, and if it
contained nothing injurious, would gladly consent to its
use.   So I'm in the hands of no water-cure fanatic, you
see.   For the rest, R. must leave me at peace with his
Aix.   I'm getting well, I know it now : my complaint
resides in the abdomen, as you are aware from the terrible
flatulence ; that must be thoroughly remedied, and therewith—by the middle of August—I hope to arrive at my
goal.—

I'm living in another part of the house now, quite
comfortably, two pretty rooms, one of which I have arranged as a little salon.   From my windows I can alight
on a big balcony which runs right round the house ;
it is a piece of luck for Fips in particular, who always

lies on the window-sill, and springs out as soon as he
sees anything—after which I always have to help him
in again.   In fine weather I mostly walk or sit in the
pretty hilly garden-grounds, which likewise is very
agreeable to Fips.   The air is quite exquisite ; headache
vanishes immediately one gets here ; I have experienced
no particular heat as yet.

So much for myself : I hope you're pleased with
it ?   Strictly, no doubt, I ought to write you on nothing
but Fips, as you appear more concerned about him —
for which I can't find any fault with you !   But it has
moved me to tears, that you poor thing should be wanting
to break off your soporific reading just for me to get the
Eidgenössische here ; for your consolation I must tell
you, I didn't mean the Eidgenössische at all ; by all
means keep it, and simply send instead the Illustrirte
(which you must renew *for me*, by the way ! !) and
perhaps the music-journal, which the Wesendoncks might
see to for me.   But every time *in wrapper.*

Now, I am heartily glad to know you're on the
lovely Seelisberg ; enjoy it to the top of your bent !
As my present hope stands, I'm thinking of another little
undertaking for late summer, in which you shall play
a fine part : would you like to ? ?   So, fare splendidly
well, greet the Seelisbergers, and hold very dear

Thy

not at all so bad

HUSBAND.

Business is looking up ; orders have come in from
Hanover and Carlsruhe !—

An organ-grinder has just begun playing, at which
Fips is furious.   He has jumped down.

Do tell me if you duly received my *letter on N.*
I have written to Fr. Müller, Weimar, as well to-day.

106.

MORNEX, 25. *June* 1856.

DEAR MIENEL !

Morning.   Last night I had bad dreams,
which I luckily can very well explain : my former
eruption has now been reduced to the ancient catarrh,
which will be easy to thoroughly get at, but meanwhile
resides in my brain too, and tries to work itself out there
during sleep.   On the other side, the last few days I had
often been thinking of the arrangement in respect of N.,
particularly of the allowance she is to have, which your
good parents formerly received, and so I also thought
a deal of them.   Add to it your last letter, which informed me you were not taking Jacquot with you to
the Seelisberg, but he was to stay behind alone.   Out
of all this, with the harassing aid of my still not
fluidified rheum, there shaped themselves the following
dreams, which unfortunately I haven't got pat in my
memory, but the first whereof commenced pretty well
thus :—You had gone away from me, and would have
nothing more to do with me ; I hunted for you (—as
really happened once, long years ago !—) and found
you rather poorly housed with your parents, which
made me more and more distressed, the more you refused
to come with me ; till at last I called to you in horror,
" But your parents are dead ! " which ended in my
shouting your name aloud and waking up.   My shout
alarmed someone above me, who tumbled about for a
long time before he grew quiet again.—Then I had
another dream : I was roaming with *Pepsel*, and seeking

you again, for you had run away from me once more;
it made Pepsel grow weaker and weaker; I looked at
him steadily, and his eyes sank the more and more in,
so that it gave me indescribable grief. At last I found
your lonely dwelling; you had gone out, and the little
room was empty. Inside, though, I heard Jacquot
whistling and chattering vastly merrily; I went in,
and was met by a strong draught: a window stood
open, which I did my best to close, without fully
succeeding; there were all kinds of slides and cross-
sashes, so that it took me all my time till I woke up.
You will easily recognise how this second dream in
particular was occasioned by what you wrote me of your
fears about Jacquot if you took him with you to the
Seelisberg.—

There you have my dreams: of my waking I've
little to tell you, except that we have had very fine
weather since Sunday, that it has made me feel very
well, my cure offers excellent promise, and I live in
the best hopes of a radical restoration. You shall give
me the cue for more through the letter I am expecting
to-day, as there isn't much to answer for the present
in your last.

Afternoon.—The hoped-for letter hasn't come; the
recent scandalous confusion is sure to be to blame for
it; you will have left Zurich before my letter reached
there, and some time may still elapse before it is sent
after you, so that you will have received my letter
to Seelisberg, perhaps, before the other. It is doubly
annoying to me, as I should so have liked to have news
from you to-day!—

Now I shall hope for tomorrow, when I may get
two letters at once perhaps, as the last time.—From

your last, by the way, I gathered that you might be changing your mind as to N. again : I am awaiting your answer to my proposal about it, but be assured in any case that I abide by my opinion. It isn't a question of N.'s forgetting herself grossly for once, and then begging pardon—but of the whole relation, which cannot *possibly* remain as it is, for *all of our* sakes. I shall write to N. myself about it, and try to convince her in all kindness and tranquillity that she has no choice. —However, I shall write you at length on this, as said, when you have answered me.—

I'm looking forward much to a report from Seelisberg, where I hope you have arrived safe and sound now.— From here, apart from the already-mentioned, I really have nothing to relate ; I go on calmly living for my health without disturbance. Yesterday I took my first hip-bath, which has rendered me extraordinarily good service [. .] : I take a little Carlsbad salt still, but nothing beyond ; we will wait for R.'s water, all the same.—In the evening (—we dine at $5\frac{1}{2}$) I usually take a long walk with Fips on *Mont Salève*, whence I return much invigorated ; I always ascend, never go down to the valley—on account of the beautiful air.—

In no case shall I go to *Aix ;* I must write to R. about it shortly.

I have to check *Fips* already from eating too much, especially small bones, of which there are a number here— owing to the frequency of cutlets ; otherwise he does very well, and is exemplarily faithful.—

Now, adieu for to-day. I hope to dream somewhat more calmly to-night, and, most to be hoped of all, that my dreams bear no ill omen. So hold me dear !—

107.

MORNEX, 2. *July* 1856.

DEAREST MINNA,

The most important thing for me to answer at once, in your letter just received, concerns your health. During my cure I have often had to think of your own condition, and especially your nervous agitation and sleeplessness ; for only now, under the treatment of my present doctor, Vaillant, have I arrived at the secret of treating such disorders with success.—I really am shocked when I see how these ailments, so frequently recurring with us, can be thoroughly got rid of by the simplest and most natural means ; and how bungling, ineffectual, even harmful, on the contrary, was the mode recommended by R. After having been so terribly upset by the shameful sulphur-baths that I had those awful twitchings of the arm again at night, one single treatment by Vaillant sufficed to procure me a peaceful night at once. Yesterday I found myself in a similar condition again, in consequence of a sleepless night occasioned by the late and noisy arrival of strangers, who had made me vilely lose my temper ; but directly after Vaillant's most ingenious treatment, I, who before had still been trembling with excitement, found myself calm and most agreeably drowsy : a good night has restored me completely.

I therefore *beseech* you to do as follows : *Each day* take one—or better, two (should you think needful) *cold* foot-baths, such as I described to you and you haven't answered me about : namely—for 20 minutes on end, and then go for a good half hour's walk to get the feet properly warm again : beforehand, too, a little walking, that the feet may at least not be cold. Every evening ere retiring to bed, moreover, get the maid to rub, or lave, your whole body gently with a folded towel (like a clout), which she must repeatedly dip in water, using up a whole bucketful ; she must alternately rub the back, the hips, then the chest, the legs (but gently !) : beforehand you must also lave your forehead. Then a sheet around you quick, gentle rubbing and drying, then into bed— and you will feel a most agreeable soothing, which is certain to help you to sleep. But you must employ the maid for it ; if you do it yourself, you will agitate yourself again. If you have a rooted objection to undressing before the maid, you must just take a wet towel, pass it gently over the back—like a shawl—the chest, and the rest of the body, for a goodish time, so that you re-wet the towel pretty often ; then dry, and to bed. You can also do this if you feel flurried and sleepless at night : light a candle at once, and use the wet towel as I have said. But it is better to let the maid manipulate you every evening in the manner stated—also by day, should there be need. If you're *immoderately* excited, though, I'll tell you what restored me yesterday at once. Vaillant spread a blanket on the bed, and over it the sheet : the latter he sprinkled with a little water, then swathed me first in it—(only as far as under the arms, however, and the same with the blanket)—sprinkled me again with water, using *two bottlefuls* in all ;—then the blanket over it, likewise tucked in *lightly*, and finally a feather mattress— *couvre-pied*—above it all : mark well, though, only to the arm-pits ; my arms and breast he simply covered with a sheet, or any article of clothing you please. Thus he left me till I felt thoroughly warm, but *not* until I sweated ; then he repeated it, uncovering me again and sprinkling me once more with water, till I got warm a second time ; thereon a slight ablution—with the wet clout—a wipe down, and a little walk about, but quite moderate and leisurely, or straight to bed. I tell you, all agitation had vanished without leaving a trace; I was so drowsy that I scarce could wait for night, which I slept through like a top.—

I *entreat* you—do not let this have been said in vain ! ! !—

I would rather get you to come here forthwith, as I'm convinced that Dr Vaillant's treatment would be of the greatest benefit to you, better than anything; for the moment, however, a few scruples restrain me :—

1. It's *very dear* (which I think quite reasonable, however, with so exceptional a physician) and I don't yet know how I am to run to it myself. 2. Not a creature speaks German—except the cook—and you would have a difficulty with conversation. 3. Candidly—fond as we are of each other—I fear our mutually exciting ourselves more often than quite suits a cure. You know that, owing to a difference of views—for all affection—it comes at times to small disputes, which it is better for both of us to escape now and then; although I cordially admit that *I* am more to blame than you, particularly when I'm flurried and fretful, which is not to be avoided with a serious cure like that in front of me, when it's better for one to be left alone.—Nevertheless, these are all objections to be overcome by the consideration for *your health*. I fancied you were safe and sound at Seelisberg, especially as regards your health; but if you really don't feel well there, and feel the necessity of a more thorough cure, just let me know by return, and means must be found; for I hold it best for you to get yourself properly treated for once. *Money* must be forthcoming, without precisely burdening anyone; we could dine in our own sitting-room, to dis-

pense you from conversation in French ; whilst peace and quiet we should have to guarantee ourselves by mutual good resolve.—

So think it over, as I myself shall think it over ; I should so like to help you !

—But I must close now, as I've another application to go through myself : moreover, I have told you the most important ; absolutely nothing else has occurred. Touching myself, rest assured I am *rid of the Roses*, and getting *thoroughly* restored in general.—

Farewell for to-day, dear old woman ! Fipsel sends greetings, and we both are true as gold.—A thousand hearty salutations from

Thy OLD MAN.

Once more :

> Set all else on one side, and answer me merely on this :
>   If you feel the necessity of a thorough cure,
>   accept my offer unconditionally ; write me
>   so that I may meet you at Geneva ; every-
>   thing else *must* give way ; one's health is
>   the main point !

108.

MORNEX, 12. *July* 1856.

In haste !

DEAR MINNA,

You see, I take your groans more seriously than you do mine ! I am sorry to have upset and even alarmed you thereby, and rejoice on the other hand that my fears about your health were groundless.

In 4 weeks I expect to have finished my cure, and then to return without stop ; for I shall have much to attend to with yourself at Zurich that won't be disagreeable to you. On that I'll write more within the next few days. For the present I withdraw my last proposal to Aufdermauer; * don't speak of our first project to him any further.—

Continue feeling so well that you give me no more reason for anxiety.

Thy

R. W.

109.

MORNEX, 18. *July* 1856.

I've nothing in particular to write you, dearest Minna ; yet your letter just received induces me at least to give you a faint sign of life.—I should hardly have thought you would have taken my brief hint so gloomily and glumly. It's to be hoped my last letter will have agreeably dispelled all your fears, and taught you the contrary ; for you will have seen by it that I'm feeling the need of a fixed place of residence more keenly than ever, and even longish summer outings have now become a nuisance to me, since they never afford what one seeks, nor that which a snug hearth of one's own, meeting all one's requirements, alone can supply. So I need waste no more words on it, as you will know exactly what I had in mind. Surely you are pleased with me ?—

As I believe I may look towards my amnestying, which will make it possible to take a trip to Germany from time to time—especially in the winter half-year—at first I merely thought of procuring ourselves a fixed summer residence, and therefore cast my eye on Brunnen, with nothing but a smaller pied-à-terre at

* Landlord at Brunnen—see *Life* vi, 157—the proposal, evidently broached in a letter missing from this series, appears to have been for permanent summer quarters at that spot ; see also next letter.—Tr.

Zurich. However, I soon reflected how disagreeable it would be for yourself in particular to go through a removal once a year, to say nothing of accompanying me on each of my possible trips to Germany and so leaving the house and our domestic pets forlorn. Wherefore I tightened my hold on the plan of obtaining the long-wished-for estate near to Zurich itself, where everything could remain in like order both winter and summer, and pursue its even course ; till at last I have hit on the right way of procuring the money in the most honourable fashion, and I am sure in any case to get from Härtels *as much as is needful for the purchase and erection*—by which I mean *twenty thousand francs.*—I have already written Wesendonck about it too.—As I am detained here by my cure, and cannot be back before the middle of August, I beg you to pave the way for me nicely by your best enquiries and commissionings, so that—if all goes well— the building may be commenced the beginning of September, and the foundation-stone laid by yourself on the 5th (your birthday). That shall be your birthday-present this time !—

Only let us come to a thorough understanding about the situation of the property. The closer to town, the better I shall like it, and—the *harder* will it also be to find to suit. As I wrote you previously, I don't set much on an extensive view : one gets that on one's walks ; but I set everything on a quiet, un-cooped situation, with big trees : and we probably shall find the latter in particular only at some distance from the city. Don't be afraid of that, however, but overcome your timidness for my sake ; for your comfort I draw your notice to the following :—Sooner or later I shall invest in a horse and carriage : when I have no more rent to pay—which stands in prospect—I can

apply the money to that purpose ; meantime the new
Zurich droschkes, with which one could make a contract,
would stand us in good stead. In any case we shall
engage *a man:* I have considered the means, and we
couldn't possibly do without one ; so you'll be well protected, even if I go away for a couple of weeks in the
winter and you don't want to accompany me. Please
don't fear solitude : *I* love it beyond measure ; and then
remember the company you'll always be having, and what
occupation the fowls, turkeys, ducks, etc., will give you
even in the winter ; so that, what with myself, N. (or
another feminine companion), a maid and a man, big dog
and little, parrot and so on, you are sure not to feel
yourself lonely. For my own part I'm looking forward to
that loneliness as if to Heaven, and after every little
outing full of toil and agitation, I shall always be only
too glad to get back to recover. —

So, do your business well ! I am most eager for your
reports, and to know if you're fortunate. The future
architect Alter *must* know of something. —

Otherwise I am doing well ; my cure is forging ahead,
and every week I feel the progress toward a thorough
restoration. As to the character of this establishment, I
can fully explain it to you only by mouth ; but take my
word for it, I had no notion before of such a careful treatment, or one that so completely suited me. The company
isn't large, and offers no temptation at all. I take my
dinner at the general table, whither *Fips always accom-
panies me:* make your mind easy about it ; he is very
popular, and unfortunately gets more to eat than I like.
For the rest, I'm living very comfortably, and you would
have thought yourself in Heaven, compared with the
Seelisberg ; whatever it is, it isn't such a band-box.

However, since your indisposition was merely transitory, as you declare, I can find no fault with you for having returned home, where you'll be able to do good service to our plan, and whither I shall return direct myself, by the shortest route, on the completion of my cure.—So farewell, good old girl, soon to be landed proprietress! Keep well, and good to me.—

Liszt has written me very amiably. Touching my Pardon, he *earnestly* begs me to *let no one hear anything of it*, though he firmly hopes I may be able to visit him so early as this winter. A general amnesty is in preparation, it appears. *Liszt comes the end of September.*—

For 3 performances Berlin has brought me in 900 *fr.* again, which I have had despatched to Sulzer.—

You say nothing at all about that charming Dr. Burkhart? (Eh! Eh!)

110.

MORNEX, 26. *July* 1856.

GOOD DAY, SILLY WOMAN!
        (I meant to say :—
                Prodigiously good, sage Minna!)

You got your dressing yesterday : * to-day I merely add a little further information about myself.

First of all, though, I beg you to go at once to *Heim*, and ask him to be so good as to reclaim his letter to me from the Post, as I haven't accepted it. The matter stands thus :—

Heim did not address "*poste restante à Genève*," but *à Mornex près Genève.*

Now, as Mornex lies in Savoy, the Zurich people put the letter in the Savoy mail, which in the first place costs

---

* A missing letter?—Tr.

40 *centimes* single weight, whereas it was only franked with 20 *cent.* ; then they had reckoned the weight at 4 times, and charged me *two francs*—including messenger ; besides which, the letter took 2 days longer. The same thing happened to me before with a letter of Wesendonck's, for which, however, they only asked *one fr.* So I thought I must put a stop to this palpable knavery, and as there could be nothing pressing or particularly important in Heim's communications, much as I enjoy them, I determined to let our friend know, that he might expose this swindle at the Post and relieve me of similar trouble in future. He mustn't take it ill of me ; I really only did it to lend no further countenance to such abominable extortion. Will Heim be so good, accordingly, as to re-address his letter, and simply :

> "*poste restante*, *No.* 111
> *à Genève*"
>
> (as you do quite correctly)—

For that matter, I'm looking forward to his letter so much, that I almost regret sending it back. Kindest regards to him and his wife !—

Well, I am curious to hear if you have received my last letter to Seelisberg yet. For the rest, I of course shall have a deal to tell you of my cure, but it is so disagreeable to me to write about it that I broke off a letter recently commenced to Dr R., and must beg you to give him the assurance that I hope to satisfy him thoroughly on my return, and receive his pardon for apparent disobedience. I know R. wasn't pleased with my refusing in advance to go through a regular cure at a Kurhaus or pension ; had I declared myself willing, and had he known all about Dr Vaillant and his institute, I am firmly convinced he would have had nothing against it if I had expressed a wish to take my cure there. As it turned out, however, I felt that *without* the daily supervision of a doctor I couldn't even carry out R.'s orders with advantage ; and this conviction was so strong that, after Vaillant had inspired me with perfect confidence, I resolved on the heavy sacrifice of starting a strict cure at a pension and willingly enduring all its inconveniences, such as total abstention from work, forced contact with often disagreeable company, and so on. As for the character of my cure, tell Dr R. simply this : Dr Coindet, to whom he recommended me himself, is in complete agreement with it, and only begged me to hold out and remain under Vaillant's treatment as long as possible. The result, though, as I firmly expect, will be the thing's best advocate. The functions of my skin are already so well regulated, that a recurrence of the Roses is no longer to be dreamt of ; my abdominal complaints are gradually decamping, and I look for perfect healing of my hæmorrhoidal ill. Added to which, my nerves are quieting down to the best of my wish, so that I can count with certainty already on at least six hours of unbroken sleep each night. Consequently, I believe I haven't spent my time in vain here, and don't repent the sacrifice entailed. But it *is* a sacrifice, and please don't think I'm dawdling here for my amusement. I must keep to it for three weeks longer : I began the 16th June, and shall have my final cure-day the 16th August ; I've promised Vaillant that, in return for which *he* gave his word to set me up completely in that time.——

Accordingly I shall return to Zurich the 19th, at latest the 20th August ; I shan't break my journey anywhere, save for a day at Karl's. On your side, dear Minna, see that I find everything ready by then to proceed to our house-building : you can't do much in it *alone*, beyond just *giving orders ;* and if Alter isn't competent, please make further enquiries as to who accepts commissions of that kind. On the other hand, spare yourself too much running about in search of estates ; it only tires you, and you will not find any. Whatever is referred to you, however, inspect it yourself, and use the new droschkes to do so. Manage in this way that, when I return, I shall have nothing to do but decide ; on my side I shall see to the needful money lying ready then. Thus, we shall share the toil between us.—

Adieu, dear old girl, for to-day. Remain in such good health, and forbid them to wake you next time. Fips is first-class, and we both are looking forward to kind faces in the Escherhäuser.

T[hy] RICHARD.

111.
MORNEX, 2. *August* 1856.

Your most obedient Servant, Madame Wagner !

So, a fortnight from to-day I leave here, and shall be a sound Monsieur.—

Karl and his wife came to see me on Wednesday ; we took a donkey-ride up Mont Salève, which I originally had saved for your arrival here ; next morning they went back, after breakfasting with me in my room after *my* fashion, when I brewed the tea myself. On my journey home, as said, I shall pay them a day's visit, and then we're to eat cakes.—

I have nothing against Kläre's and Mathilde's [Frl. Schiffner's] visit ; only I should have thought that Kläre, who cannot well repeat the visit for some time, would have found herself better off with us next year. It suits me thoroughly, however, to go on lollopping awhile at first on my return ; only it mustn't cost me much more money, I may tell you, for I have the less idea how my exchequer will hold out this time, as it naturally has been drained already through my very expensive cure ; for *your health* it would have been another matter. However, we shall see.—I expect you'll have made some tidy savings during my absence—presumably (?) hm ! hm !—

That good Franz Müller also will come from Weimar about the same time ; but I shall be glad if *Liszt* doesn't come till mid-September, as I begged him, for during *his* visit I am sure to have a lot of excitement, which wouldn't be good for me so soon after the cure.—

Semper can't be quite so wrong regarding Tichatscheck ; of sheer thoughtlessness—*certainly not* from *ill* will—he is certain to have damaged Semper. For he [T.] resorts daily to a certain club which includes two police-councillors among its members, as he told me himself—one of them a regular chieftain. Naturally Tichatscheck and his like do not remark that they are being spied on by these gentry ; in his simplicity he will have told the story of that evening, without knowing what he was doing—and perhaps he doesn't know even yet that it was he who blackened Semper. Thus children often do one just as much harm as actual rogues. Please pass on this guess of mine to Semper, and give him my best regards.—

For the rest, I naturally have nothing more to report to you from my monotonous cure-life, beyond the assurance that I shall not get the Rose again.—The Heim letter affair is annoying enough to me, but there was no other means of obviating similar cases ; all one should do, is to reclaim the letter at Zurich and demand an explanation of such swindles.——

Now, God the all-bountiful shield you ! Fips is blooming like a cabbage-rose ; both of us greet you
most respectfully and humbly.

I am curious to know when you will have even a commencement of explorations for the plot of ground to report to me ; you should have been able to send to *Alter* long ago.——

An enquiry from *Vienna* about *Tannhäuser*.——

To-day I combed and flecked Fips single-handed ; he had something like a dozen.——

112.

MORNEX, 5. *Aug.* 1856.

Very good, Mietzel, I won't be stubborn !—So put on your best clothes at once, and pay a call on Frau Bodmer-Stockar. Tell her you would like to know if she believes I should have any success if I wrote to her husband about the estate I have in mind : she is pretty sure to know if there is any possibility of their giving the Trümplers notice. What I should propose, would be to take this property on a life lease—or for 10 years—to do up the interior and make it comfortable for winter. Tell her how much I need to live in solitude, and that I meant to go away from Zurich at last if I couldn't find anything suitable. In short, do all you can to get a favourable decision from the lady—who appears to me the leading person. All else shall then depend on it, and in a favourable event I shall be quite content to satisfy my need in *this* way, by which I should get what I want for less money.

So play your part well, and tell me the result at once.

Indeed I've nothing more to tell you, excepting that it's 9 o'clock at night, and I am soon going to bed.

A fortnight from to-day we shall be hammering away again!

Adio, cara amica !

Il tuo

Riiicardo.

Am I not lamb-like ?

113.

MORNEX, *Monday,* 11. *August* 1856.

MY SPOUSE,

So, a week from tomorrow I shall reach you again. On the Monday I still have a rendezvous with the Wesendoncks at Berne, for which he pressed me, as I had declared I couldn't visit them at Thun.—Will Kläre really have arrived by then ?

My God, I have nothing at all to write you of my terribly monotonous life here ; I'm at the end of the cure now, and merely have still to recover from the exhausting treatment in its middle : by mouth on all that. I now enjoy good sleep and an agreeable calming of my whole nervous system ; I've no more terror of the Rose, as I have my health completely in my hands now, and simply need to live accordingly, to be secure against relapses.—

By chance I knew all of your news, even the story of Bohland's going mad in Dresden. I have my sources, you see ! Many thanks for the Illustrirte, though I could have dispensed with *that* also now ; Lord knows, I've grown entirely indifferent to everything that's going on.—On the other hand I have to inform you that *Härtels'* definitive answer arrived to-day ; it confirms all my hopes, and through the contract soon to be concluded I am placed in the position to proceed to the execution of my project without any fear, as I shall obtain all needful means for it thereby. I must admit I have gained great respect for Härtels.* I am to receive from them *fifteen thousand francs cash* in 3 instalments, and the *interest* on another *fifteen thousand francs* throughout my life and yours ; so that I have 30,000 *frc.* at my disposal, which ought to suffice, I imagine, if the property were sought and found a little farther from Zurich—not quite in the immediate vicinity (where it certainly is dear —indeed impossible).—

Nevertheless I honestly hope the Bodmer business may come off ; if I can get a life-lease of their property, one could fit it up quite nicely for oneself, and we really have no use for a *hereditament.* So do your share ; I shall write Frau Wesendonck this very day, and follow your advice. But time presses ; the season is already advanced, and I should like to know where I am, not to lose the chance of being able to work away in the quiet of a pleasant home next summer.—

So you see I'm doing all I can, and have already succeeded in drawing money from my work ; rejoice me in exchange with thoroughly good news on my return.

Fare excellently well ! If you write me once more *by return* (assuming that to be Thursday) the letter will still catch me at Geneva. Adieu, dearest old woman !

Thy R.

I've flecked Fips again to-day !

---

* Nevertheless the entire arrangement (*re* the whole *Ring,* of course) fell through in less than three weeks, for Otto Wesendonck is informed at the end of the month that this " all but instant certainty is foiled once more " ; see *Life* vi, 146 *et seq.*—Tr.

114.

MORNEX, 13. *August* 1856.

DEAREST MUZIUS,

Really you are very wooden people, all of you ; you cannot even start a thing without me. Surely Herr Dr R. might have had a talk with Frau Trümpler in the first place ; others can often speak up for one with more importunacy than oneself. But all these people seem to have a dread of one another !—So I shall have to go begging from Pontius to Pilate again, and that means a loss of time. Can't you get introduced to Frau Trümpler by Heim, then—or Dr R. ? You could speak better in my interest yourself, than I.—Not one of you can do anything—isn't that true ?

It is awful to me, to hear that you've had to take opium again ; it's to be hoped you will listen to reason, and let yourself be supplied with rest and sleep by *me* for once, which I promise you if you only will follow my orders a bit.

For the rest, I'm waiting for the day of my departure now with great impatience ; probably I shall not write you again, unless anything very important should happen unforeseen. I expect to arrive from Berne on Tuesday morning by the Baden train, as I prefer travelling at night in this heat.—Please *do not* have my bathtub filled with water, but leave it *empty* in the alcove : I shall only use it to do my washings in. But go at once to the Post and tell them to send on no more letters here from *Friday morning* onward, but to give them to the postman. True, I wrote to the bureau yesterday, myself, but it will be as well for you to ascertain if they duly received that letter.

Now let me hope for a kindly reunion ; I expect

you'll be satisfied with me and my health. What I have lost by the sweating, Fips has picked up, so that you can abide by him if I don't please you. If you want a few good nights' sleep ere my arrival, carefully follow the advice I have given you ; but of course you don't appear to think of it, and would rather take that curs. opium. At the least take a couple of cold foot-baths.

Adieu, bad woman who gives me so much anxiety ! To a speedy good Wiedersehen !

Thy R.

[*Between this and the next group of letters husband and wife do not appear to have been parted even for twenty-four hours ; in the meantime the famous " Asyl " had been acquired at Enge, a suburb of Zurich, and entered in the spring of* 1857, *the Wesendoncks taking possession of their adjoining " Villa " the ensuing August.—Tr.*]

115.

PARIS, 17. *January* 1858.

DEAREST MINNA,

You gave me a miserable night with your unlucky *Hôtel de Lyon*, which had another landlord 8 years back, and appears to have come down in the world since. I arrived at ½ past 11, and hunted out a passable room for 3 francs at last : when I examined it closer, the door gaped half an inch ; the chimney smoked. Very good : finally I get to bed, and the rattle of traffic literally doesn't cease the whole night ; stupid fool that I am, I hadn't reflected that this is the noisiest spot in all Paris, immediately off the *Rue Richelieu*. I scarcely closed my eyes, and the first thing in the morning I went to the new big *Hôtel du Louvre*, where I simply asked for a quietly situated room at 3 francs. I was given one on the 3rd floor at once, looking on to the courtyards ; small, but everything very clean and solid ; a large fauteuil, even though no sofa. No din of traffic, since the adjoining *Rue Rivoli* is not paved ; in short, just what I want. Every visitor to Paris should go to the *Hôtel du Louvre ;* you simply ask for what you seek, and get it, from the most sumptuous apartment to the plainest and cheapest. And then one isn't gêned in any way ; if one likes, one can dine in the hotel restaurant *à la carte*, which I much prefer ; I can always get my fish and veal-cutlet there. In brief, I am glad to see peaceful nights before me ; also I have no neighbours.—

As I have only just unpacked, am fearfully tired, and naturally have been able to make a commencement with nothing as yet, I really shouldn't have thought of writing you to-day if it hadn't been for the address. Kietz met me at *Epernay*, at the station ; he can't come to Paris at present, which is a pity for me and seemed to cause him great regret. He entreated me by all that's holy to spend a day with him and Chandon on my journey home.—

The letter from yourself and Präger * I fetched from Kietz' portière this morning, and had to pay 16 sous for it, as the postage was insufficient, and it had been treated as unfranked. Please enquire at the Post exactly what a letter costs to Paris ; it goes much by the weight. If you come by any money, I would rather you franked every time till I have some ; naturally my exchequer isn't at its best. From Strassburg itself, however, I took fresh steps to provide us with money, and I think the pinch will soon be over.—

Präger's letter was very important to me ; it gives me useful addresses, and saves many enquiries.—

Now I must write to Dresden again, to prevent their dawdling with the despatch of my operas.—I shall make a

* Meaning a letter from Präger sent on by Minna ; see *Life* vi, 332. —Tr.

start with my affairs tomorrow, and shan't write you again till I can report how things stand and when I may hope to depart.—

I'm delighted you have slept so well ; only continue going to bed early, as soon as ever sleep comes on. Fips's not eating *for my sake* shews him from an entirely new side, and makes his character doubly precious to me. Shake his paw ! Send me word soon that you have received money and your heart is beating tranquilly. Farewell and hold me thoroughly dear—in spite of all the faults and turpitudes I have. We must really try and pull along together now ; and at bottom things are going quite passably, even though I unfortunately have more fame than money. And you have seen for yourself now, that it isn't the . . . * alone : all the securer can you feel about me. The embarrassment on account of my journey really has preyed on my mind, and indeed I'm more a man of feeling than you think !

Now keep well, and soon rejoice me with good tidings !

Thy

Address : RICHARD.

Monsieur Richard Wagner
Grand Hôtel du Louvre
(No. 364) *à*
Paris.

---

* As these dots exist in the German edition, it will be as well to reproduce the whole enigmatic and idiomatic context : " Wir müssen's nun doch miteinander vollends durchmachen ; und im Grunde genommen geht es jetzt doch ganz passabel, wenn ich leider auch mehr Ruhm als Geld habe. Und dass es die . . . nicht allein macht, hast Du nun auch gesehen : desto sicherer kannst Du über mich sein. Mir stak wirklich die Beklommenheit wegen der Abreise in den Gliedern, und ich bin eben mehr Gemüthsmensch als Du glaubst ! " Under the circumstances, with almost every word presenting ambiguities to the outsider, any translation can only be tentative.—Tr.

116.

PARIS, 21. *January* 1858.

MY GOOD MINNA,

I fancy you will prefer my writing you something in brief at once, to my waiting to write at greater length tomorrow, when I shouldn't have much more to tell you either. For your letter only reached me close on 3 o'clock, and if I am to get my answer off by post-time, I can't be long about it.——

Matters stand in this way, that I expect to be able to go back the end of next week for certain ; but I fancy I shall have completely attained my aim then, and better than I could have hoped, in spite of several misadventures now detaining me.

My Mr *Amat*, to wit, had gone away the very night of my arrival, to give concerts in the provinces, and isn't expected back before next week. His wife gave me very good information, though, and—as it seems highly probable that my Tannhäuser will be taken up in earnest here sooner or later—it is becoming certain that, *together* with the declaration of my copyright in the pianoforte scores etc., I shall also be able to secure myself the sole right of performance. And the latter really is of great importance ; for, not only will it place me in the position to prevent any performance I do not approve of, but, if it does come off at the Grand Opera, I shall also be able to demand full author's rights with tantième etc., which should amount under circumstances to something decent. With *Mr de Charnal*—the translator, at whose house I am to dine to-day, and who is plaguing me to co-operate with him in a new opera for the *Théâtre lyrique* (the ass !) —I have agreed to make no further present enquiries of the management of that theatre, but quietly to register my declaration of copyright ; which will then give me the right to lodge a valid protest even on the day of an intended first performance. My strict concern accordingly consists for this time in acquiring that right, and entrusting someone with authority based thereon to prevent any such performance ; and Amat will do quite well for that, as it will be to his own advantage in course of time. So I must wait not only for this person's return, but also for arrival of the copies of my operas from Dresden, for which I've written pressingly once more ; with the end of next week I hope to have them both behind me.—By the way, this business will bring me into contact with the Saxon ambassador, who is needed for it ; which should afford me much amusement. —

Surely you must have received the small sum from Berlin by now ? My having left you so in the lurch gives me more anxiety than you believe. It is to be hoped the Vienna affair will be also put straight now. *Liszt* writes me, he'll send me some money in a few days ; in any case I shall send you some of that, as I already know how to help myself here at a pinch. Härtels certainly make me a very different counter-offer [for *Tristan*]—only the *half* of my demand (400 louis d'or) down, the other half from profits later. However, I shall have to agree to it (for they advance really plausible grounds), and am certain thus to get 100 louis from them at Easter (even if not sooner). Moreover, I have been hawking the *Rienzi* like sour beer (Hanover, Frankfort, Breslau), urging its *prompt* production and consequently also a prompt remittance of the fees. If only some of this comes off, we shall be all right, and then—just let me look ahead ! The thing shall not repeat itself so soon.—

I have written to England at once, and set forth every ground for my excuse ; also begged—in case of confusion arising—to excuse me to Prince Albert [*vid. inf.*] These Zurich Post officials (may Sulzer forgive me !) are really utter . . . !—

Concerning letters, *don't frank them at all in future :* the fat letter cost me 4-fold postage—your double stamp being too little. For letters to France have to be terribly thin (at the utmost like this one), and if they are not franked sufficiently, the *franco* isn't counted *at all*, but the whole postage must be paid again (according to French rates). Believe me, I didn't let myself be taken in by any portière : that is so !—in return I shan't frank my few letters to you.—

Liszt's other daughter only returns from Germany also this week ; her husband (Ollivier) I haven't been able to catch yet (Paris !) ; I shall call on him tomorrow, though. —Yesterday I dined with Lindemann etc. at the *Taverne anglaise* (almost nothing but fish !)—

I am writing letters nearly all day long, and expect they'll bear fruit.

—What does Eckert [Vienna dir.] write ?—

Now, God be with you for to-day ! After dinner I'm to go to the said *Théâtre lyrique* (but *not* Euryanthe!) with Charnal !—Fare wellest of well, and hold as dear as you can

Thy immensely loving

HUSBAND.

The Strassburg incident has already got into the news-papers.—The attentat [Orsini] has not affected me at all : make your mind easy about it ; I hear nothing of it what-ever.—

117.

MY POOR MUZIUS,

You cannot think how it distresses me to have left you in such straits for money ; so, even the small Berlin return has not come in yet ? Really it's incredible ! I wrote to Hoffmann forthwith, enclosing the letter to Haslinger, though, as it is the latter who is to send the money at once, and—in case of need—to make it up to a round 1000 *fr.* Thus you will receive a bill of exchange on Paris, which you must sign for me—I hope it's allowed —best at Schulthess and Rechberg's ; the brother of Squire Wyss is there. Perhaps it will be necessary for you to beg it as a special favour, for strictly the bill ought to be signed by myself (unfortunately I didn't think of that yesterday). In the worst event, I shall probably be coming back at the same time myself, or shortly after.

To go on with, however, I send you at once what Liszt has sent me : namely, the enclosed 500 *fr.* He was thoroughly averse to demanding the fee for Rienzi before its production, and therefore advances me on it for the present these 500 *fr.* from his own—as he says—very empty pocket. I send you the whole of this, that you may have something in hand ; for my own part, as I wouldn't rely on even Liszt alone (quite right !), I provisionally borrowed 200 *fr.* from London, off *Präger*, which I only need repay at my convenience. That money will take me back to Zurich.—

Best thanks for your tidings. Though I strictly had no further intentions here than what you know of, already something more might come of it perhaps. Naturally *I* am hunting no Director, but must lie in wait for their hunting *me*. That has been done now, under the rose,

by the Director of the *Théâtre lyrique*, who—notified by
Charnal—had me invited to a performance at his theatre,
and begged for the honour of presenting himself to me.
I was very stand-off towards him ; he, on the contrary,
couldn't contain himself for civility. I don't quite know
what to make of his intentions yet regarding Tannhäuser,
and therefore keep silence ; but thus much is certain, he
wants something of mine. After having seen his theatre,
under circumstances I might decide to give him the
Rienzi—but not Tannhäuser ; as my only object with
the affair is money, I am cautious myself. There are
several other considerations here inclining me to Rienzi
as my first opera for Paris, all of which I'll tell you soon
by word of mouth : it isn't so easy to ruin as Tannhäuser,
and I would even let them make some alterations in it ;
touching that fatal dialogue [however], the Grand Duke
of Baden would have to use his influence with the local
Emperor, and get him to give special commands for
permitting an exception. For an opera like this would
be regarded by the theatre in question as a decided stroke
of luck, and I should only give my consent under a
contract ensuring the most unusual exertions and the
engagement of singers who thoroughly pleased me, as also
and finally, under guarantee of *very considerable pecuniary*
advantages. All this *may be*, dear Minna, and is quite
possible ; but do not pin your faith to it just yet.

I am dining at Ollivier's to-day, who has received me
uncommonly cordially and placed his services as advocate
entirely at my disposal. He is a personal friend of Mons.
Carvalho (director of the *Lyrique*), and has offered to set
everything in order with him when the time comes.
That is really something like !—

In that way there would be an earlier result than I

anticipated here. I must leave the directorate of the *Grand Opera* completely on one side for the moment; Meyerbeer still has influence there, and no doubt that theatre must first have its hand forced through Rienzi's success at the opera-house of second rank. But then it *will* be forced, and I shall be able to lay down any condition I please; nor would Rienzi itself be lost entirely for the Grand Opera later.—

Now don't excite yourself too much; all these are merely plans as yet, but their possibility reposes on the visibly strong desire of the *Théâtre lyrique* to have an opera of mine. Only through my personal presence could such openings have deen descried and seized; consequently I have no reason to repent any sacrifice incurred for this journey even already.

The above was the chief thing; for the rest, I spend almost the whole day in my cubicle, writing letters and reading. May my small remittance of to-day set you up a little; and forgive the stupid fix in which I placed you. Let Müller only wait till I come back, or for the Vienna money to arrive; I shall write him in a day or two.

So the best farewell, dearest Minna! Salute the household for me, stay good to me, and wish plenty of luck to

Thy

truly good

HUSBAND.

118.

PARIS, 28. *January* 1858.
Grand Hôtel du Louvre
(*No.* 365)

Chère Épouse,

Comment vous portez-vous ? Avez vous bien dormi ? Que fait votre cœur ? Que fait Mr Fipps ? et Jacquot ?

Ja so ! I must speak German now ! I should have
written you the day before yesterday, dear Mutz, had I
really found time for it. In the first place I've a lot of
business correspondence still, and in the second my
engagements here are ever on the increase. Even to-day
I don't propose to write you much, though, to save up
for us both, in reality this time, the pleasure of having
quite a deal to tell by mouth ; which one always spoils
through too great circumstantiality by letter, leaving one
strictly nothing more to say when one gets home. Merely
the following general outline, then, to give you some
notion of the character of my present stay.

Neither could it have been the object of my journey
to bring anything to a definite conclusion, nor would it
have been possible during so brief a stay. Before next
winter, too, there can be no idea of a production of any
of my operas here, as the season is too far advanced
already. For my part I can make overtures in no
direction, but must wait for folk to come to me. Well,
the director of the *Théâtre lyrique* has come so far to me
already, that—with 1000 bows and scrapings—he has
expressed his wish and hope to acquire an opera from me
shortly, and to visit me at Zurich with that aim.—Regarding the Grand Opera, it is *everyone's* opinion that the
management must and will make offers to me soon. I
could hardly have believed how much they're occupied with
me in Paris ; certain proof of which I have received, as you
shall hear. But my greatest good fortune is the acquaintance
and friendship of Ollivier, about whom I shall have much
to narrate to you. He entirely sides with Liszt, and has
broken with the d'Agoult ; he is a most delightful man,
and eminent in many respects. For the present only this
much : he has taken to me in a way that makes me quite

secure. Here is an instance, which will shew you at the same time how the eyes of people here are turned on me. The evening before last, on my going to dine at Ollivier's, he informs me he has seen a poster of the *Concerts de Paris* the same day, on which the first Paris performance (erroneous !) of the overture to Tannhäuser was announced for Friday in enormous letters. As, if I mean to guarantee my copyright for performances also, I must make even a concert execution of the overture depend on my own consent (since it might otherwise be regarded as a waiving of my right, and lead to serious consequences later), here I have to take an immediate step. So Ollivier at once dictated me a letter to the director of those concerts, declaring that I would not frustrate the proposed performance of my overture this time, yet should only permit it on the express condition of the maintenance of my rights, of which such permission must involve no abandonment ; at the same time, moreover, that a rehearsal of my overture must be instituted in my presence, to convince me that its execution will correspond to my wishes.—Then we drove off to an *avoué*, a friend of Ollivier's, whom the latter commissioned to deliver this letter to the director in due legal form next morning. And to-day I have received the politest invitation to give myself the trouble of attending a special rehearsal of my overture at 1 o'clock.—Look you, *that's* how one must act here ; Ollivier knows it, and is very keen on it. How good it is, once more, that I was in Paris myself at the moment ! All this, for example, would have never been heeded, and my rights have thus been viewed as half abandoned in advance and difficult to re-establish. Moreover, as people are so impatient for my compositions *now*, an inferior performance of precisely this overture would have been most injurious to me; whereas I now shall have it in my power to bring about the best result. These are beginnings, but of decisive weight. After the performance you shall learn the result. General conclusion :—fair prospect of seeing two operas of mine—Tannh. (at the Grand Opera) and Rienzi— produced next winter at full tantièmes. And as regards the latter point—the receipts—it's something quite stupendous !—

For the rest, I have made very agreeable acquaintances, who shew me Paris from a side I never knew before. Last Sunday—through Ollivier—I was at a real Conservatoire concert for the first time in my life ; seated next me Mad. Herold, widow of the composer of Zampa, such a pleasant, charming, genial and distinguished woman, that I have fallen quite in love with her, notwithstanding her grey hair and fifty years. We spent the evening at her house, among her children and acquaintances. Last autumn Mad. Herold was in Vienna with her daughter and son-in-law, on their honeymoon, heard my Tannhäuser there (with a guest named Altkäs in the title-rôle), and was just as enraptured with the freshness and fire of the performance, as she was revolted by the flabbiness and chill of the Berlin performance she heard thereafter. This really was news to me ; I had my doubts, but her descriptions and her serious enthusiasm convinced me it must be as she had said. So I wrote next day to Hoffmann's Kapellmeister, told him what I had heard, and thanked him.—I made other notable acquaintances there, on whom by mouth.

Yesterday I also drove to Madame Erard, who is living at Passy in a princely château. She and Madame Spontini (her sister-in-law) were delighted with my visit, and—to cut the story short—my first Paris receipt this time consists in the present Mad. Erard is making me of a grand piano, which will shortly reach the Asyl on the Gabler. In return I have begged her to accept the dedication of my first opera that appears in Paris ; what do you say to it ? Perhaps—with your permission—I shall have to bring a sacrifice to Mad. Erard ; she very much wished me to spend an evening there, and (as we shall be at the Herolds' again on Sunday evening, with Blandine —Ollivier's wife—who only returns from Berlin this evening : an engagement I couldn't well refuse Ollivier) she has appointed Tuesday next week. I haven't accepted yet, but after her costly present (it is catalogued at 5000 *fr.*) I think I ought to shew her that attention ; in which case I should have to abandon the visit to Epernay. For the rest, my departure hinges on the expected arrival of the Dresden pianoforte-scores of my operas, with which those odious people still are lagging. In any case, however, I irrevocably fix next *Wednesday* (*i.e.* a week from to-day) as the day of my departure ; therefore, as I mustn't arrive on a Friday, expect me midday *Saturday*, and by all means invite our oyster-party for that evening. Then I shall either spend a day at Epernay after all, or remain another day at Strassburg, where I have half promised to call on the conductor, who probably would like to make use of my presence for his benefit concert. In any case I shouldn't care to knock myself entirely up by travelling day and night, but to reach home nice and fresh ; whither I indeed am strongly drawn—particularly for reason of my extremely pressing work.

My health really had somewhat run down, the long course of un-nutritious diet I needed has been a great drain on me in the end; I am fearfully thin, and feel rather weak.

Therefore I'm going in for more nourishing food now, which on the other hand always stirs up my blood troubles again ; so that poor I am constantly between two evils. I am bearing up, however, and strength is returning already ; so have no anxiety. The surprising weakness of my constitution is revealed to me now ; never before have my wants been so small.   Well, we'll see how that turns out at Wagners'.—

For the reason given above I omit any further account of my experiences here, merely telling you that I shall call on Rossini (if only for his physiognomy's sake), that Berlioz read his operatic subject [*Troyens*] to me yesterday, etc., and I'll just pass on to our immediate affairs.

How the devil did such a confounded address get into your head, as that under which you imagine I sent my notes to England ?   *Anderson—Sydenhampalast !*   Stuff and nonsense ! the address was :

> " *To Her most gracious Majesty*
> *The Queen*
> *Buckingham Pallace*
> *London.*"

To the care of
the H^r C^l Phipps

Let there be no mistake about it—and cause no fresh confusion.

How can Spyri be so idiotic as to say that Tannhäuser has been accepted at the Grand Opera ?   That's going the round of all the German papers now, looks like brag, and will draw down on me all kinds of fooleries.

Your wonder at my sending you some money really pains me.   My God, for whom do you persist in taking me ?   I don't deny that at times, and under circumstances, I am inclined to extravagance ; but you never have found me indifferent to the dilemmas thence arising for yourself ;

on the contrary, my one sole care then is to beat up money to remove your difficulty, which I now am attempting again in every quarter. I have no answer from Frankfort and Breslau as yet (good sign !) ; from Hanover, where they would like to see Rienzi at Dresden first (people are a little distrustful of my earlier operas), they also beg me to let them defer it awhile, as Armide was to be given next : at any rate, then, it will be coming off shortly. As soon as Rienzi has made its due sensation at Dresden and Weimar, I hope to be able to put this opera's vending in commission, against the deposit of an advance of 1000 thaler ; toward that, too, I've already taken steps. From Härtels I expect to be able to draw 2000 *fr.* the end of February. So—just a little patience ! Meanwhile Vienna will help, which must have put its tribute on the road by now. Next month, too, probably something more from Weimar. For the present, then, please lay out the 500 *fr.*, and pay off our most pressing debts with it ; I shall find some other means for *Müller*, I promise you.—

There now—you have a proper letter. Possibly I shall not arrive at writing you much again ; I've a number of business and other letters still ahead, whilst the nearer I approach to my return, the less need I have of written communications. But you, please write me regularly ; I'm pretty sure to remain here till Wednesday, so you can send me yet another letter on Monday. I have changed my room, as it was far too cold and had no sun at all— I haven't got rid of my cold yet—so no. 365 (exactly the days of the year).

Farewell, good, charmante old girl ! Salute the animals, and remain fond of

Thy

feeble old RICHARD.

Afternoon. They fetched me to the rehearsal before I could close this letter. Lord, what a good father I am ! This overture is 14 years of age now, and yet I couldn't let it run alone. The band might have been better, and the conductor, who had no full score, was obliged to leave many important points obscure : what luck that I was there ! I couldn't stand it at last, and placed myself at the desk for *two* hours' drudgery. The orchestra gave me a thundering ovation—but couldn't satisfy me much. I was so knocked up by this unexpected fatigue, that—all in a heat—I had a closed carriage sent for quick, to take me home. Consequently I have left the conductor to finish his affair alone ; let us hope the orchestra and he have made a note of everything. For that matter, don't attach too much weight to this performance ; these concerts aren't of much account. As I was unable as yet to prevent the performance, at least it was worth while making it as good as possible ; and that I've done.—Now farewell. I have ordered a veal-cutlet and bowl of Julienne ; then I must be off to Ollivier's again ; but I shall go to bed early this evening. Wishing you a really good night !

119.

PARIS, 1. *February* 1858.

BEST MUZIUS,

I have to create a confusion again ; I can't get home till midday Saturday—toward 2 o'clock. It was impossible to leave the kindness of Mad. Erard unrequited, who had firmly reckoned upon me for Tuesday ; she had invited a big assembly in my honour, among whom *Rossini* himself may be present. So it will be late at night before one gets home, and it would be too fatiguing for me to rise at 6 in the morning and travel all night again (to arrive on Thursday). Further, Kietz and Chandon have pressingly begged me once more to give them a day at Epernay; which I now shall do, and travel home quite leisurely, so as not to arrive on a Friday. I am bringing money too. The Vienna people sent the 1000 *fr.* bill of exchange to me here, after all, as it was drawn upon Paris; it doesn't make much difference, and saves in fact a trifling loss.

You will receive no further news from me, except perhaps a hasty confirmation of my departure. So bespeak the party for Saturday evening; I shall bring the oysters with me, and thus be following your advice.

I had hoped for another letter from you to-day; you aren't unwell by any chance?

Adieu, good old Madame! Stay good to me till then; when you can reprove me again if I behave badly.

To the very finest of welcomes!

Thy

much-loved

HUSBAND.

[*Two months after Wagner's return to Zurich Minna intercepted a letter of his to Frau Wesendonck, leading to a now notorious "scene" between the two women—see* Familienbriefe, R. Wagner to M. Wesendonck, Life vi, *etc.—immediately after which occurrence Minna temporarily departed for a nerve-cure at Brestenberg in Aargau.—Tr.*]

120.

ZURICH, 20. *April* 1858.

You made me very uneasy, dear Minna, with your silence. I telegraphed about it yesterday to Herr Dr Erismann, prepaying an answer; remarkable to say, none has reached me, and I mean to make inquiry into it. Luckily I received your letter in the afternoon, however, and that relieved my mind. Eh, eh, I told you you'd experience wonders from your cure ; that a suppressed catarrh came out at once, e.g., was quite in order, and you may simply congratulate yourself upon it. Many another thing will likewise come out, that has only been repressed by the eternal feverish agitation of your nerves, but on the other hand so sorely aggravated your complaint itself. I could never prevent your exposing yourself to a chill ; you took no notice of the consequences—but they were partly to blame for the increase of your illness.

Well, your having such good trust [in it] gives me the most hope of the cure's successful issue. Just keep to that, and so give *me* the relief of having a sound and right sensible wife again soon. I know I've to overlook much in you for the state to which your ailment has reduced you ; so may everything turn for the best !— I'll hope so !—

Now keep to it, think of nothing but your health. Without it there's no hope for any of us !—

Nothing special has arrived in the way of letters ; what pleased me most, was the kind reply of Dr R., who really had been much offended : I enclose this letter for your heartening. Nevertheless the old gentleman did indeed more harm than help you, and one is really too considerate towards such people. But we'll let that drop for this once. —

I have received a second message from Erard's, that the piano went off yesterday.—For the rest, I am in no particular humour yet, as you may easily imagine ; I haven't the least disposition for work. Perhaps I therefore shall accept Wille's invitation to spend a couple of days with them ; I suppose you'll have nothing against it. Perhaps it will distract me a little ; the agitations and exertions since the beginning of this month have been a shade too great, you know.

As I haven't otherwise been much about yet, I can only tell you of our household : that Friedrich is behaving exemplarily and doing an enormous amount in the garden ; it really will be very pretty. Lisette had to get cupped yesterday. Both of them serve me very well, and accordingly it's quite endurable at home here.

I have nothing further to tell you concerning ourselves ; so soon as anything occurs, you shall hear of it at once. Now give the Herr Doctor my hearty regards, and thank him most profoundly for his care. For yourself, dear old girl, don't be slack about writing, but go on sending me a perfect diary of your treatment. Only patience and courage ! Everything will come right, for sure, and after all troubles and storms a peaceful, contented old age will appear in the end !

Farewell, behave yourself, and give me tranquillising news as frequently as possible.

Thy

good RICHARD.

121.

ZURICH, 23. *April* 1858.

POOR DEAR MINNA,

Once more I cry to you, repeating it a thousand times : Have *patience*, and above all else, have *trust !* If you knew how you torture me with your want of the latter, I feel sure you would repent it. In brief, when you assured me you really did love me, I adjured you to prove it me by forgoing any encounter, any arraignment on that side, at least until after your cure ; in return for which I promised you to fulfil *on my side* whatever you wished for your pacifying. But the Tempter mastered you a second time, and this time you openly broke your love and faith in me. I forgive you that, to begin with, for the awful state of health which made you almost irresponsible ; and more : I forgive it you for all the future. But I now implore you, put forth all your strength of mind henceforward to *preserve unshaken* your belief in my sincere and lifelong sympathy, my heartfelt wish to promote your welfare, my steadfast will to harbour no ulterior hopes whatever for this life. If you are unable to do so, you will make yourself and me unhappy ! I should have no need of this entreaty if you had yourself had so much mental composure from of old as to judge me justly, and in particular to form a clear idea of that relation which fills you with idle fears, as I perceive, even after your procuring yourself full satisfaction. From the other side but *one* reproach has been addressed to me, namely that I had ever omitted to make the *purity of those relations* clear to you, so that it would have been impossible for you so to insult the lady concerned. These reproaches were made me by the husband, the man who, admitted from of old to the minutest confidences of his wife, yet could ever bear himself with nobleness and friendship toward me, just *because* he was convinced of the purity of our relations. The only excuse I could offer in reply, was that I held it a sheer impossibility to convince *yourself* of such a thing—and that, alas ! in spite of all my declarations, appears to be intending to prove true.—

So once again, and for the last time (since you will destroy *yourself* if you continue thus !)—have *trust !* Forget in what has happened whatever seems to remain inexplicable to you (such as my familiar expressions in that letter)—and cleave alone to my explanations reiterated to you to-day ! That also is what I meant by wishing to have a right *sensible* wife in you soon, which I hope you'll take amiss of me no longer.—

For that matter, I may simply tell you that I was really invited to Wesendonck's again last Sunday [18th], and quite *alone.* I have been at the Willes' two days. Next week the Wesendoncks go away for some time. I am longing for my work again at last, and think of resuming it tomorrow.—After this serious and truly well-meant letter, I have nothing further of importance to communicate to you to-day.—

Your *sufferings* have touched and thrilled me much again ; God is my witness how honestly and sincerely I wish you speedy convalescence. Persevere ! Your illness once alleviated, you'll look at everything again more calmly, and recognise that the causes of life's sufferings do not only lie *outside* us, but mostly also *in* us.

So, good recovery !

We soon shall meet again !

Thy

faithful Husband

RICHARD.

122.

ZURICH, *Tuesday* 27. *April* 1858.

This, dear Minna, is the date on which I've determined to get myself put, not in a hydropathic institute, but in a mad-house—for that now seems the only proper place for me ! Whatever I say or write, even with the best intention, I stir up nothing but misfortune and misunderstanding. If I keep silence on certain things, I make you distrustful and suspicious that I want to circumvent you ; then if

I write seriously and openly, and at the same time thoroughly composingly—as I, poor ass, believed—I learn that I have been hatching a fiendish plot to hurry you under the turf! In the same breath I'm told to be a *man!* Good : not *a* man, but *thy* man I'll be. Tell me exactly how I am to speak, think, and look on the things of this world : I'll shape my course accordingly, and say, think and see nothing that doesn't suit you :— are you satisfied ? Lay down for me, also, what and how I'm to indite and compose : indeed I shall conform to you in everything, that you no longer may have a moment's doubt about me. For whatever I do of myself, in *my own* way, you still believe it doesn't spring from me, but from someone or other who has an object with me. Very good : that shan't occur again ; I'll look to left or right no longer, and if you then can still doubt that I live for no one but yourself, that I love and dote upon you, at least *I* shall no longer be answerable.

God knows if the above has put you in good humour, as my object was, or if I appear to you the refinement of malice afresh. I'm so in doubt concerning all I say or do, that I shall shortly get carried about like a child. No matter, though, if only you will bid good-bye to these terrible fancies, and recognise that at least I have the best, most honest will to shew myself good and grateful to you, faithful and attached, affectionate and thoughtful. Or am I to end by following Sulzer's example, before he married, hating " women " in the lump, and wishing there were none but males upon this earth ?—

God in Heaven, what *am* I to do then, to make you content ?—

Now listen ! Thursday I shall write you exactly

when you are to fetch me from the station Saturday; then we'll come to some arrangement. Meanwhile abide by the *best* you can think of me, and you always shall find me still better.

Nothing has occurred. I shall bring with me a letter from the Fürstin to yourself. Its intention is good; she is much affected by the description I gave her of your state of health and mind.

I am going to Wille's with Herwegh to-day. I had really repented accepting, as I was in the vein for work; but your letter of to-day has made me so confused again, that the distraction will come in just right.—God only grant that I'm not exciting you again with this letter; I literally no longer know what I am doing! You extract a black meaning from everything. However, we shall see, and hope for the best when your mind has somewhat quieted again.

I'm taking terrible walks with Fips, e.g. across Kilchberg, Sihlwald etc., yesterday. He eats very little; he must be fretting. He, too, will be highly delighted to see you again. Moreover, my visits may become much more frequent when the railway is opened [the whole way], and taking all in all, I really feel as if the worst were got over in every direction. In truth it cannot be but things must mend; if they continued thus, neither you nor I could stand it.

So, on Thursday full particulars about the Wiedersehen!—

Everything that is best, heartiest, and most reassuring, as greeting from

Thy

age-worn

HUSBAND.

123.

The Erard, good Minna, has just been unpacked and set up in spite of rain and weather. What a delight it is to play on such an instrument, only the player himself can fully appreciate : the lightest pressure, scarcely touching, at once brings out that gentle bell-like tone which becomes a full clear, rich, but always mellow chime if one presses somewhat harder. I can play on it so softly that nobody in the next room would hear me when composing.—*One* joy at least, then, has stolen like a friend into my life !

Now *you* must soon give me the great joy of knowing you're on the high road to improvement. That is the sole joy whatever still in store, and then we'll thoroughly enjoy your full recovery, and take good care that things don't turn so bad again.—

Last night I returned to our house with great sadness and sinking of heart :—it is indeed a sore trial !

It filled me with sorrow to find you always falling back, as at our taking leave, into your black self-torturing fancies. For Heaven's sake don't fasten on single words and expressions of mine, which you indeed always understand wrong. Do reflect, with some approach to justice and consideration, that I myself can't always keep an eye alert, with everything I utter, upon its possible impression on yourself. If I point out to you what a serious frame of mind my own has been, please always go by my eventual actions, i.e. my ultimate resolves when the inner conflict is ended. You really need a thoroughly intelligent, experienced and heartily well-wishing friend of your own sex just now, who on many points could give you such advice and explanation as *I* cannot possibly give you without starting fresh misunderstandings which truly never lay in my intention. Perhaps that may also be found, and then you will be radically tranquillised. But do put some faith in my character; on my last visit did you not remark the genuine, ay, cheerful calm I now have won? Surely you noticed no unrest, distraction, or dissimulation in me; let that reassure you on the state of matters in my inner self. Without, too, all is set in order, and my sole remaining care is for your health; a care that fills me with sincere concern when I see you still so ailing. Think of nothing beyond your cure; firmly and steadfastly believe I'm keeping nothing from you that might give you reason for anxiety on *my* account; be sure of me, and rest assured I hope and long for nothing more upon this earth and in this life, than peace and quiet to be able to fulfil my task that keeps me on my feet. So let us jointly bear the lot appointed us, be lenient toward each other's foibles, and honestly assist each other to fulfil life's heavy task with cheerfulness unruffled!—

So once more, and ever more :—Get well! Sleep calm and free of any care for me! I too am calm, and in my breast there dwells a peace so deep that nothing save the care about your health can shake it now.

Enjoy our Fipsel also, whom I truly left you at a heavy sacrifice; I miss him terribly, and when I drew his basket on one side to go to bed, tears came into my eyes. But you shall keep him; I will eke out with the Erard and my work now. Help me yourself as well, through good news of your health!—

Kindest regards to the Herr Doctor and family! Be brave, as I am; behave yourself, and thereby prove to me you really love me! Thy

RICHARD.

124.

How goes it with you on Ascension day, good Mutz? We have rain again, and so far as I'm concerned, I shouldn't care to join the flight to Heaven ; I'd rather fly beneath the earth !—

God, what a melancholy time it is ! *You're* in clover ; the cure gives you plenty to do, you have dog, bird, and agreeable male society.   Since Monday, when I saw Herwegh, *I* haven't caught sight of a soul ; which quite suits me, all the same.   At least I have declined another invitation to the Hubers to-day ; to me it isn't any jollity. Yesterday she called, in my absence, to enquire after your health ; I shall look in for a moment tomorrow.   If only the Herwegh would get confined at last, at least there'd be a human being the more in the world.   She has been in labour for 2 days, and Friedrich brought word to-day it had got no forwarder.   It must be a truly hard job for her !—

I'm not at all the thing myself.   Those Brestenberg visits in bad weather have left their tracks in rheumatisms of all kinds ; also I am troubled with my lower parts again, apparently in consequence.   Probably you will not get sight of your husband next Saturday : I really should like to fetch back a little good humour for once ; but the weather will certainly have to do its share in that.   Moreover, I'm just getting true zest for my work [comp. *Tristan* ii] and all manner of delicious themes are occurring to me, which I easily might lose 'twixt wind and weather in that open chaise.   Should it turn out very fine, however, I'll come for sure ; rely on that.

And not a cock crows, not a dog barks, not a cat mews for one ; never a sound from abroad.   It's really getting on my nerves ! Na, send me good tidings *yourself*, that one at least may have one prospect of things mending. Your having got accustomed to the complete packings so soon, is a good sign. The first time at Vaillant's I felt alarmed in them myself ; so don't let that upset you. On the whole I see progress, and hope it will continue.

Unless I were tempted before by fine weather, probably you won't see me again till my birthday, when I hope you'll already be feeling much better. Müller will come with me then, in any case ; he promised it me solemnly at the parade.

I really do not know at all what else to tell you. I am so living in my inner world now, that I literally do not remark if aught is happening in the outer. It is possible I may look in on Sulzer to-day, though ; perhaps I shall hear something there.

Now, God and Dr Erismann preserve you ! I will attend to your commissions ; if I do not come Saturday, I shall send you the biscuits for Jacquot. I'm also getting a new ring set with a green stone expressly for you ; there was nothing of the sort in stock.—Farewell, be patient and hold out, that you may give joy to

Thy
RICHARD.

(Fipps is a good fellow.)

125.

ZURICH, Sunday, 16. May 1858.

DEAR MINNA,

There it goes, raining the whole blessed Sunday again, and though I'm not particularly delighted with it here, it's well that we are not passing the rain-sunday

together at Brestenberg in mutually affixing our crotchets
again.   When the weather looked so promising yesterday
I felt quite sorry I hadn't come, but indeed I also think
the doctor is right that my visits excite you ; at least I've
never yet been able to bring home a true belief that I had
soothed you, however willing my intention.   That also
will come in good time ; but the greatest equability and
true relaxation of spirit are doubtless the first essentials
for your present cure.   Indifferent society, and particularly
reading, are very good then ; I know it from experience,
notwithstanding that my creative fancy always keeps me
in a certain agitation—which is not unpleasant in itself,
but gets made painful by clashing with other vibrations
of life.   Accept my heartiest congratulations on the
" splendid night " of which you wrote in your last letter ;
it did me worlds of good myself, to receive such good
tidings from you.   Yes, simply rest ! rest ! both of us
need it so badly.   And that will come, too ; only be kind
and continue reporting your faintest improvements.—

I have not been at my best myself this week past.   I
always feel worst of a morning ; it is the old abdominal
disturbance, connected with my blood trouble.   I have
tried making an alteration in my breakfast, but remarked
no difference.   It has its times and seasons, but I know
only too well on the whole where its seat is : I live too
much within myself, and have too little diversion without ;
which has been brought about, in turn, by my situation
since ever so long.   Naturally, even the love for my work
suffers under it ; good God ! from whence can I expect at
last to draw my inspiration ?   For two days I had made
no headway with my work at all ; yesterday morning I
quite fell into despair, and—just to see human beings and
let off a little steam—I promptly set out for the Willes',

where I remained until late in the evening. After hardly speaking a word for a whole week, I properly unloaded myself there of all manner of artistic plans. To-day I've really felt a little better, and my work has gone well. Yes, the body is not accountable for everything ; the soul needs its excursions also !—

This evening I'm invited to Sulzer's, where whist is to be played with Müller. I called upon Sulzer the other day, but couldn't do much with him ; what interests him is most indifferent to myself, at bottom. He seems badly put out, moreover ; the shooting business cropped up too. —But now for a principal item : the day before yesterday, at 3 in the afternoon, the Herwegh was at last delivered of a strapping boy ; so you may congratulate her. —

I have had one joy : young Hirzel came back from Leipzig and left me, as he didn't catch me, the wished for photograph of father Geyer's portrait ; which really touched me very much. It has turned out quite passably ; the face excellently. With it there also lay a pencil copy of the same picture, executed by Clemens Brockhaus, which certainly leaves much to desire.—That is all that has occurred to me, tho' ; otherwise nothing but nonsense, stupid letters from musicians, and so on. Consequently I still am left in expectation of something decent turning up at last.—

If you write me of nights slept well through, it will be what I should like best ; and if ever you feel bad and wretched—which I do not wish—just think of your husband, who often fares no better too.—

Friedrich forgot the biscuits, and has got the sack for it from me. His only passion is the garden, and the housekeeping book is always blossoming into a mass of plantings, to say nothing of $4\frac{1}{2}$ fr. for bean-poles ; I must really put some check on his enthusiasm. Otherwise he is quite a model of steadiness, so that I've really nothing to complain of. Lisette is a—cow !—

Now best greetings to your honoured company, and give the Herr Doctor my kindest thanks for your good nights ; you require plenty more of them !—

I shall be with you in good time Saturday, and Müller too.   The rascal hasn't even shewn his face here, though !

Now farewell, greet the animals, and Fippsius in especial ; hold me dear, and continue rejoicing

Thy

HUSBAND,

who deserves it !

126.

ZURICH, Tuesday, 25. May 1858.

O Minna !—very, very bad weather ; rheumatic pains, and all the rest !   To work it off, I climbed up the pear-tree again yesterday.   Heims came in the evening ; they send you kind regards : I had to tell them a lot about you.—But what shall I tell yourself ?   Whence take, without stealing ?   Stay, tho', here's something I have stolen from the Tagblatt, but which had already appeared in the Eidgenössische yesterday : Friedrich brought it up to me with great importance—it would interest me, he thought.—

I have received no further letter of congratulation at all, except from Herr Regierungsrath Franz Müller of Weimar, but another surprise in the garden, and we are quite unable to find out to whom one owes it.   On the morning of my birthday an extremely choice rose-bed was planted in the garden ; indeed, it was already there at 6 o'clock, when Friedrich got up.   At first we believed

Lorck had received orders for it ; but then I remembered having never expressed such a wish to the Wesendoncks,— albeit to Herwegh, whom I asked a month ago for his opinion whether it wasn't too late to plant such a bed, whereon I let the subject drop. Friedrich now declares he knows for absolutely certain that Lorck did not lay out the bed, neither he nor his men ; what is more, they hadn't any rose-trees of that sort. They are all ticketed and appear to be very expensive, consequently I presume that Fröbel [nurseryman?] supplied them ; and as I also know that last year's cushion was *not* from Wesendonck, I'm half inclined to think some unknown being is making game of me. I really didn't want to tell you of it till I found a clue ; so—don't get angry over it, old dog in the manger !

Concerning the strawberries, I have to tell you that they really have *all* come to flower. So soon as Lisette finds some good asparagus, you shall have it sent you. Everything else is in order, only Friedrich is grumbling about the snails. I haven't been to town yet, to see after the ring.

My little Tausig (Tausendsappermenter) played to us magnificently yesterday ; almost a second Bülow. He gives me great delight, affording me distraction, entertainment, and incentive. To-day, too, I have again been able to compose well.—

There now ! But how goes it with yourself ? Slowly —very gradually ! I know all that : but only *so* can you be re-established in the end. Simply *force* yourself to repose and indifference ! Rest assured it will work ; I know it from my own experience. Often, if I have a fit of the blues, I suddenly tell myself : " But if that really is the case, cannot you prevail against it by sheer composure?" So much will then pass over one with no particular impression, and finally one sees it wouldn't really have been worth the while, and everything would only have worsened, if one had flown into a passion. How should I have the heart left for any work you please, for instance, if I dwelt on nothing but its future bad performances?—

Apropos, Tichatscheck has sung Tannhäuser at Berlin with éclat ; consequently there will be good tantièmes in July. We can do with them !

I'm expecting news from you tomorrow, and hope for thorough good ones. The doctor has firm trust ; so you must let him prove it !

Fipps was quite haughty when he got home, and wouldn't deign a glance at Friedrich, so that the latter felt quite hurt. Last evening, when there was company, however, he thawed. Unfortunately I cannot take long walks with him in this bad weather.—

Now be right good and patient. My heart has really great misgivings lest you should suddenly lose patience and do yourself some injury through fretting. Simply remember what a good husband you have ! So farewell ; be good—and sleep a lot !

Thy out and out

GOOD MAN.

127.

ZURICH, 28. *May* 1858.

DEAR MINNA,

I really would have gladly come to you to-day, if a conveyance could have been anyhow arranged. So I am waiting till 8 days hence, from which time forward I shall be able to visit you regularly once a week and fetch myself good evidence of your performance.—

In place of your broken ring I am sending you to-day a whole it's to be hoped will wear better than the old one, which was rather flimsy stuff. You shall have that back as well, though.—

I should have dined with the Wesendoncks at Huber's to-morrow, but had already declined for the Willes. This evening I'm expecting Herwegh and Semper here; let us hope I shall find the bottle of rum. Nothing has occurred since yesterday; everything is quiet and in order. It is only with great emotion that I watch the garden, since you cannot enjoy it in its waxing beauty. Friedrich is exemplary in his care; he has finished sowing the lawn all alone, as the gardener never came; whilst everything is nicely planted, and transplanted.

The house is quite in order otherwise. When I cast my eye around, I really must rejoice in the beautiful Asyl prepared us. It is and will be saved to us; we have to do with pure and noble people. Yet the winter shall be lightened for you, even next one; in any case we'll pass it somewhere that offers more distraction. About that in due time!—

For to-day, all that's best and fairest! and the heartiest wishes for your mending!

Thy
R.

128.

ZURICH, Friday, 28. May 1858.

This moment I've received your letter, dear Minna, and am much rejoiced at its good humour, which leads me to infer good health. I meant to surprise you Sunday morning—weather favouring—but if you will and can come yourself, the better shall I be pleased; for even in bad weather—of which there's a prospect—it is easier to rub on here than at Brestenberg. So, on the chance of your really executing your proposal, I shall write you nothing more to-day ; neither will I despatch your finished ring—as I should otherwise have done—but simply beg you to leave Wildegg by the 1 o'clock train tomorrow, Saturday, when you will get here exactly at dinner-time, and all needful cleaning up here can also be taken in hand in the morning.   Asparagus has been sent off to you already, but I shall see to your finding some here as well. —That you may get these lines to-day itself, I must hurry Friedrich to the post ; therefore nothing beyond—Come if you can, and it will greatly delight me to shew you everything in good condition.

Auf Wiedersehen !

Thy
RICHARD.

129.

ZURICH, Sunday evening, 30. May 1858.

DEAR MINNA,

Fear nothing !   Be calm !   I'm greatly suffering ; yet you touched me greatly [see pp. 340-1].   Perhaps everything will so take shape that we can quietly await the amnesty.   Even a temporary separation will scarcely be needed.   Let your only care be for your health ; if you recover that, and tranquillity of mind, you will alleviate this time of trial for us.

It will be the last ; and perhaps enduring calm will light the evening of our life.   In the worst extremity God helps, if the heart is pure and kind !—

Thy
RICHARD.

130.

GOOD MINNA,

I have had a lovely night, peaceful, refreshing sleep ; what a blessing ! How I wish it were bestowed on you again in ample measure !—So I feel tranquil again, clear and strengthened. The sight of our beautiful garden, of this agreeable Asyl, affects me ; your having suddenly lost all taste for it yourself, after that grievous night, has pained me. Reflect what sufferings *I* had undergone before ; I who, to spare you for the present, during your cure, had had the garden tended ! Yet—I am calm and collected. We will consider nothing altogether settled yet ; God will help to make our hearts clear and composed ; and out of the heart come all things, good and evil. Take courage ; and whatever may some day prove inevitable, forget in no ordeal still haply in store for you that for you there beats a good, a grateful, and a loving heart in mine. Be just, and acknowledge that in this truly awful time—for me as well—my every action has been finally dictated by that heart. What I have suffered, moreover, you simply may measure by this : not only have I felt my own, but fellow-felt the sufferings of others also. Consequently I may regard myself as greatly chastened, and now, after being unable as yet to spare you many a hard word the last time, my calm is returning to me fairer than before, and I can be nothing but kind. A great seriousness has come over me, however, and will abide with me for good. Win you this noble seriousness, which constitutes true human dignity, and we shall easily agree at all points. In that case, if I may argue from my inner feelings, I hope for a benignant issue to whatever trials may be still appointed us. To begin with,

though, it remains unalterably fixed [between us *] that
I give up all personal intercourse with our neighbours ;
only thus has it become possible for me to retain the Asyl
for us till the fitting time.   In the long run that will and
must seem best to all concerned.

Now, best greetings !   May these few lines of mine
have helped to calm you !

Farewell, behave well !   I shall visit you very soon.

Thy

R.

131.

ZURICH, *Monday,* 31. *May* 1858.   *Evening.*

Can you explain to me, dear Mutz, the meaning of
this telegram I have just received from Dresden ?   I cannot make it out, and don't know how to answer it ; so I
presume you must have written to Frau Tichatscheck and
invited them.   Please help me out of the dilemma.   It
looks as if we had been expecting the Tichatschecks
shortly, and the wife would like to know if she may come
alone.—Please answer me at once, if you know about it.

And be plucky and calm !

Thy

RICHARD.

132.

ZURICH, *Thursday* 3. *June* 1858.

Dear Child, you haven't quite correctly understood
and estimated the seriousness of my communications ; but
doubtless that is not given to you yet, and in any case it
alters nothing in myself and course of action.   So abide

---

* " To pacify her, at last I broke off all association with our neighbours
during that time "—to sister Clara next August : see Introduction to
R. Wagner to M. Wesendonck ; see also letter 132 below.—Tr.

by the latter, and infer my sentiments from that; you will never have to complain of it. So—now above all, and for ever, Peace! No more brooding; everything is above-board, and the resolution, ay, the hope stands fast, that all may take a smooth and favourable turn. So—no more about it now!—

The Dresden telegram explained itself the following day—in the evening. Frau Tichatscheck came to visit us with her daughter (on an excursion from Soden, where the daughter is taking baths); she was very distressed not to find you, as the telegram, about which I had to tell her at once, called her back in hot haste. After passing the evening at our house with Müller, she travelled back at 5 next morning.—Tichatscheck (as you will see from the enclosed playbill) sang in Tannhäuser at Berlin a second time, by desire; so—good receipts!— I shall bring you a little souvenir she left behind for you.—

Otherwise nothing has happened. The Wesendoncks arrived the evening before last. He called upon me yesterday and invited me to tea; whereon I very delicately explained to him in writing that we would remain on friendly terms for the future, but without personal intercourse. Let it stop at that, and I most earnestly beg you to abstain from *any* kind of interference : which would only have results I should be obliged to regard as a fresh breach of your trust! This must be entirely my affair; and I hope you will obey me this time at least. Here it is no question of strength or weakness upon my side, but solely of this : that it has appeared to me the sole resource for avoiding possible unpleasantnesses, provided we mean to *remain* here.—

I have been invited with Tausig to Wille's to-day.

Baumgartner came yesterday afternoon, and opened his mouth to his ears at Tausig's piano-playing.—

Well—we've weather now and no mistake ; it's bright and hot, and you'll enjoy the water. Only see to going nicely through your cure again : true, it can't do every-thing, and the mind must help ; but the mind becomes less irritable when bodily comfort increases. The one must help the other, and just as the very best mental distraction would have done you no permanent good if the basis of bodily health were not first re-established, so I hope that both may march hand in hand henceforward to the advancement of your well-being.

I'll hunt for the key. Sunday—for certain, I think— we shall see one another again. Farewell, and—firmly rely on   Thy

good HUSBAND !

I have only just received your last letter ; so the Immediate didn't work ! You are enlightened now, tho'. I will tell you more by mouth about the unlucky visit [Frau T.'s].—Sleep well—and accept best remembrances from all the household.—

133.

Wednesday,
(the such and such of June)
(: ZURICH, 9. *June* 1858 :)

Dearest Mutz, I have nothing at all to write to you, and really am in a fix about it, as you will be expecting a letter from me all the same. No letter for me, no tidings, no occurrence, no call ; only bad nights, as I have a sort of crisis again, and am constantly driven from bed and sleep for several hours, when I make studies of dawn effects and other fine things of the kind. In the daytime I am not of much use then, nor in the best of humour; which is a hindrance to my work in particular. Thus each has his torment, though mine is transient this time, and it becomes me ill to vent my lamentations on you poor tormented woman. For that I surely might have awaited news from yourself; for state-of-health is indeed the supreme question with you now, and everything depends on how it promises. Is it progressing a little? Have you anything satisfactory to tell me?

My God, I'm really growing somewhat impatient myself, though I was fully prepared for a lingering cure. However, once you've recovered your equilibrium after its last disturbance, I believe a marked improvement will soon appear. Good nights; that is almost the chief point!—Well, Fipsel is helping you again now; I miss him very much again myself.—

Stay, tho', a letter: Bülow has written—about the arrangements [*Iphig.* and *Tristan*] and accepted once more with his wife for the end of July. That fits in quite well, and the agreeable distraction of having the house a bit full will serve you very happily as after-cure. *Tausig* is gradually worming his way into my heart; small bad habits apart, he really is a very intelligent, sympathetic and good-hearted youngster; he seems much attached to me, and often surprises me with a torrent of thanks for my kindness to him. So he forms a very agreeable little companion to me and blues-conductor. Owing to the great heat in his room, he often works in yours beneath me now, where he makes his nest from 12 o'clock without a sound. I hunted out your mantilla and ribbon to-day, and have given them to Friedrich for despatch to you. On the other hand, despite the most diligent search I've been unable to find the lemonade extract and my small umbrella.

That must suffice you for this time ; I kept thinking something might occur, to make this letter presentable—but nothing has chosen to come ; so please put up with it.

Be thoroughly industrious with your cure ; be at rest *within* your heart, and then the heart itself will soon become more restful.   Salute the Doctor, and tell him that I hope to find you quite phlegmatic when next I come.

Farewell and send fine tidings soon to   Thy

good

HUSBAND.

I have had strawberries for the first time to-day ; only a few, though.   So soon as there are many, you shall get some too.—

The Grand Duke of Baden is winning my heart more and more ; he has actually dismissed the *Intendant*, so I read, and Devrient accordingly remains.

134.

ZURICH, *Friday*, 11. *June* 1858.

My poor Mutz, only be calm and don't torment yourself with fancied evils !   Be gentle, kind and patient ; you can't believe what power it gives you over me !   Your tears and laments that last night in our house touched me more than any other argument.   Even before that, however, I had nothing hostile to you in my mind with my plan for the winter ; I even believed it must do you good to divert yourself in Germany, whereas this retirement here, in present circumstances, could bring you nothing but continual fret and worry.   Neither did I consider Paris a happy thought for both of us, under straitened conditions—if I produced nothing of mine there—and since you speak no French. However, I've told you that already ; so enough of it here ! Now I know how differently you regard all that, rest assured I shan't urge you to anything you do not like, or in which you don't concur with me. Do let that suffice you !— I am not going to turn you adrift, please don't think that !—I am entire master of my actions ; whether I go or stay, depends upon myself alone. She whom you hate so wishes nothing more than that I should retain this pretty Asyl, even if she never sees or has any other intercourse with me ; the only condition, upon the other hand, on which I deem it possible to remain here and wait for my amnesty. Just comprehend, then, with *whom* you have to do ! In truth—as I told you before—by kindness, gentleness and magnanimity, you might have contributed much to making everything easier and more bearable here. It was not given to you then, and I forgive you ; but please reflect that only *so* can you move me to all that is good, just as only *so* can things in general take a supportable shape in the future. I feel sure it will dawn on you in time, how sound is my advice to you, and how well it would have been if an experienced and sympathetic feminine friend had stood at your side from the first.—I simply tell you this for your encouragement, to corroborate you in your present milder view of things, and at the same time to shew how you thereby prevail over me.—

So do not fret about your journey, either, any more ; everything in that respect shall depend entirely on yourself, and I demand nothing of you, just as I likewise have made no fixed plans for myself.—

Tranquilly wait for the end of your cure : I do not expect a sudden total change in your condition ; if only the foundation be laid for a gradual improvement,— and you are now on the high road to that.—Your body, which has been quite undermined by the mass of opium and physic, must first renew itself completely ; you must get fresh blood and nerves, and that is not done so quickly. Luckily you haven't fallen back on the old treatment, and so are gradually regaining your former strength ; whatever you do, tho', you must hold any excitement aloof with all your energy, and to that end—believe me, good Minna—you must also hold your heart itself in rein ; in short, become—what I call sensible, realise your position, and remember how entirely different your part in life would be if we had children, perhaps even grand-children. Plainly imagine yourself in that position, and you will soon find that true repose and dignity which will benefit you so much. Be at ease about myself, however : no doubt you can't quite look into the bottom of my nature, but—believe me—I am not as every person, but have something higher in me whereon I live and feed, and do not need the common, trivial sustenance and distraction of the world !—

The quartettists are to come to me tomorrow evening. I shall coach them nicely up, and when the Bülows are here I'll give you all a real surprise. I shall visit you also next week ; until then just keep restful and steady. My complaint, which is never more than periodic, has abated somewhat ; I'm hard at work again, and should dearly like to set something in front of me, for which it is time. About the hip-baths another day. Farewell for to-day. Don't touch on the subject discussed any further, if you can help it, but pluck up courage and assurance !

Thy
RICHARD.

135.

DEAREST MINNA,

Your answer to me is a pack of nonsense : perhaps I ought to have been prepared for it and rather not have written you my letter. Let it pacify you if I give you my word that you haven't understood me correctly, but much too materially. Grant Heaven that this may have an end now ; really it gives me no pleasure, and my only consolation is the consciousness of having meant well and intended better.—

So the quartet was here last evening. The fellows scraped and squeaked so hideously again, that Tausig bitterly bewailed me. Nevertheless I'll have another try next week.—

Härtels have sent me 25 louis d'or for the Iphigenia [revision] ; consequently we're a little secured again on that side too.—

I am scrambling you these lines after work and before dinner ; after dinner I can never bring it off. I have nothing else to tell you ; my health is going better again. I'll have another hunt for the umbrella ; the citric acid can't be found.

The *sly elephant*—see enclosure—will delight you as much as it delighted *me.*—Tell the doctor, If you don't sleep well soon, I shall turn abusive, but in any case I mean to contribute to it by never writing seriously to you again, as it always seems to cause you great confusion.

Adieu for to-day, silly Mutz ! We shall see one another this week ; may I find you quite corpulent then, as the labourer found it, and I shall rejoice myself thin !

Thy

good old MAN.

136.

ZURICH, *Wednesday*, 16. *June* 1858.

DEAR MINNA,

The Grand Duke and Grand Duchess of Weimar, who have been at a Savoy spa until now, invite me to a rendezvous at Lucerne for this day week. We'll see if anything may result from this personal acquaintance, and consequently I shall go. But I also intend to combine it with my next visit to yourself, as I otherwise should have to leave my work too quickly in succession, which would much disturb me—now that I am thoroughly into it and should like to get something soon finished. So you will be relieved of my presence till a week from tomorrow, when I shall come to you straight from Lucerne—viâ Aarau—and tell you all fresh what I've contrived with the Grand Ducals. You agree to that, I suppose, and won't get any thoughts into your head ? After the longer parting, I hope to find you've got a good step forward.

I learnt very sad news from the papers yesterday through Heim. Tichatscheck is really dangerously ill : at least, he overtaxed himself and had a hæmorrhage after his return to Dresden from Berlin ; scarcely recovered a little from that, he attended rehearsals—apparently for Tannhäuser—and came by inflammation of the spinal cord, which naturally is a matter of life or death : good God, the suddenness of it ! Certainly there still is hope, with his good constitution, but he naturally will have to be very careful for a long time in any event ; so it's all up with Rienzi again ! !—

And now for something passable. The Basle theatre has just been taken over by a local heir to a fortune, named Neukirch, who has got it into his head to produce *Lohengrin* there with myself, cost him what it may. He is afraid of no expense, an enthusiast, and absolutely bent upon the reputation of having been the first through whom I ever heard my opera. Orchestra, scenery, singers— everything as I decide. Well, that's a case for biding, not thrusting out one's horns, especially as I'm thinking of the possibility of winning this rich enthusiast for the Strassburg undertaking [*Tristan*] in case my amnesty itself hangs fire beyond the year.—

Now you have had all of my news. Digest them well ; they're rather mixed.—

Four days ago—to the alarm of little Tausig—I went up the Uetli, and haven't regained proper use of my shanks even yet. Everything else here goes passably, quiet and lonely. Take care you're able to return soon, or the garden will all blossom away from you with this heat. You shall have strawberries in a day* or two ; yesterday I had green peas.

Now farewell, and send consoling tidings to

Thy

Grand Ducal

GUEST.

137.

ZURICH, *Sunday*, 20. *June* 1858.

GOOD MINNA,

I must hunt out a sheet of pink paper to-day, although I'm so full of affairs that I don't know whether I am standing on my head or my heels. Fresh proofs arrived from Härtels yesterday [*Tristan* full score, act i] and gave me great delight, since it all looks so nice now it's engraved. To-day—all manner of agreeable novelties. In the first place a telegram from—Tichatscheck : " Sunday. Tannhäuser to-day. Have slowly recovered.

Three conscientious band rehearsals held ; performance will go admirably. Johanna—Elisabeth.'' Could I do anything else than let it cost me a twenty-franc piece ? I telegraphed back my thanks, delight and greetings.

Then came an order for Lohengrin from Düsseldorf, which doesn't precisely count for much, but still is another beginning.

And then a letter from Hülsen, about Lohengrin for Berlin. I must see to extracting another advance from him ; when I shall create no further difficulties. Who knows if the King will not abdicate for good by the commencement of winter?—folk say October—when I shall apply to the young Prince of Prussia to let me come there. If that doesn't succeed, why, I must leave it in the lap of Fate once more.

I should soon be getting an answer to my demand from Vienna also.

See now, that really looks a trifle promising. I mean to have a serious talk with the Grand Ducals about Berlin as well.—

The only thing that lacks now, is my having a passably healthy wife at home again. How stands my hope of that, Mutz ? You, lucky soul, have Fipps at least ; I've absolutely nothing fondling here. Is he helping you to sleep well now ? The heat has somewhat diminished, you know, and I'm in hopes you'll shortly send me joyful tidings. Does the porter go on delivering you my greetings from the station ? All our numerous grand pianos are newly tuned, and when you come home I expect to hear you brilliantly extemporising every morning ; anyhow you will be able to help in my composing now.

Friedrich and Lisette are quite despairing of your return ; it takes me all my time consoling them. By the way, Lisette says you've made a mistake about her wages : you hadn't engaged her at 100 *fr.*, but at 130 *fr.* yearly ; if that is so, of course I must pay her the additional 7½ *fr.* for the quarter. That can soon be set straight ; but money keeps flying away, and it's a good job fresh prospects are shewing. They will be giving Rienzi, too, at Dresden after all ; for Tichatscheck's illness, though serious, doesn't appear to have really been dangerous. What a man he is ! not the Devil's strength itself can lay him low ! I hope it will be the same with you, and in spite of all your present sufferings you'll bonnily pull round again and duly help me celebrate my resurrection in Germany. The giving of my operas again at Dresden is really a very good thing, and bound to contribute in the long run to my amnesty ; one can hardly conceive otherwise.

Well, we shall see. In any case to-day's telegram was highly momentous to me, and my answer will give the good fellow great joy. Perhaps he is receiving it this very instant.—

It is Sunday to-day—a beastly day. I think of driving, swimming, or wading out to Wille's. Strictly, I ought to have gone to Sulzer again ; but it gives me the horrors.

I shall write you full particulars of my Lucerne journey later, and beg you to send the carriage to the station on Thursday.

God preserve you, good old Wife ! Be of good cheer, hold me dear, and build on

Thy

good old

HUSBAND.

138.

ZURICH, *Monday early,* 28. *June* 1858.

MY GOOD MUTZ,

I really meant to write you yesterday, but couldn't get to it although I was invited nowhere. The consequence, however, is that I have something extra good to tell you this morning. For yesterday afternoon I received a call from the Vienna Kapellmeister *Esser*, who had been expressly sent by the management to arrive at an agreement with me concerning Lohengrin and go through the opera itself with me at the piano, that I might instruct him in my minutest intentions. And all the way from Vienna!—That really is deserving of all honour, and [Director] *Eckert* has risen mightily in my esteem ; it is a truly signal and handsome distinction, such as I had never yet been treated to. The management at the same time propounded its counter-proposals : Tantième is impossible, since the Kärnthnerthor theatre is too small, has no high prices, and in the very best event can only take 800 gulden [a night], from which the company's enormous salaries must be deducted ; not before a new big theatre is built, can the tantième system be expedient.—So they asked me to accept 1000 gulden down for the first 20 performances, another 500 gulden after the 20th, and the same after the 30th ; more they could not offer me, in view of the present insignificant takings, and anything nearly approaching this had never yet been done. I considered that quite reasonable, and was particularly delighted at their having sent me their Kapellmeister express ; so I signed the contract, and immediately received from Esser my 1000 gulden cash. There's Sunday trading for you ! We went through the first act the same evening ; this morning the second is to take its turn, and the third this evening. His dinner he's to take with me, this *Esser*, who let us hope is no *Fresser*.*—

One thing is certain : the Viennese production may, indeed must prove excellent. They really have the best singers there ; *every* part can be almost perfectly cast ; and since the Kapellmeister also promises so well, I'm looking forward to Vienna very much, and only wish I could be there.—From the accompanying you will see that the Kaiser of Austria is also said to have intervened in my favour at Dresden ; it's very possible, and in that case I owe it to the Grand Duke of Weimar, who was at Vienna quite recently and must have tackled the Emperor there. How it stands with King Johann, on the contrary, you will likewise gather from this notice ; not a bad joke, forsooth, for me to submit to being tried and condemned at Dresden first ! However, the affair is bound to take a turn now. True, I have had no further news from Dresden, neither from Tichatscheck nor from Fischer ; but Tausig's father, who had just been there, has written his son that it [*Tannhäuser* revival] was something extraordinary, unprecedented, the enthusiasm not to be described.—

I have written my political epistle to Berlin as well. There the scenery and horses will have to do the trick : the singers are too miserable, so that I should be unable to do much with them myself. Lucky, on the contrary, that I may expect such gratification from Vienna.—But if Hülsen also forwards that advance, we shall be nice and straight again for once, and I shall pay off all remaining debts, furniture, shoemaker, bookbinder, and so on. Heim, too, can promptly have his money back, and we shall have enough left to wait for the future in safety.

* *Esser* = " eater," *Fresser* = " glutton."—Tr.

With such good prospects, then, the only thing still lacking is that my poor dear Mutz should soon feel better, and return to house and garden with firm trust in her further convalescence. Mind you employ the brief remaining time well, however long it seems to you. You're in a good way now, I convinced myself of that on the last occasion, to my great relief ; only pluck up heart and confidence in your improvement, then it can't be long deferred. If you don't come soon, the birds will hatch everything away from us ; another white-throat has built her nest in the vine under my balcony ; ay—think of it !—one has even built and laid eggs in your apple-shaker. The white-throat in the rose-bush has made great friends with me already ; she is brooding, and no longer flies off when I pass, but just peeps out complacently as if to say, You'll not molest me, will you ?—Here in my room, tho', I have a blue-bottle that rinses its mouth out ; at least it sounds so : surely I am not to put up with that ?—

I have to pay 1 *fr*. 80 *c*. for chickens to-day ; isn't it scandalous ? But that comes of having visitors from Vienna !

Now farewell ; be of good courage ; have trust ! Everything is straightening, and will straighten still better and better. Adieu, you good Minna !

Thy
RICHARD.

139.

ZURICH, Friday, 9. July 1858.

DEAREST MINNA,

But tell me, why don't *you* write to *me*, then ? Surely there is more of importance to tell me about yourself and progress with your cure, than I can tell you when simply nothing is happening to me ! However, I have been daily expecting a line from the Bülows, concerning whom I had heard through Herwegh that they intended getting here as early as the 10th, which put me on tenterhooks ; whereas they haven't written to this day, and if they did not first announce *to me* their advent, I should really think it somewhat too ill-mannered. Consequently I suppose they are coming at the time originally fixed ; in which I am supported by the latest tidings, that B. has engaged himself for several soirées at Baden-Baden. But it has kept me in suspense from day to day, since—if they had been coming earlier— I shouldn't have known whether I ought not to fetch you earlier myself. Moreover, absolutely nothing has occurred, and I'm living with Karlchen here as forsaken as if in an enchanted castle. O yes, one thing : Tausig's papa surprised us by arriving yesterday ; a nervous little manikin, who will probably depart again tomorrow.—

I have settled everything quite capitally with Frau Ochsner ; they hadn't really noticed that one good washstand, whereas the night-stand was already gone ; so I agreed to accept 55 *fr.* for the things returned, instead of 15 *fr.*, which is quite another thing. She will also make good to you the cover that has disappeared, if you will only tell her what you claim as compensation.—

The first tantième account from Berlin has come, 255 thaler ; but no answer from Hülsen as yet about the advance—which rather annoys me. All I hear, is that Hülsen wishes to resign, and had an audience lately of the Prince of Prussia, who insisted on retaining him, however. Something appears to be going on there.

There you have all my news, which no doubt won't seem peculiarly important to you. I shall fetch you

Thursday morning, then ; I have already spoken to Furrer himself. Your return really eases my mind in every respect, for thus much is certain : the cure is *greatly* pulling you down now, as I judge from the fatigue you complain of. Remember, however, what I told you beforehand : that one token of the efficacy of the cure would be a feeling of tiredness and bruisedness in your limbs ; it really is a proof that the great excitability of your nerves is laid : I feel it every time when rest at last returns—especially through sleep—after any commotion. So don't be concerned about it ; it only proves for certain that the time has come when you require a *rest*, and for that very reason it is well that the exertions of the cure are drawing to an end. Be equally unconcerned for your repose, under every aspect, after your return ; here nothing reigns but calm, and any further agitation is unthinkable. But you will soon convince yourself of that ; perhaps it will be *too* quiet for you !—

I intend to make you well and comfortable ; I mean it—and all accordingly is well ! Whatever may be agreeable to you, you shall find ; only you also must take proper care of yourself. Frau Schürli is working day and night at your clothes, and you will be pleased—I hope—with the other presents ; I have been fairly particular with their choice, only that choice itself is not particularly great.—I will also see to the rug and napkin-ring being quite according to your wish ; so what more would you have ?—

Lisette is scrubbing and scouring, polishing and sweeping. What more would you have ?

Friedrich is plucking the tiniest weed from the path, and toiling away left and right. Both are looking forward to Thursday. What more would you have ?

And your good husband ? ?

He would have——repose ! repose ! ! exactly what you want yourself. So come, be heartily welcome, and— contentment no doubt will soon appear.—

Farewell for to-day. Write about your condition ; slacken the cure, and prepare for a good rest.

From his heart

Thy dear HUSBAND.

140.

ZURICH, *Saturday,* 10. *July* 1858.

DEAR MINNA,

Pardon ! I had really won an easier mind about yourself, than you had trust in me. I did not believe the brief postponement of a letter from me—now—would plunge you at once in disquiet again. I see I was mistaken, and unfortunately recognise that your idea of me is still the prey of every wind that blows. Well, I never thought I had deserved that now, but, relying on your trust in me, for once I deferred writing you for 2 days, simply because I had nothing to write and deemed mere protestations of my own reliability superfluous. Moreover, I really was prevented at the time when I usually write, namely between work and dinner, as I had to go to town twice over to attend to presents for yourself. I could willingly forgive your little plaguing of me thus ; only your not ceasing to torment yourself as well quite makes me sad, for I hardly see *how* it will stand in my power to reassure you in the long run. But enough of that now !—

I am writing these lines on the eve of X's [Tichatschek's] expected arrival. Touching this visit, I may tell you very candidly that I would rather have seen it omitted. Many people are fond of me whose affection I am unable to return, and what I have to say to him is so soon exhausted that his daily companionship may become fairly trying to me. This woman's-brawl, moreover, has disgusted me in the last degree, and I should almost have preferred your having passed such a scandal by more quietly yourself ; knowing you were at a cure, the wife would have done better to spare you such muck. I hate this whole common pack, one as much as another, for they're all of a muchness. In my retirement I have long since found uplifting over such vulgarities, and any dragging of me down into that odious stew affronts me past all measure. I wish everyone of that sort would only leave me alone.—

The B[ülow] also writes me to-day that they were just starting from Berlin, but not when they'll arrive at Zurich ; I presume they'll make a stay at Baden-Baden first.—

Now, my good Mutz, do drum it into your head that the expected visits are not to upset you in any way. Only let *me* provide, and I'll try and keep everything off your shoulders. Should I remark that a visitor isn't *doing you good*, I'll bundle off the lot forthwith, and take a proper pleasure-trip with you instead. But—don't let that alarm you either ; I mean merely what I say, and have my eye on *nothing* save your quiet, your recovery. So let us hope for the best !

Whether I shall pay you another visit first with X, I must leave unsettled. On the contrary, I don't think of detaining him, and the sooner I am rid of him, the better I shall be pleased. I tell you candidly, I should prefer to come comfortably alone to you on Thursday with the big carriage, and hope it may be so. Pull yourself together, then ; anticipate nothing but what is good and pleasant. I am looking after you ; so put your trust in me, and don't let yourself be bent by every passing breeze, do you hear?—

So—to our speedy reunion ! Before then you shall have had further news from me, especially concerning X.

Farewell, and prove yourself reliant and reliable to me !

Thy

RICHARD.

141.

ZURICH, *Tuesday*, 13. *July* 1858.

So I'm writing you for the last time, dear Minna, to-day. From your yesterday's letter I reaped at least the boon of reassuring news about yourself and your condition. It was needed ; for I have been and am greatly fatigued. Imagine it, on Sunday came *Niemann* besides, and indeed with his fiancée, the famous *Seebach.* They spent Sunday evening here, when I read aloud, and the whole of Monday, when *I* had to keep at it of course, as these people will hear of nothing but myself and my new works. Early this morning the Niemanns departed. By all means he is just born for Siegfried ; yet—I have no more hope of anything, and all I know for certain is the unheard-of exertions I'm always strictly squandering.

But on all that by mouth the day after tomorrow. Most likely X will come with me, though I gladly would leave him at home ; there really will not even be convenient room in the carriage. We'll see.—

Very well, no rug. Instead a very beautiful cigar-box at 30 *fr.*, and a napkin-ring at 16 *fr.* ; nearly 50 *fr.* together. That is neither too much nor too little. [Present for the Brestenberg doctor ?]

To-day holds out a prospect of fine weather ; the barometer is also standing high : accordingly the hope that you will make a thoroughly cheerful re-entry here. I expect to arrive by 11 at latest, and hope we shall be home by 7. Now shew that you understand the making of a proper cure ; may God give his blessing ! I'm so run down to-day, that I have sent X out awhile ; Müller, to whom I took him at once, unfortunately is on duty at Küssnacht this week, of all others ; he will drop in for dinner to-day, though. It is getting time you also came yourself ! May the distractions you will find here do you good ! You will also find letters—from Fräulein Schiffener the faithful, and from Clara ; I don't think there's any hurry with them.—

So, a thousand best greetings ; strengthen yourself by good sleep for my coming ; and then be kind and calm toward

Thy

good HUSBAND.

["*Since a month ago, when Minna returned while we had guests in the house, it had to come to a final decision. . . The most unheard-of scenes and tortures never ceased for me, and out of consideration for the one as for the other, I finally had to make up my mind to give up the fair asylum once procured me with such delicate affection*" (*to sister Clara, Aug.* 20). "*However insensately and passionately she behaved in the most delicate situations, I cannot after all be really wroth with her. Everyone suffers in his own way, and she suffers—in hers ; but she suffers, and did suffer most acutely. Only think of a heart continually beating as never with an ordinary person save in instant terror of death ; and added to it, almost total sleeplessness for a whole year ! It is impossible to make anyone who suffers such agonies responsible for what is done in semi-mania. But it had at last become unbearable for us to be together. To be able to exist, I was obliged to draw a fresh supply of strength from solitude ; and Minna, too, I knew that change and possible diversion must do her good*" (*to sister Cäcilie next January*). See Life *vi, etc., etc.—Tr.*]

142.

GENEVA, 19. *August* 1858.

MY GOOD MINNA,

I have just received your telegram of to-day, and at once fulfil your wish that I should write to you.

O my God ! had I only the power to let you look into my inner heart and clearly see my sufferings and battlings of this year to win repose for my life-task ! In vain : all stormed and tossed around me, all passion and blind rage ; and whatever I laboriously built up to safeguard peace and quietness, came toppling down again.—You, my dear child, can make light of all that : you help yourself out with reproaches, perceive none but your own misfortune. I am juster : I lay reproaches on no one, nor—of a truth —on yourself. Much was required of you, and in your terribly tormented state of health, *too* much. So let us part in peace and reconciliation now, each to go his own way for a season, to win composure and fresh mustering of strength. For my own part, solitude, removal from all company, is now an indispensable condition of my life ; the dearest society, even such as we lately had at home [the Bülows], only tortures me.

I am bleeding from many wounds, and heartfelt concern for yourself is not their slightest. Further, I feel the urgent need of winding up a whole life ; I must clear my mind on much that has passionately moved me in this latter time, and above all I must take undisturbed counsel with myself how to find peace and quiet for completion of those works I still may be appointed to deliver to the world. Where last year I believed that I had found asylum, it is impossible any longer ; years would need to elapse, before everything had cleared and subsided. For the present, I have but one need, as said : to be left alone and long in undisturbed possession of my inner self; any contact from without confuses and confounds afresh. A little outward distraction, such as the visiting of a remarkable city and so forth, can only be a help toward that : I can more easily be alone and without company there ; whereas it would have been impossible in the long run where we were last. Thus I hope for—inner convalescence and emancipation ; and once the mood for work returns to me, I shall be rescued, since my solace in this life *can* only flow from my own inner being.

Lay this to heart, my dear Minna, and if you wish to support me in my necessary and salutary resolve, please do not make my heart too heavy through your cries and lamentations. I know you are more dependent upon what comes to you from without, so to speak, and consequently more a plaything of the chance and change of outward fortunes ; therefore you have a very hard time with me, who am often so indifferent and callous to life's outward relations : but do obey me now, and hope with me for improvement in your state of suffering by the thorough change of scene which stands before you. It is natural that you should refuse to believe it at present, but I know better, and all who have the least experience of such a thing know that your stay in Germany, the renewal of old acquaintanceships, the distractions and art-enjoyments now in store for you, will have a more beneficial effect on you than anything else conceivable. For this reason, too, I can now depart from you with a grain of comfort : *I know* I shall receive good and better news from you in a little while. Any other expedient would have proved inadequate ; a radical step such as this had to be taken perforce. So may God bless you, my good old Minna ! Be strong and win self-control ; bear this trial nobly and as befits the character of Woman ! Thus shall we be able soon, I hope, to send one another good news of our inner condition.

Let us patiently leave the rest to Fate ; if we only can rescue our inner peace, the world without will also shape itself quite peaceably. —

And now I beg you once more, shorten this worst hour of yours as much as possible ; only with great grief can I think of you as still within those walls which saw us at the last so frequently in passionate dissension, and I therefore also was so glad to quit. Set forth as soon as possible.

As to my own farther journey, I can't well settle anything as yet. The great heat is against one's going straight to Italy, where I should like to be soon, however, to find the point to fix myself as speedily as possible and get to work. I intend waiting for Ritter's opinion. Meanwhile, I have letters to write, proofs to correct, and a copy of my text to see to ; which gives me a certain amount of occupation. I should be unable to tax myself much just yet, there's an aching weight in all my limbs ; but—rest will come ! Ah, if you would only help me to it also ! You can, if you will write me shortly with a little self-control, and tell me you are on the road I deem so needful and alone essential now for your inner recovery. Believe my word, dear Minna, had I not been inwardly convinced that the decision I have had to come to will be wholesome and beneficial to yourself as well, I gladly would have hit upon some other. But everything had been exhausted, we were wearing each other away, and a break was obliged to be made for its promise of thorough healing and improvement. If you are not totally unlike myself, you must also come to feel that in the end : I cannot help it, only *thus* do I expect good for us both !

And now farewell, you good old Mutz ! Greet Fipsel a thousand times ; I left him to you willingly, although I miss him very much. But—*miss* I must now ! Greet Jacquot too, and tell him good of me. Farewell ; control yourself, and tell me, for my consolation, that you are calmer. Adieu : with God !

Thy
RICHARD.

143.

GENEVA, 25. August 1858.

DEAR MINNA,

I telegraphed to you yesterday that I should be starting for Italy to-day ; that is now about to be executed, and I hope to be already at Venice by Sunday [29th]. In and for itself, my chief desire is to make straight for the spot where I think of settling for some time, arrange myself a tolerable abode, get the piano sent, and find at last a frame of mind for work again. Geneva could in no case have been that spot for long, and Venice principally attracts me through its notoriously being the only city that hasn't the smallest noise of traffic, to which I have become extremely sensitive. Well, you know I was only delaying on account of the heat of the sun ; but Karl Ritter implores me afresh not to make that an obstacle : Venice has an exceptionally healthy climate, he says, and most people go there precisely at this season, etc. That suited me perfectly ; for I couldn't have remained here much longer without setting myself up with piano etc., which I didn't want to do twice over. Now I'm curious to see how this Venice will appeal to me ;

God grant I may find it supportable, for I shouldn't care
to travel farther, and mental repose, such as my work
alone can give me, has become my supreme need.

I have been feeling particularly wretched for some
days past, especially after receiving your letter, which
shewed me that it probably will forever remain impossible
to you to see clearly and correctly. With you, a definite
blame must and should always be borne by a definite
person ; you do not comprehend the nature of things and
Fate, but simply think that if this person or that thing
had never been, all would have happened otherwise.
Upon that I can say nothing more to you ; others must do
so for once : Heaven grant you may find the proper person
to enlighten you. It also is repugnant to me to make a
fresh attempt, and I merely declare once more to you
emphatically that nothing drove me to abandon Zurich beyond the recognised impossibility of continuing in that close
neighbourship. Things could be requested of the husband
by his wife which you and I can request of him no more :
so long as silence reigned between the *four* of us, under
well-understood conditions of propriety, one could jog
along ; but so soon as it had come to speech between the
four of us, that would work no longer. He accepted my
announcement of removal with the greatest friendliness
and gratitude—but he *did* accept it ; and I also was in
honour bound to go, since every other road to a good
understanding shewed itself harder and harder.—But
enough, and already too much ! You'll go fumbling at
this again, I fear, and fail to find your way. Best we
should drop it entirely and each seek to conquer his past
for himself, thus to find for the future the only path that
promises repose and healing !—

Regarding yourself in particular, I abide by it that

you will gradually feel better after your total removal from Zurich ; it will be slow in coming, but come it will. Your heart-complaint is terrible, and I can't tell you how I pity you in these sufferings ; but everybody knows that change of air and surroundings is the first means to improvement. Remember how it is when a certain position in bed begins to irk you : if you remain in it, the oppression increases, and may even become fatal ; but as soon as you change your position, and so bring the blood into proper circulation, it is relieved of a sudden. It is just the same with moral situations ; believe me, and hope for improvement !

By the time I reach Venice I hope to have to address you at Zurich no longer. Therefore as soon as the day of your departure is fixed, write to Venice *poste restante ;* my first letter to you from there will then catch you, I hope, on your birthday in Saxony—at Zwickau, if it must be : against which place I have nothing in particular, though it would have been better if you had gone direct to Dresden, taken a small apartment there, and let N. return awhile—on trial—to leave someone in charge of the animals in the event of your making excursions and visits. But I shall dictate nothing further to you on that head.

What Tichatscheck may have understood when I wrote him we were leaving Zurich, packing up and selling trifles, I cannot comprehend ; he wrote to me as well about the pictures and the Erard. Do you think he isn't quite all there ? I shall answer him as soon as I get his report on Rienzi. Of course you'll take no notice of this stupid query ; I particularly want our departure from Zurich not to bear the look of a breaking up, but simply of a removal with everything kept together.—

Now farewell, my good old Mutz ! Would to God I had been able to provide you with quieter days ! I am very sorry for you, and my compassion is heartfelt and great ; I indeed have a singular life of it : that it brings you so much trouble, I deeply deplore ! But put your best foot forward now : act calmly and with dignity, shew self-command, and soon give me good news of yourself. Farewell ! Bear patiently, and—God be with you !

Thy
RICHARD.

Many kind greetings to Heim : tell him he mustn't be cross with me for throwing so much upon him, and I hope to be able to lighten his load before long. Please also give orders at the Post that newspapers and the like, such as theatrical journals, be either altogether counter-manded or sent to Heim ; in no case forwarded.

Give Friedrich and Lisette hearty greetings too ; say I want them faithfully to help you. O God, to think how everything might have gone better ! It was possible ; but—I won't expostulate. To good Fipsel a thorough good shake of the paw.

Conceive the present feelings of a domesticated, homely man like me ! And yet—it must be so awhile ! Farewell !

The poor bed-clothes I always meet with, pampered mortal, inspire me with the wish that you would send my bed-linen along with that packet of music I asked you for. Please think whether it can be done. The piano mustn't go off before I have obtained a free pass for it at Venice, which I then will send to Heim.

Perhaps the wadded quilt also, and feather-bed. Just as you think.—

(Yet perhaps *not ?*)

144.

LAUSANNE, 26. *August* 1858.

DEAR MINNA,

I am on the road, and can only just manage to write you a couple of lines ; I shall be on Italian soil tomorrow evening. I forgot to tell you yesterday that Tichatscheck had written me he would allow Friedrich 10 thaler travelling-money. What he writes about the pictures etc. is pure nonsense in any case.

—Yesterday I received another letter from Kapellmeister Esser of Vienna, reporting to me on the second representation of Lohengrin already ; he says *Eckert* telegraphed me directly after the first performance. Did you receive that telegram ? I know nothing whatever about it.

And now farewell once more. I am travelling with Ritter alone ; his wife is going to Dresden also for the winter. Farewell ! be calm, and bravely surmount this evil time ! Many best and heartiest greetings !

Thy

RICHARD.

145.

VENICE, 1. *September* 1858.

MY DEAR GOOD OLD MUTZ,

Here I am in Venice ; where are you ? I confidently assume at Zwickau, but my having no tidings at all from you yet makes me very uneasy. After my telegraphing to you from Geneva, couldn't you at least have written me a couple of lines, as I asked, to Venice *poste restante ?* I arrived here the 29th of August, and really hoped to find a letter from you, but have enquired each day in vain. To-day I'm at last getting really alarmed. You have a bad time to surmount now, and certainly for you a very sad one ; I begged of you to shorten it as much as possible, so I still think you must have started on the 29th, since you had that day in remembrance from your [first] arrival in Zurich. God grant I may have a letter from you tomorrow confirming this, and at the same time telling me you have pulled your whole strength together to face everything well. I have nothing fresh to tell you to console and cheer you ; all I can cry to you is, Hope and don't lose heart ! See here, poor Wife, your destiny—which surely should have been appointed you on calmer and more even lines—was linked with the destiny of a man who, much as he also wished for placid happiness himself, yet was appointed to so extraordinary a development in every respect that at last he believes he must even renounce his own wishes, simply to accomplish his life-task. All I now seek is inner self-collection, to be able to complete my works : renown no longer has effect on me ; of succeeding in representing my works [*Ring d. N.*] I even despair : nothing—nothing—but work, the creative act itself, still keeps me alive. It is natural that so extraordinary a destiny should also rouse extraordinary sympathy ; there are many persons who have turned to me with deep and intimate regard. If *you* must suffer for it, those sufferings will some day be accounted to you too, and your reward must be—my prospering, the prospering of my works. Just now, however—let us not be thinking only of the future ; let us try to get over the present, and hope to find rest for ourselves and prepare for one another kindness, reconciliation.—

Allow me not to write you much about Venice to-day ; I'm terribly upset by the journey, and particularly through the search for an abode. Before I've set myself up so well and comfortably as to make it possible to hold out, I cannot recover my senses ; you know how much the dwelling question counts with me, and I *must* aim at staying glued to one spot for the present, to be able to continue my work. Naturally I am living in furnished apartments ; there are no others here. My landlord is an Austrian, who was very happy to give shelter to my famous name. All such lodgings here are in big palaces relinquished by their former patrician owners, and arranged by speculators for letting out to foreigners. But I will write you on all that next time. For to-day only thus much : I hope to hold out at Venice ; really the city is interesting beyond all measure, and the positive still-ness—one never hears a vehicle—quite priceless to me. I am receiving no callers, and hope to live entirely with-drawn upon myself here. For the present I see Karl at dinner every day, for which we have made a restaurant on St. Mark's Square our rendezvous ; should that prove inconvenient to me later on, I can also have meals fetched at home. Things do not really seem dear ; only the lodging is not proportionately cheap. I am just writing to Heim, to send me the piano forthwith ; there will be no imposts to pay on it, were it only because Venice is a free port. No doubt I shan't require the sheets and bedding ; naturally I must content myself with coarser.

Now, my dear Minna, accept my heartfelt and sincere congratulations on your birthday ! Poor Wife, I could have wished you a better ; yet it is some consolation that at least you're spending it with your relations, as 4 years back. That did you then a heap of good ; may it be a comfort to you on this occasion also ! Give them my kindest regards ; divert yourself among them, and en-

deavour to forget as far as possible ! Look up, and hope
that we shall meet again in Germany ere long. I am
sending you a true Venetian present, as souvenir of this
birthday ; I hope it won't arrive too late. So, courage,
composure, regard for your health ! If you want to send
a truly handsome present to me in my banishment, give
me tidings that you are somewhat amusing yourself
and deriving hopes of an improvement in your sufferings.
Farewell ; be a thousand times heartily, heartily greeted !
And greet good Fipps, and eke the silly parrot, *Mr*
Jacquot ! I, on the contrary, am living in a world of
utter strangers ; nothing around me save my manuscripts,
to shew me what I've still to do and—suffer ! You have
taken our home-brownies with you ; look after them,
they're very dear to me as well. Adieu ! Adieu ! Stay
good to me.

Thy
RICHARD.

Here's my address, which you must always get written
in a thoroughly legible hand.

> Herrn *Richard Wagner*,
> *Canale Grande, Palazzo Giustiniani*,
> *Campiello Squillini No.* 3228,
> *in Venedig*.

146.

VENICE, 14. September 1858.

MY POOR DEAR OLD MINNA,

Rest assured that your condition and fate concern me
closely and deeply. Before I got your first *poste restante*
Venice letter (still from Zurich) I was in the most painful
anxiety about you ; how glad I was when I gathered from

that letter that your practical labours and worries were keeping you up! Yes, with true relish I read of your scene with that rascally man-servant, and even your reflections upon certain others ; all this shewed me at least that you were passing through the terrible time of your departure with that strength peculiar to yourself : which is certainly not to say, however, that the vulgarities you encountered on leaving—as you tell me in your last letter—did not revolt and thoroughly ashame me. But who can foresee anything with an individual like this fly-man Furrer ? Others at least remained decent, in the confidence that I should not cheat them. Perhaps it would have been better in many respects, if we had simply closed the house and provisionally left everything in it just as it was. I should then have been able to attend to the packing up etc. later on, and even if I hadn't been so practical as yourself in the sale of various articles, and had lost something over it, yet you would have been spared more drudgery and bother now than the loss would have been worth, and above all there would not have arisen such a fuss as necessarily must come now ; which would also have been much more favourable for my [future] settling down. You will remember, too, I once proposed this to you ; but you preferred getting it all done with at once. As for the chatter among those who have still to present their accounts for the current year, I hope to stop their mouths soon ; now that Rienzi has come out [again] so happily at Dresden (Tichatscheck wrote me he had been called 14 times in one night !), I have no doubt of speedy good receipts [from other theatres], which I already am busy about and soon will place me in the position to wipe off everything. I was just rejoicing that a small increase had befallen your exchequer through the

proceeds from what was sold ; but you must have had
to dip pretty deep into it now, poor woman, and perhaps
even make a hole in the rest ?   Please tell me how much
you have left, and whether you can manage comfortably
till the end of October, when you shall have money again
in any event.   I shall pay that Furrer out for this ; don't
you bother any more about it.

My dear good Minna, when I thus review the uneasy,
almost mournful lot to which you've so long been exposed
by my side and through your union with my own uneasy,
changeful fortunes ; and when I ask myself, What if you
could provide and guarantee the poor sorely-tried woman
for the rest of her life a sure, abiding haven unexposed to
change—it seems to me that I could only do it this way :
that I should beg you to take plenty of time in seeking
out the place of residence most pleasing to you, set yourself
snugly and cosily up there with all our goods and chattels,
and then regard it as your own fixed habitation.   Thither I
would come to you as often as I needed a home ; and for
the rest, quite apart from my personal needs of sojourn, it
would be *your* peaceful nest to which I also could withdraw
at last when all the storms of life were weathered, to find
my lasting rest beneath your care.   In any case that
dwelling-place should remain completely unsubjected to
my fate's vagaries.   I cannot help thinking this arrangement the most sensible, ay, the only one to give you
certainty of permanence.—However, I know that it isn't the
dwelling-place that counts for everything with you either ;
you want to have your husband with you just as constantly : ay, that has been your sole reason for enduring
all life's hardships of the past.   Consequently I neither
can nor will make you this proposal seriously, for I
want to wound you in nothing I can avoid ; you have had

hard enough lines to endure from me, for which I am heartily sorry !

I too, I won't deny it, at bottom am fond of a permanent homestead ; and how to procure it, has been my chief preoccupation of late. Neither can I believe that a strictly vagabond life would suit me in the long run. Our going different ways was really needful for the present, and I haven't a moment's doubt that our passing separation, with the complete change in our position, will have had a truly curative effect on our minds, and also on your health in particular. I made a very lucky choice with Venice : I shall write you circumstantially about my mode of life and installation here next time ; for to-day merely thus much : the singular melancholy-cheerful repose of this place, with the absolute retirement in which I'm able and intend to live here, already begins to strengthen and smooth me out, and in any case I hope to pass the winter here. By the winter's end I definitely hope to finish *Tristan* quite ; till then I shall not stir. But once that's finished, I shall look around a bit to see how the world is standing ; and I hope to find it standing favourably for me. Whatever may be the case with the full amnesty, so much is certain : the Grand Duke of Baden in particular has received from Saxony the assurance that I shall be allowed at any time to come to Germany for a reasonable time for the production of a new work of mine ; Liszt himself writes me so. That would mean the gaining of the most important point already, and the production of Tristan somewhere about next Easter at Carlsruhe in my personal presence would be a certainty. Isn't that already something ? And once I am there for a couple of months (for that's the suggestion) no rational being will doubt but that the rest can be

managed meanwhile ; toward which I even imagine my
personal acquaintance may contribute its share. This,
good Mutz, might have been happening *now*, had I only
got through with the Tristan. But perhaps even the full
amnesty may have arrived by next Easter, for I recently
heard that the Saxon Government harbours a project of
provisionally commencing the amnesty by permitting
fugitives to re-enter any part of Germany with the solitary
exception of Saxony. I no longer have much thought of
Saxony, however, for that country best would suit me
for a lasting foothold where the Court is best disposed
towards me—and this, beyond all doubt, is Baden. This
young Grand Duke is said to be really unceasing in the
most energetic of efforts for me, and it is *he*—not the
Weimar one—who is said to have concerned himself for
me at *Vienna*. With his widely-famed great personal
amiability and staunchness, he attracts me the most ;
whilst worthy Devrient's family would also be very agreeable to me.

See now, good Mutz, that really is a definite prospect,
and surely a great comfort to yourself as well. You thus
may count with certainty on seeing me again next Easter,
and—God willing—we shall then have no difficulty in
also finding the spot where you may plant the abiding
tent of rest for this roaming life of mine.—Very well !
Recreate yourself till then. I have no doubt you will
soon feel better ; rest and retirement will heal your spirit
also, and valiant Tröger's treatment will help you pick
up your health. It is certain that your bodily condition,
as with all nerve-invalids, is very closely connected with
your frame of mind ; once there's a tendency to improvement in the one, it goes hand in glove with the other,
and I am sure of receiving good, comforting reports on

your condition soon. Therefore remain at perfect rest with your relations as long as ever you find yourself comfortable, and don't go travelling before you feel a decided need of distraction, which will itself be a good sign of improvement.—

Touching myself, in my next letter, as said, I shall tell you a lot about my life here. For the present merely this—to complete my Tristan, that's the main thing! With the completion of this work I shall have survived a remarkable period; I foresee the clearness, calm and equanimity, which that will win me.—Farewell. A thousand hearty greetings to good Tröger and your people; squeeze Fipps' dear little paw, and get Jacquot to say:

" yet a good Husband

RICHARD WAGNER."*

147.

VENICE, 28. *September* 1858.

MY POOR GOOD MUTZ,

Hearty thanks for your letters, the first of which crossed my last to you. You still have to report unpleasantnesses that have occurred to you, and thereby afford me great regret and continual cause for legitimate self-reproaches. May that soon alter, and you have nothing to report but soothing and agreeable impressions! That is my heartfelt wish, and what *I* can do toward realising it, I certainly shall. Only in one hardship endured I cannot pity you; for your travelling third class on that long journey I am at a loss for words! Don't take it ill of me, but I consider that more than absurd:

---

* Apparently an allusion to the parrot's traditional " Böser Richard, arme Minna !" which it must have picked up from that superfluous Natalie.—Tr.

your motive for such self-tortures and abasements makes no appeal to me; I know I'm not to blame for such exaggerations, but am doing all I can to hold privations of that sort aloof from you, which, comparatively speaking, don't even yield a perceptible saving. In such-like things, and there are many of them, I cannot truly pity you; for a certain stubbornness on your side, in which there lurks a dumb rebuke of me, is solely to blame for them. Forgive me, you deserved the tiny sermon!

As for that scoundrel Furrer, I demand that he shall ask your pardon; I hear from Heim that his conduct roused universal indignation.* For that matter, the whole town behaved pretty disgustingly; Heim told me that, to account for my unexpected departure, they stumbled on the idea that I had left Zurich on account of excessive indebtedness. Well as it might suit us for people not to guess the actual reason, really this belief was stupid and low enough, especially as various tradesmen might have stepped forward to whom I had paid considerable sums in full this year for our furnishing. But a perfect panic seems to have seized those who had yet to present their annual accounts, and Heim couldn't send me the piano because legal distraint had been laid on our things by these asses. Naturally it only needed my simple declaration that I acknowledged the claims in question, and should pay them at New Year, to put an end to the proceedings; particularly as it had been discovered meanwhile, of course, that no one else had claims on me and the whole thing was a blind alarm. Consequently public

---

* The man is said to have driven Minna to his own yard, instead of the railway station, and refused to deliver up her luggage till she had settled a former account of a few pounds; at least that is the local tradition, and something like it evidently occurred.—Tr.

opinion has been corrected also, and the damage rebounds on the rascals who had bled me of so much money and of a sudden behaved so abominably that, as Heim tells me, they're being soundly rated for it now. So next week I expect the piano, the music, and the bedding, which I missed, to tell the truth, and should have missed. I got the key all right ; best thanks.

My having to go without the piano so long, was very provoking to me, for my best cordial had been the recovery of a good mood for resuming my work. Of late, however, I've been occupied enough with letter-writing. Naturally I'm trying all I can to coin Rienzi's great success at Dresden into takings [from elsewhere], and accordingly have been inviting all the theatres I'm friends with to acquire this opera speedily. On the whole they seem to be stand-off and distrustful toward this older work of mine, and consider its success is merely due to local interest and Tichatscheck. Still, a few good examples will encourage the rest ; Breslau wants it shortly, also Darmstadt. Hanover I haven't bagged yet, but there's a prospect of it ; and by the new year I may hope to have polished everybody off at Zurich.

And now to speak about my life here. Linking on to the last point, I won't exactly say it's very cheap ; which can scarcely be expected *en garçon*, when the setting up of a whole establishment always costs such a large amount at first. A small unfurnished lodging was out of the question ; they are only to be found in the business quarter of the inner city, from which God preserve me ! Apart from those, there are none but the furnished apartments in palaces bought from the impoverished old nobili and fitted up by speculators for foreigners who visit Venice for a shorter or longer time.

After long search I had to think myself lucky to find something of the kind to suit me at last, and to submit to paying more than I had anticipated.

Like all such apartments, it is in a big ancient palace, with wide halls and spaces. For my living room I have an enormous saloon looking on to the Grand Canal; then a very roomy bedchamber, with a little cabinet beside it for a wardrobe. Fine old ceiling-paintings, splendid floors inlaid with magnificent mosaic; badly distempered walls (once richly tapestried, no doubt), antique furniture, very elegant in appearance, covered with red cotton-velvet, but very rickety and miserably stuffed; nothing quite in working order, doors not shutting properly, all somewhat the worse for wear. I had a big state-bed removed at once, and replaced by a smaller iron bedstead with spring mattress. Linen so-so; pillows stuffed with wool; for the colder season a foot-quilt weighing 3 hundredweight. The landlord, an Austrian, is delighted to have me in his house, and does all he can to satisfy me; I have contrived a few conveniences myself, arranged a passable divan, fauteuil, etc. Things now will do quite well, and the piano is sure to sound glorious in my big saloon. The want of air-tightness in windows and doors is said to be no serious drawback even in winter here. The climate and the air are really heavenly; a regard in which Venice is said to be one of the most favoured of places, far more so than Florence, Rome, or even Naples. An agreeably refreshing East wind constantly blows from the sea, moderating any excessive heat, keeping the sky always clear, and furnishing beautiful air. For a whole month we've only had two rainy days, and only one at a time. Of course, one never sees a trace of drought, as the sea keeps the air always moist. I still go about in full summer clothing, and that of an evening, not until when do I make my promenade.

My manner of life is as follows : The whole day till 4 I work—at whatever there has been to do yet—then I get ferried across the Canal, walk up S. Mark's piazza, meet Karl there at 5 in the restaurant, where I dine *à la carte*, well, but dear (I can never get off under 4 to 5 francs !— without wine, too) ; after dinner, so long as the fine season permits, out in a gondola to the Public Garden, promenade there, and return either afloat or on foot through the town ; then another promenade on shore for the length of the Molo, a glass of ice at the pavilion there, and then home, where the lamp stands lit for me at 8 ; a book picked up, and finally to bed. So I have been living for 4 whole weeks now, and am not tired of it yet, even without real absorbing work. What affords the never-flagging charm, is the strange contrast of my dwelling with the part that serves me for a promenade : here all still, supremely tranquil, a broad track of lapping water from the sea, with ebb and flow ; instead of carts and horses, gondolas moored to the houses' very doors ; wonderful palaces in front and everywhere, all lofty, silent, melancholy. Then of a sudden, on one's stepping forth, mean alleys of the strangest twists and crossings, often scarcely wide enough for two to pass, all flanked with open shops and stalls in which one feels as if upon the pavement ; continually flooded with a stream of people one only needs to join, when without the smallest notion of topography one either arrives at the Rialto—the business quarter—or the Square of S. Mark, where nobody does anything but promenade.

The amazing, unique and quite unparalleled splendour of this Square, and everything connected with it down to the water's brink, is not to be described; each time I reach it from my house, the whole thing staggers me afresh. By all means I must send you some good pictures of it soon. One would never believe one was in the street, if only since it all—there being no horse traffic—is paved with slabs of marble just like some great prince's court. (I've a bad foot, and for many days have been going out in my slippers.) Everything strikes one as a marvellous piece of stage-scenery. Here it is one continual surging up and down, everyone doing nothing but stroll and amuse himself. This peculiar gaiety never fails of its effect on the newcomer; one feels at ease, and the eye is perpetually entertained. For myself the chief charm consists in its all remaining as detached from me as if I were in an actual theatre; I avoid making any acquaintances, and therefore still retain the feeling. The gondola trip out to sea always has an extremely soothing and beneficial effect: the battle in the sky twixt day and night is glorious; ever new isles in the distance to keep the fancy alert with their gardens, churches, palaces.

In brief, I believe the choice of Venice was the happiest I could have made; for there was everything to fear for me if I had not lit on such an element, if I had felt uncomfortable, not come to rest, lost patience, roved about, and never got to work—which in fine is the one and only thing to enthral me sustainedly. Now that is overcome, and hope thereby won for a turn in our fortunes.—

At the outset my landlord spread the news of my arrival, and it got into the papers at once; but I won't let him admit anyone, and am enjoying the most complete retirement. People in Vienna naturally jumped to the conclusion that Lohengrin had prompted me to an

attempt to get permission to go there ; but everything
that has come to your ears to that effect, of course, is
mere false rumour without the smallest foundation. On
the contrary, I am only too glad to be left at peace here.
True, they demanded my pass a second time, and I began
to fear lest demurs would be raised to my remaining
longer ; but the police returned it to me—very flatteringly
addressed, in fact, " to the renowned Herr R.W."—with
the assurance that no objection had been discovered to my
unmolested residence in Venice.   Consequently I am now
enjoying full asylum.

So much for my life here, good Mutz.   Tell Fipsel
also, there are dogs here too, quite good ones, both
spaniels and poodles.   They set out marble basins everywhere for the dear good beasts to drink from, and I often
catch the good chaps at it.   Tell Jacquot I haven't yet
quite found his like ; but when I open one of the windows
in my bedroom of a morning, I always pay my respects to
a pair of canaries placed in front of a window at right
angles to mine, so that I can almost reach across to them.
They know me already, and no longer are frightened.
But—I'm providing myself with nothing, neither bird nor
dog, but remain faithful to our own good beasties.   So I
hope Fipps in especial will keep faithful to me, and give
me a hearty good lick when I see him again, which shan't
be such an eternity off.

To yourself, dear Minna, I have to say that you do
wrong to make light of compassion ; which can only arise
from your understanding something erroneous by it.   All
our relations with others have but one foundation, either
sympathy or decided antipathy : community of grief and
joy makes out the true essence of love ; but community
of joy is something most illusory, for there is little

reasonable ground at all upon this earth for joy, and our fellow-feeling has a solid footing only when directed to another's grief. For my part, in all my relations to whatsoever persons, I no longer wish for anything excepting that they shall not suffer on account of me ; but where I feel this, it peremptorily drives me to sympathy. Neither do I ask anything more, than to be able to assuage the sufferings of others for me. Nothing, nothing —beyond !

Enough of that. Carlsruhe, of course, was a mere project ; I'm very pleased at your intending to set up in Dresden. I wrote to Tichatscheck about it yesterday ; Dresden, after all, is the only place where I'm at home, so to speak—everywhere else I'm abroad. Do so, and write me all about it soon. And give my heartiest remembrances to your people, make your mind easier and easier, sleep well, and console with reports on your feeling better your good Husband who greets you most heartily and with sincere fellow-feeling. Farewell, and send good tidings soon !—

148.*

VENICE, 22. *October* 1858.

MY GOOD MINNA,

I have this moment received your letter, and hurriedly sit down to answer you forthwith on the most urgent point—our things.—

Simply write at once to Zurich ; whatever you want, you will promptly receive. I told you the last time that that injunction was merely a passing stupidity of the creditors involved, set aside as soon as ever I heard of it.

---

* At least one letter must be missing between this and the last ; see the allusion on page 381.—Tr.

I only needed to commission Heim to acknowledge the
bills in my name—so far as they should be found correct
—and the injunction was removed at once.   Believe me,
I wouldn't conceal anything from you.   It was annoying
enough ; but it's over.—So, get sent you whatever you
wish.

—I'm curious to learn about Furrer's behaviour.   I
sent Heim an open letter, which he was to read aloud to
that low person—perhaps through Spyri—if possible in
presence of the men concerned : a letter in which I
demand of him that he shall beg your pardon ; but Heim
hasn't let me hear anything further yet.   I wrote for my
coverlet also ; I need it much, as my bedroom is splendid
for summer, but not for the winter, and I wouldn't give
much for the heating.—

When you arrive in Dresden, you shall find a longer
letter from me at Tichatscheck's, which will supply you
with further news about myself and Venice.   If my
pocket permits, I shall accompany it with views of sundry
parts of Venice.   Anyhow I have already been hunting
some up at the shops for you.—

Really it's too cruel of you in our old age, to be
wanting to divide up our estate ; it will end by your
letting me starve when my other operas cease paying and
I've nothing but Rienzi to fall back on.   For the present
I must beg you to allow me from your undisputed property [*Rienzi*, jocularly ; see pp. 386, 395] enough to pay off Heim
and Zurich bills, and to be able to live on till Tristan.
When the Tristan comes along, I'll hand you over some
of that in turn, and thus, I fancy, we shall keep each
other going.   But joking apart, I hope for good takings
ere long from my ancient Rienzi ; which will really come
in very handy.   Breslau has paid me already.   What I

get from Hanover, will go to Heim straight off. Presuming on my new friendship with Lachner, I have got Munich also after it now, and am hoping that will come off ; then others will soon follow suit. No one has sent me a refusal yet, merely puttings off; I hope to get Frankfort and Prague after it yet, though, whilst Darmstadt also has to send its fee.—

Well, no doubt you can manage awhile with the 1000 *fr.* from Ritters for the present. Just pay Frau Hänel, but don't let that make you buy yourself anything inferior to what you ought to have, I beg you for my sake. I really don't draw any hard and fast line for you, and whatever you need you may be sure of obtaining at once from me ; don't be so absurd !—

Your throwing that Rottdorf " houselet " in my face is just what I might have expected ; it came from my merely thinking of our former little flat there, and your meaning to take precisely such another in it. Forgive my belittlement of the big house !

For that matter, I could earnestly wish you—once more—to come to rest at Dresden, the sooner the better. I quite understand that, with Klärchen's familiarity with our [moral] relations, a harping on recent occurrences was less to be avoided than at Zwickau ; but that is just what I should like to see prevented. There is nothing more foolish and cruel, than the constant tearing open of such wounds, and only with reluctance do I allude to it in this letter myself. Dear Mutz, come to rest ; endeavour not to think of what has tortured you and is to be overcome for good. Believe me, I now am living [solely] for my art and the heartfelt wish to make your life as supportable and agreeable as possible in future. Nothing shall shake my resolutions, not even yourself when you try to

provoke me.   I shall even overcome your contradictions.
—I regard the world otherwise now, than but a few years
since, and can truly say, I feel that I've been tested in a
higher sense at last.   Let this be evidence to you of what
I mean : that I can report how much better and calmer I
feel now, in every respect.   For some time now I have
unintermittently had such beautiful sound sleep as I've
hardly ever known before.   Oh, if I only could lend it
you, how soon you would get well !   But believe me,
this health and recovery doesn't come from without or
through physic ; it comes from nowhere but within : my
retirement and profound collectedness refresh me, give me
deep tranquillity and peace.   If you look without for anything, hold fast to *me* alone !   And if you would console
yourself for all you've suffered, hold fast to it that my heart
has stayed good to you, and—surely you can see it !—
will stand unflinching by your side. —

Enough !   I hope for the production of Tristan at
Carlsruhe toward Easter ; then we shall meet again, and
all the rest will arrange itself kindly and well.

Farewell, and rely on

Thy good HUSBAND.

149.

VENICE, 28. *October* 1858.

MY GOOD MUTZ,

I sent off the views of Venice yesterday ; I hope
you will find them on your arrival in Dresden, where I
also hope you will come to a little rest soon.   I've had no
further tidings of you since your last ; I should have been
glad if Tröger had written me,* but shall henceforth go

---

* His prognosis reached Wagner three days later ; see the entry in
the Venice Diary for November 1 (*R. Wagner to M. Wesendonck*).—Tr.

by Pusinelli.—Everything within me is becoming so calm now, that I keep hoping you must also share that happiness ere long.—

To-day, however, I intended to amuse you a little with Venice. The pictures will do the best for that. I have sent the chief views coloured, although they're not exactly works of art ; only, with Venice the vivid colouring has so much to do with the effect, that one can really form no notion of it from mere black outlines. The Doge's Palace and church of S. Mark look just as bright and dazzling in reality, as in the pictures. I have marked the photographs on their backs ; a portion of my palace comes into one of them, though unfortunately not the part in which I dwell : still, it will give you some idea. On the big bird's-eye view of Venice I have made a red cross where my palace stands ; going up the Grand Canal you must keep to the left, and at the first big bend you'll find it.

I also have enclosed a folk-group that pleased me most ; these are the feminine water-carriers, who really have a very original look. The other women of the people do not shew up to their advantage, and in particular would be improved by some sort of head-gear, which I miss in them greatly. True, they expend very much art on their coiffure, and that is why they go about bare-headed ; but unfortunately the good girls can't tidy up their hair except on Sunday, and never again in the week, so that of a Saturday they look like tousled hags. Among the men, the sailors are often very interesting ; striking physiognomies, with red caps *à la* Stumme von Portici. But your subscriber chiefly mixes with the gondoliers, who naturally play a big rôle in Venice ; they try to overcharge you when they can, but I am already

well known in my district and no longer treated by them
as a foreigner, which makes it easier and cheaper for me.
They all have fine, clear, powerful voices. Nothing is
more thrilling, than when one hears a solitary gondolier
on the Canal at night suddenly begin with plaintive
accent " O Venezia ! " etc. ; it's quite unique. Then
one hears them answering one another from the distance
with a kindred chant, until it dies away ; which has
quite an indescribable effect. Moreover, there is a regular
Gondoliers' Vocal Union, with a workman at the Arsenal
for conductor and composer ; the voices are wonderfully
sonorous and robust. For the upper part they have altos,
which lends their singing quite a novel character ; and
then they sing the most diverse kinds of ballads in the
folk-style, all with incredible precision, purity of intonation
and nuance. They usually get hired by strangers to make
a slow tour of the whole Canal on a gondola lit with
coloured lanterns ; which is followed by a lengthening train
of boats with listeners, amid great silence, and actively
applauded from the windows. They have often entertained
me, on my balcony, very finely in this fashion.—

That sort of thing here constitutes the limit of my
enjoyment from without ; otherwise I adhere to my
retirement, and see no one but Karl. I have to keep off
[would-be] friends by force ; the other day, however, a
prince pursued me down the Square, and regularly buttonholed me. This time I didn't regret it : it was the Russian
Prince *Dolgoruki*, who really is a very clever and highly-
cultured man ; he told me a lot about Lohengrin, which
he had seen in Vienna, and gave me many very interesting
details. As he is soon going away, I make an exception
of him, and have allowed him to call. Otherwise I'm
merciless ; I have had a Count Kalenberg dismissed twice

over. Already I am as well known to the Austrian officers as a spotted dog ; they always make for Karl to get my news. Unfortunately I have been unable to avoid coming into contact with the local military bandmasters. Perhaps you know that the Austrian military bands are excellent ? Well, there are *three* of them here, which take it in turns to play in S. Mark's square of an evening, when the whole of Venice is on its legs. One of these bandmasters got round my landlord, but I had him turned away. In the evening I heard the Tannhäuser march performed by him, however, and the dragging tempo vexed me ; so I sent him word that the next time he gave anything of mine he must let me know first, that I might shew him the correct tempo etc. He promptly fetched me to a rehearsal of the Tannhäuser overture, for military band ! That was in barracks, and all the officers dropped in. It really went quite well, against all expectation.—But then the bandmaster of the Royal Marines got hold of Karl, and begged him to persuade me just to honour him as well : he wanted to perform the overture to Rienzi. What else could I do ? I had to go off to the Marine barracks, where a regular high-ceremonial reception awaited me, all the officers *en masse*. The overture went very well ; I heard it from the restaurant with Karl, over dessert and half a bottle of champagne [Liszt's birthday, Oct. 22].— Next day the bandmaster of the Hungarian regiment announced himself, with pieces from Lohengrin : but I dismissed him for the nonce.—

    There—those are about all my adventures ; otherwise everything is going very uniformly. I am glad to be back at my work ; I'm at it hard, and even take the evenings now for instrumenting. It is all becoming very beautiful !

    I have heard nothing decent from abroad for ever so

long ; for some time past no news at all, or else unfavourable. Unfortunately, things will not go so swimmingly with " your " Rienzi as could be wished. They all would prefer something new of mine ; but the worst is, that the curs. subject gives such trouble. The day before yesterday I received a great shock through it ; I was already expecting the fee from Munich, and rejoicing in the ability to forward Heim his cash at once, when Lachner writes me : Unfortunately the reading committee has decided that, in view of the present rigorously Catholic trend at Munich, the production of Rienzi would be quite out of the question on account of the religious topics occurring in it, and accordingly the score cannot be accepted. That was a knock-down blow, and I fear it will be exactly the same in Austria ; even of Prague I've no more hope now. What makes things worse, is the subject's having a political, as well as an ecclesiastic splinter. That, at any rate, is to be feared no more with my poorer, later and latest works (a rub for you !). Even that wearisome dolt Ed. Devrient has treated me to a refusal ; he is again on the eve—so he writes me—of breaking with Carlsruhe ! What a chapter of absurd confusions ! I must try and pull through, however, and so am very busy corresponding ; but thus much is certain—I cannot count *much* on Rienzi, as you will see. My Tristan, on the contrary, will go off next year like hot cakes ; even now I am continually having to mollify theatres all clamouring for the *first* performance. Thus *Darmstadt*, also *Munich ;* I've had to promise *Prague* at least to give them second place with this opera's production.—For Rienzi my main hope now is Hanover ; but I've had nothing from there as yet. Don't you get anxious, however, and deny yourself nothing ; it will all come right !—

And now be heartily welcomed to Dresden! Lord, how delighted I shall be to hear that you're getting a little rest and some comfort in your provisional small abode! It will come for certain, poor dear Mutz ; your health, so much dependent on your frame of mind, will gradually improve ; the most distressing symptoms will vanish step by step, and you'll draw courage and pleasure from life again. I build great hopes on Dresden ; much will suit you there, for sure, and if only you regain sufficient strength to pluck yourself from troubling fancies, you'll already have so much to reconcile you to the present, that at last you'll also pluck up courage for the future.

To begin with, give my heartiest greetings to Tichatscheck and Frau Pauline. Lord knows how gladly I'd be with you all !—You ought to be pitying *me*—and yet I have to keep consoling *you !* Tell Tschekel it's a bargain that we're to be chiselled for Dresden.* And greet Heine and Fischer ; I'm going to write to Pusinelli. And good, good Fipsel, greet him a thousand times ; he's not to over-eat himself! A good thing the red-tail [Jacquot ?] is coming—else ! !—

Now adieu, farewell, good Mutz, and you shall have a thorough good buss for the first night's good sleep you can write me of ; so do your best, and hold me dear !

Thy

R.

Please tell me the house-number, and whether your lodging is left or right of the parterre.—A good thing you have no stairs to mount !—

---

* To Tichatschek, in joke, Sept. 27 : " I mean to leave directions in my will for setting up a monument to the pair of us in front of the Dresden theatre," etc. ; see *Life*, vi, 375.—Tr.

150.

VENICE, 14. *November* 1858.

MY DEAR GOOD MUTZ,

To-day I'm merely sending you the most essential answer to your letter just received, and reserve to myself to write again tomorrow in case I forget too much.—

I have been ill since the first of November, and only the last two days have I gone into the air again a little, about dinner-time. For three days I was confined to bed ; a gastric-nervous fever threatened. The private physician of a Prince Gallitzin has been treating me. Now I'm on the mend, and think of resuming work in a day or two.

Dear Mutz, I won't conceal from you that your last letter from Chemnitz had its share in the development of my illness. The grief of seeing you forever falling back upon that chapter, where every fancy does you harm, convulsed me deeply. Have we taken opposite paths for a while, merely to renew from a distance those conflicts which, alas, were so injurious to both of us when last we were together ? Your letters from Zwickau touched me so much, whereas those from Chemnitz only shewed me how recklessly and insanely your wound was being probed again there.

Do please discard the fatal notion that I'm keeping something up my sleeve and mean to break away from you insensibly, or anything like it. For the sake of a clean slate and calmer future for the pair of us, I deemed it best that we should separate at present for a season, precisely to avoid the very thing you keep relapsing into, to my sorrow. Whatever I have said to you, and .all I've adduced in support of it, was honestly and truly meant. I reproach myself most bitterly for having let the irritation of the moment betray me [at Enge] into joining issue with you harshly and saying wounding and offensive things ; it is *that* for which you have to forgive me, just as I heartily repent it myself. But nothing more shall shake me in my present resolution to keep all that is wounding or slighting aloof from you. I therefore tell you, please don't challenge me again : 'tis waste of breath, you will not draw me ; I shall simply pay you back with gentleness and kindness. But with that on which I'm silent, it is not because I need to circumvent you, but solely since it is not meet (*nicht taugt*) between us, and must be absolutely ignored and forgotten. This is my only reason for not answering on that point, believe me ! I have sworn it to myself for good and all !—

Only take heart, my dear good Minna ! Overcome, and steadfastly believe in the intense sincerity with which I now aspire to nothing—nothing on this earth save to make up for what has been inflicted on you, support and guard you, preserve you in all loyalty and love, that your suffering state may also mend, you may regain an interest in life, and together we may then enjoy life's evening as cheerfully and cloudlessly as possible.—Dear good Mutz, what more can I say to you ? Would not all else be utterly superfluous and vain ?—

Can it be humanly conceivable that they are putting serious difficulties in the way of your residence in Dresden ? I'm dumbfounded at it !—Still, I keep hoping it is nothing but a mere scruple of the local police which may easily be set aside. I am writing Pusinelli a couple of lines, which please convey to him at once ; my next step shall depend on his answer. I am determined to pursue it [if need be] right up to the King ; in any case

I shall write to Lüttichau about it, perhaps within the next few days. My God, what does one really care, tho', for this Dresden? In the worst event I would beg you to join me at Venice immediately, if it were not so dreadful to let you and your pets make a fresh stiff journey in the heart of winter, and to tear you again from a rest scarcely entered. The sole object with Dresden, accordingly, is to afford you a point of repose for this winter, for your [medical] tending, diversion and recreation, until I can return to Germany myself; when we can't perhaps so well choose Dresden, after all, as unfortunately that stupid old publishing tangle (with Kriete's) hasn't spun itself off even yet, making Dresden still a little awkward to me. I rather think of our settling in Berlin or Vienna; you yourself shall have the casting vote in that, as I am indifferent on the whole to the exact place, provided only it's a large city with good artistic means. The time for us to make our minds up isn't far off now; as soon as I have done with Tristan I shall in any case be able to go to Germany *for a while*, and the settling of the larger question must necessarily be knit with that. But I anticipate with next-door to certainty that the new change of Government in Prussia will expedite everything; at all events a Prussian amnesty will soon be promulgated there, and if they do not think of me themselves, I am determined to address myself personally to the Prince of Prussia and beg him to sanction my residing in Berlin. I can't help fancying I shall receive an invitation to Lohengrin even as it is, which would almost plunge me in perplexity—firstly, because it would detain me for long from the completion of my new opera (which we really need to live upon), and secondly because, after these 10 years, I shouldn't care to obtain my first hearing of Lohengrin precisely in Berlin, turned to a weariness by their miserable singers, when I would far rather choose Vienna, where the representation is said to be unsurpassably fine.—But more about all that tomorrow ; for to-day only thus much : I definitely assume that we two poor married folk shall come together again from next summer onward, no matter where !

But just you behave ! For God's sake don't play havoc with yourself like a maniac ! Neither be afraid you might never be able to see me again ; Tröger has written me, and the only thing to fear for you is a *very wearying malady* if you do not yourself help to abate, improve, and make your sufferings bearable through tranquilness of mind, which is the only thing to help here. But you have just got to be a bit stronger and sounder when I see you again !—

And now farewell. I see I've still a deal to write to you ; so a second letter tomorrow !

Farewell, good, good Mutz. More tomorrow from

Thy

RICHEL.

Get a *warm carpet* for your lodging at once ; *I command it !*

151.
VENICE, 14. *November* 1858, [*Sunday*] *evening.*

So, my good Minna, now I am quieter I'll write you again at once, that nothing may remain forgotten, and everything, if possible, be made still clearer.

Once more, I meant to have written you a couple of days after your last letter, as I hoped to have overcome by then the truly disheartening impression your terribly excited letter had produced on me. Meanwhile, however, my own illness became more and more critical; I lost all appetite, could keep nothing down at last, had fever, and was utterly wretched. As soon as he heard of it through Karl, Prince Dolgoruki sent me Prince Galitzin's private doctor, when we parried the outbreak of an apparently very bad illness which seems to have been brewing in me for a long time ; and at the end of 14 days, as said, to-day I've been out for the third time already and feel set up again, only that I must still be very careful with my diet. So that is done with, and let us hope, for long !

Then at the beginning of this week came good, good Frau Pauline's answer, for which I am deeply obliged to her. She wrote me about yourself as well, saying you intended to write me next day—quite calmly and nicely, she hoped. I confess I waited gladly for that promised letter, which would certainly have made my answer easier ; but it did not arrive, alas, until a few days later. You poor good Wife, for Heaven's sake don't plague yourself so shockingly ! Never again will you move me from my fixed determination, which distance itself makes the easier for me in its first stage, since I there am master of my mood and able to consult nothing besides my duty to you. Only believe me, all else is quite useless, and— as I already have written you to-day—if I keep silence on certain points, it is not that I have anything to conceal from you, but simply and solely because I know too profoundly how foolish and unprofitable it is to keep returning to such a subject, whereas oblivion is the only anodyne even for yourself. Enough of it, I beg and implore you by all that's most heartfelt and earnest ; *never* another word on it ! Attest to me *thus* that you really are fond of me.

Think of nothing but our reunion, and to make that a thoroughly great and enduring boon to both of us, attend to nothing else whatever now beyond your health ; toward which you can do nothing, nothing in the world, unless—you tranquillise your mind ! Fulfil my prayer, and believe me, nothing now can grieve me more than the knowledge that your malady is positively being increased by those gloomy thoughts ; whilst nothing can more rejoice me than to hear of your improvement, since it at the same time is proof to me that your mind is finding ease about me and you are according me belief. That you can only do by firmly carrying out the instant resolution not to speak *another word* on that which still is so unsettling you, and that to *no one;* then it at last will happen of itself that you won't think so much about it, until it finally will vanish from you like a murky shadow, and in its place the Present shall approach with fostering, uplifting, liberating hands. Open your eyes, and look unprejudiced on all that can afford you joy, amusement, occupation. Gladden yourself with the performances of my operas, and—if you really must have something to unsettle you—be thoroughly impatient in your expectation of my license to return at last, to present my works in person and restore myself to the exercise of my art. At Zurich we were far too buried and thrown upon our own resources ; in the long run that was bound to act injuriously and set us grousing. Once we are back in a big city, where I can busy myself with performances, and you can tend me after tiring labours and rejoice with me at their success,—it will seem to yourself all a dream that we ever were tucked into a crib like that and only with an effort could get a reasonable guest or two into the house from time to time. Well, well, all that will alter and a whole new life begin, full of honours, fame and recognition, as much as ever I desire ; so get yourself in trim to enjoy this harvest with me after a long and arduous seedtime. Keep this future in eye, and if you will, be thoroughly impatient for it to come about at last : that sort of impatience won't harm you at all ; on the contrary, it will heal and regale you !—And it won't be long in coming now ; only give me free leisure to finish my Tristan—which, if I'm left undistracted, will be done by next Spring—and my return into Germany is ensured me already. Perhaps it will come even sooner ; but should it chance that I'm not let return *at all* (which of course is inconceivable !)—why, then you must return *to me*, and we should have to say Valet to the pleasant prospect of Germany. *Then* we should have to transplant ourselves to Paris, where I should push the presentation of my operas with all my might, and in the meantime Tristan must provide us with the means to live agreeably there. So, if I am not amnestied by next summer, you would come to me again with dog and bird, and we'd definitively emigrate to Paris ; which I should never quit again, however, even if I were amnestied later.—

Well, only don't grow *too* impatient, good Mutzinius ; that also is not well.—No, my own temper is so calm and steady now, my outlook on the world so clear and void of hate, that I shall get on very well with it henceforward ; only you, poor Wife, disquiet me : nothing—nothing else ! —so calm yourself, too, and nothing then will lack me any more.—

But it is imperative that I should get done with this confounded Tristan ; it must bring us in much grist next year. Rienzi unfortunately refuses to go down at all ! I really had been reckoning on Hanover for certain ; but, apart from Breslau, not a theatre has taken it in earnest yet, and we should have a very poor look-out if I had written none besides this opera of *yours !* You know I had to pay Heim back his 1000 *fr.* last month ; I had counted on Hanover, but nothing came in,—then my good Tannhäuser (already a long way off being so good as Rienzi!) helped once again : the *Stuttgart* people addressed themselves to me for it at last. You know that I had strictly meant to keep them dangling, but I grappled to and wrote that if they sent me 50 louis d'or at once, they could have the opera, so far as I cared ; I received their cash at once, and was able to repay Heim in the nick of time. Good old Tannhäuser! rotten Rienzi!—At Pesth, too, they want to have Tannhäuser. I've offered Lohengrin to Cassel. Dingelstedt writes about Rienzi for Weimar—naturally only with Tichatscheck ; probably that will remain my last transaction with Rienzi.—But that is not to say that things are standing badly with us ; Tannhäuser and Lohengrin are still inexhaustible. Only the other day there was another Berlin performance of the former ; consequently another tantième, which the entirely good Minna shall have for New Year's gift. Lohengrin also is bound to be coming out there soon, and even though the advance must be worked off first, still there will be good receipts to expect from Berlin again by Easter. And by then I shall have finished my Tristan (God willing !) and pocket another 100 louis d'or from Härtels. I also hope to get a supplementary 500 gulden for Lohengrin from Vienna this winter itself ; there have been 12 performances already, at the least, and they have to pay me again after the 20th. Moreover, Tannhäuser is set down for next season at Vienna ; consequently I must be getting my 1000 gulden again for it in the summer.

Then will come Tristan, which everybody wants to be the first to have, and doubtless will bring me in a tidy sum in no time.—

It is *Vienna* that gives me most delight, though. *Kirchberger* [Alex. Winterberger], the pupil of Liszt's who was with him at Zurich two years ago, has arrived here—with a Russian princess whose sons he is teaching. He has seen *all* the Vienna performances of Lohengrin, after hearing it often at Weimar, and says it would be quite impossible to imagine anything more perfect and entrancing,—compared with Weimar (in spite of Liszt !) he absolutely would not have recognised the opera : all, all were so excellent, from the first to the last, that it was one continual transport ; *Ander* as Lohengrin bewitching, and everything, orchestra, chorus and all, unsurpassable. Prince Dolgoruki confirmed that also. And above all, the success ! How would that have formerly been possible in Vienna with Lohengrin straight off? The audience is said to applaud like mad, and each representation to be a perfect festival.—I confess, it would give me joy, at last to hear a thing like that. Naturally I have acquired a great predilection for Vienna, and the place—I think—would also please yourself. Well, we shall see ; only not too impatient ! But one of these fine days all will suddenly become magnificent, and we shall stare at each other and ask in amaze, Where, wherever have we been all this time ? Were we dreaming ?—

There now, I've picked up nearly all I know about myself to tell you ; may it please you to some extent !— Just as winter has descended on the whole of Europe, so on Venice too. What as a rule one experiences very seldom even in the hardest winter here, actually came at the beginning of November : snow lay on the ground for

several days ! Not bad. And then the poor protection
of abodes here, ridiculous stoves, etc. ; it was awful. I've
been having fires all day long, especially during my illness,
and wood is the reverse of cheap here. It's really getting
time ' that we were done with it ! Now I have had
windows and doors duly protected with list, the stoves
repaired, and at last it's quite comfortable ; moreover the
weather has turned mild again.—For God's sake, do keep
yourself sheltered ! I expected it, those d—d parterre
apartments aren't fit for winter. Mind you have a
thoroughly warm carpet laid at once, else you shan't have
that New Year's tantième !—But that fearfully good
Pauline, *isn't* she good ? It's almost more than one can
bear, so good as that ! What you write me about her has
rejoiced me exceedingly ; moreover it has done me an
amount of good it can scarcely have done even yourself,
to know that you are surrounded by such kind people.
Only see a lot of the Tschekels ; they'll soon drive away
all your doldrums, and help [to divert] your impatience.—

So you haven't been to Heine's or Fischer's yet ?
Soared straight to Lüttichau ! Well, I'm glad to hear
that he expressed himself so nicely. O, if the man had
only treated me a shade more delicately then, as is fitting
with an artist of my stamp, how much might have
happened quite differently, or never have happened at all !
But, oblivion of that as well ! I harbour no ill-feeling
against anybody now.—For sure he'll send you decent
tickets ; otherwise Devil take him, and you'll proudly pay
your money for the amphitheatre—that is self-under-
stood.—

I *cannot* yet conceive their raising serious difficulties
against your stay in Dresden ; but your having to go to
the police-court yourself is really shocking ! The Devil,

is there no one who at once will see to all this rumpus in your stead ? There I recognise the seamy side of Dresden at a glance. Pusinelli must undertake it ; he is the most suitable person : in case of need he is to recommend you a good lawyer who will take the whole thing off your hands. It quite revolts me to think of your going yourself !—

For the rest, the fact of Zschinsky's place as Minister of Justice not being filled yet is a good sign to me : they are waiting to see what Prussia means to do about the amnesty, to shape their course accordingly.—

And now farewell for to-day ; may you very soon give me the unspeakable joy of your writing me quite calmly, trustfully and hopefully ! Greet Fipsel and Jacquot, the good, good beasts ; I often dream of them as well.—I shall write a couple of lines to N. myself.—And in conclusion, another hearty salute and kiss from

Thy good
HUSBAND.

END OF VOL. I